BF
311
F35

Symbolic Regression

Psychology

Paul D. Fairweather
Donovan Johnson

SCHOOL OF
CALIFORNIA PROFESSIONAL
PSYCHOLOGY
LOS ANGELES

✳ IRVINGTON PUBLISHERS, INC., New York

Copyright © 1981 by Irvington Publishers, Inc.

All rights reserved. No part of this book may be reproduced in any manner whatever, including information storage or retrieval, in whole or in part (except for brief quotations in critical articles or reviews), without written permission from the publisher. For information, write to Irvington Publishers, Inc., 551 Fifth Avenue, New York, New York, 10176.

Library of Congress Cataloging in Publication Data

Fairweather, Paul D.
  Symbolic regression psychology.

  Includes bibliographical references.
  1. Consciousness. 2. Regression (Psychology) 3. Symbolism (Psychology) 4. Family. 5. Psychotherapy. I. Johnson, Donovan D., joint author. II. Title [DNLM: 1. Symbolism (Psychology) 2. Regression (Psychology) WM193.5.R2 F172s]
BF311.F35   154.2'4   80-22915
ISBN 0-8290-0420-3
ISBN 0-8290-0421-1 (pbk.)

Printed in the United States of America

CONTENTS

Chapter		Page
I	CONSCIOUSNESS	1
II	SYMBOLIC REGRESSION	41
III	IMAGINATION	81
IV	PERSON	115
V	FAMILY	143
VI	PATHOLOGY	187
VII	GENUINENESS	213

Chapter I: Consciousness

> The ripening and the proving of man's spiritual powers
> may be accomplished through individual tasks and
> interests; yet somehow, beneath or above, there stands
> the demand that through all of these tasks and
> interests a transcendent promise should be fulfilled,
> that all individual expressions should appear only as
> a multitude of ways by which the spiritual life comes
> to itself.
> Georg Simmel[1]

THE PROBLEM OF CONSCIOUSNESS: MAN'S DENIAL OF HIS PSYCHOLOGICAL BIRTHRIGHT

Each person is born with an implicit sense that life is to be a garden of harmony and delight. This sense, or promise, defines man's deepest aspirations. It finds expression in the "state of innocence" celebrated in the poetry of various cultures as a paradise, or place of primordial felicity and fecundity. Each person lives in relation to this ultimate sense of felicity, and it is embodied in the ordered gardens of poetic tradition as well as in the primitive paradises of worldwide myth. William Blake's "Songs of Innocence," first published in 1789, portray this condition just as do the ancient Biblical Garden of Eden and the classical images of the Golden Age and the Elysian Fields.

The garden is a place of order and spontaneity, of innocence and fecundity. It is a symbol which corresponds to each person's desire to know that his place in the cosmos is secure and meaningful. It corresponds to each person's desire to believe that his relationships with others will be grounded in enduring love and human caring. And it corresponds to each person's desire to experience an untrammeled inner sense of peace and harmony.

This sense of promised felicity is a birthright which each person receives when he comes into the world and which he interprets and reinterprets throughout the course of his life. This sense is referred to in a limited way in political language as the human right to "life, liberty, and the pursuit of happiness." This sense _is_ man's spiritual substance.

But there is a fundamental problem with this innate sense of "the good life." Man's experience is at odds with this promise. The promise by which each person lives is thwarted, degraded, and insulted. The individual is torn from the experience of felicity by the traumas of his life. He becomes disillusioned with the promise and comes to question its reality. A chain of traumas--beginning as early as intra-uterine experience and birth and continuing along the perilous road of personal relationships--undermines the individual's sense of his birthright to the point where he finds himself estranged from it. That which he believed to have been promised by the very right of birth comes to seem like an illusory dream. Something feels wrong about it. He questions why he has so much trouble experiencing the reality of his pristine promise.

The person especially feels this uneasiness in his family, where it becomes most obvious that intimacy is only partially experienced. His parents teach him that he should feel at peace with life, but in their very way of living there is an implicit demand that he, the child, dispel their own doubts about the promise of life. In this he is asked to perpetuate the very uneasiness which throws doubt on the meaning of his own existence. Thus he learns no longer to recognize the promise as his own. Moreover, he begins to question its reality. At the same time, he has a deep, perhaps unacknowledged sense of its loss. His life has become a contradictory response to this sense of promise: he at once desires it and distrusts it. He finds himself confronted by the problem of consciousness, for the discrepancy between the individual's sense of this promise and his experience of life is the problem of consciousness.

William Wordsworth expresses the growing person's developing sense of estrangement from this birthright in his poem, "Ode: Intimations of Immortality from Recollections of Early Childhood":

CONSCIOUSNESS

> Our birth is but a sleep and a forgetting:
> The soul that rises with us, our life's star,
> > Hath had elsewhere its setting,
> > And cometh from afar:
> > Not in entire forgetfulness,
> > And not in utter nakedness,
> But trailing clouds of glory do we come
> > From God, who is our home:
> Heaven lies about us in our infancy!
> Shades of the prison-house begin to close
> > Upon the growing boy,
> But he beholds the light, and whence it flows,
> > He sees it in his joy;
> The youth, who daily farther from the east
> > Must travel, still is nature's priest,
> > And by the vision splendid
> > Is on his way attended;
> At length the man perceives it die away,
> And fade into the light of common day.   (ll. 58-76)[2]

Blake too traces the process of man's estrangement from his original birthright. He contrasts the child's original state of "innocence" with the later oppressive state of "experience."[3]

The image of the garden and man's sense of his estrangement from it work together as the two elements which constitute human desire. Man has to have a sense of the place of felicity in order to know that he has lost it. When man's essence is defined in terms of this ultimate desire as it is embodied in the image of the garden of felicity, he is seen as a spiritual or cosmic being. The condition of estrangement, loss, and desire makes it necessary for man to envision the garden as being distant from him. Thus the garden is often located by its remoteness from experience in space and time. The garden is placed at both the beginning and the end of the world in Judaeo-Christian tradition and it is placed at the beginning of the world in Greek and Roman traditions. But man instinctively knows that it should be more accessible to him than this. Thus, man is sometimes offered an experience of this place as a gift or as an attainment in the midst of his life. Aeneas is allowed a glimpse of the Elysian Fields when he visits his father in Hades before beginning his conquest of Italy.[4] Even Milton's Adam, when he is being ejected from Eden by the stern justice of the Puritan God, is given a special promise of the spiritual garden which will always remain accessible to him through obedience:

> [In obedience] wilt thou not be loath
> To leave this Paradise, but shall possess
> A paradise within thee, happier far.
> (Paradise Lost XII, 585-87)[5]

Milton, in this softening of the wrathful God, goes beyond Puritanism by making the promised inner garden comparatively more enjoyable than the Eden of Adam's primal experience.

But if the promise of life is embodied in the image of the garden, the sense of estrangement from it is embodied in the image of the desert. It is the meaning of this estrangement that makes T. S. Eliot's poem, "The Wasteland," so haunting:

> Here is no water but only rock . . .
> Dead mountain mouth of carious teeth that cannot spit
> Here one can neither stand nor lie nor sit
> There is not even silence in the mountains
> But dry sterile thunder without rain
> There is not even solitude in the mountains
> But red sullen faces sneer and snarl
> From doors of mudcracked houses
>   If there were water . . . (11. 331-46)[6]

When a man senses the discrepancy between his primal sense of promise and his experience of life and then chooses to believe in his experience of deprivation rather than in his birthright, he becomes full of bitterness and despair. He finds he has lost the poignancy of his will to live. And he finds himself resigned to what he takes to be hopeless paradoxes, such as those expressed by W. H. Auden in "For the Time Being":

> For the garden is the only place there is,
>   but you will not find it
> Until you have looked for it everywhere and found
>   nowhere that is not a desert; . . .
> And life is the destiny you are bound to refuse
>   Until you have consented to die. (11. 153-54, 157)[7]

The discrepancy between the intuition which we have described as each person's birthright and the experience of estrangement from it is the condition which all persons know to a greater or lesser degree. We have seen how this discrepancy can lead to cynicism and disillusionment and confusion. But for some, it can call forth a project of recovery as well, one which faces the despair in this state and goes beyond it to the state of recaptured innocence, even as Auden's lines suggest, if we reread them with determined hope in mind. It is Wordsworth and Blake, among others, who, by taking their sense of loss seriously, have actually been able to create poetic projects which result, with more or less success, in the recovery of their original birthright. Both poets take on the task of consciousness in order to come to terms with this discrepancy. In this project of recovery, Wordsworth assigns a special function to his role as a poet:

>   Paradise, and groves
> Elysian, Fortunate Fields--like those of old
> Sought in the Atlantic main--why should they be
> A history only of departed things
> Or a mere fiction of what never was?
> For the discerning intellect of Man
> When wedded to this goodly universe
> In love and holy passion, shall find these
> A simple produce of the common day.
> --I, long before the blissful hour arrives,
> Would chant, in lonely peace, the spousal verse
> Of this great consummation:--and, by words
> Which speak of nothing more than what we are,
> Would I arouse the sensual from their sleep
> Of Death, and win the vacant and the vain
> To noble raptures; while my voice proclaims
> How exquisitely the individual Mind
> (And the progressive powers perhaps no less
> Of the whole species) to the external World
> Is fitted;--and how exquisitely, too--
> Theme this but little heard of among men--
> The external World is fitted to the Mind.
>   ("Preface to The Excursion," ll. 47-68)[8]

Here the promise of birthright from which each person becomes estranged in the experiences of life is to be recovered through the poet's song. The poet gives voice to each man's task to recover his original birthright. The recovered birthright, the reunion of mind with nature, the unification of the individual with all of Being, is the decisive experience by which nature is to be again transformed back into the original garden of promise.

Fundamental to this project of recovery is the belief that there are solid grounds for one's expectancy that he can be in harmony with himself and with the world. In experiencing the discrepancy, the individual tends to use indirect tactics to try to protect himself from the pain of his loss: he becomes cynical and denies his own access to his birthright; at the same time he constructs idealizations that rationalize his deprivation and allow him to accept little bits of joyous experience instead of a more comprehensive harmony with the world. Such self-made oases in the desert are part of a defensive strategy which protects the individual at once both from the feared despair and from the potential joy which would be his if he were enabled to face his loss and to accept the reality of his true birthright.

The basic assumption underlying symbolic regression psychology is that within each person's inner being is a point of natural harmony with all Being. The individual's continuing quest is to discover and unite himself with the reality of this primal birthright which he received at the beginning and which has been present with him though hidden throughout his life. The conflicts of life seem to convince the individual that the harmonious living which he senses through both this promise and his desires is in fact unreal, and that all of his dreams of the good life are actually some great, groundless hoax. Thus, individuals spend their lives only half-heartedly trying to discover and to validate their primal birthright of harmony and love which is embodied in the image of the garden. The individual's task in this quest is to conceptualize life so that somehow he can keep the truth of his birthright alive along with his experience of personal and organic disharmony. The task of life and the task of symbolic regression psychology is greater consciousness: the recovery of man's experience of his pristine promise. The individual needs to integrate his promise within his psyche at its latest stage of development so that the promise becomes usable for him and so that he expresses its reality in the ordinary pursuits of his life: in the way that he thinks about life, in the way that he feels about life, and in the ways that he acts in response to the requirements which life imposes upon him.

Ken is a middle-aged man whose experience of this discrepancy between his original birthright and his actual experience is typical of many who come to the psychotherapist with the desire to find access to a greater portion of their original birthright. In a visualization, a technique useful as a fundamental means of access to this birthright, Ken imagined himself to regress in time to the point where he once again became a fetus in his mother's womb. As a result of this experience, he was able to articulate the theme which lies at the heart of the psychology of symbolic regression:

> I always wonder where or how, but somewhere I've been promised a rose garden. As a fetus, I am completely looked after. But the world outside has been limited. It imposed conditions on me. This has made me angrier than hell. This wasn't the original contract. In my life I have felt outraged. I was taken from a garden and placed in a desert. I was given away. I was placed from home to home. I was shuffled around and I ended with a psychotic woman who was to raise me as my mother. The insult to my garden was epitomized by the Christmas when I saw a new bicycle under the Christmas tree. It was then taken away and put in the garage because of some misdeed I had done. This experience has been the opposite of my experience as a fetus. In the womb I am simply there. I have nothing to earn. There are no performances which can bring me into the state of well being or take me out of it. The circumstances are ideal to survive. I am quiet.
>
> I am now in a new relationship to the rose garden, for it _was_ mine. It was not an illusion. I haven't been crazy for looking for some kind of ideal in my relationships. This really happened to me. I was not hoodwinked. It wasn't given to me in my pablum. I _was_ in a rose garden. There is a rose garden in me, and I am cosmic. Now it is easier to give it up, because it is real. I can choose to give it up because it is my ideal reality, and it is there. I can experience it although I can seldom achieve it. I know that it is real and now I cannot deny it. I must not consider myself strange for seeking it. Nobody did this to me when my back was turned. This is the primal contract of being and it has been handed to me. I cannot stop until I recover what is mine.

Ken's discoveries about himself and about his own reality in this experience of symbolic regression were instrumental in orienting his aspirations and his tasks in his quest for greater consciousness. In this experience he was learning to relate to himself as a symbolic being. He was discovering his integrity as a being who has cosmic dimensions. He was discovering the meaning of his birthright.

THE CLUE TO CONSCIOUSNESS: MAN'S ACCEPTANCE OF HIS SYMBOLIC NATURE

According to Ernst Cassirer, man is an *animal symbolicum*, a symbolizing animal.[9] From this assumption it follows that symbolic representation is at once the essential function of human consciousness and the object of human knowledge. Symbolic representation constitutes a totality that both transcends the perceptual sign and provides a context for it.

When we take seriously what Kant calls his "Copernican Revolution,"

> myth, art, language, and science appear as symbols, forces each of which produces and posits a world of its own. In these realms the spirit exhibits itself in that inwardly determined dialectic by virtue of which alone there is any reality, any organized and definite being at all. Thus the special symbolic forms are not imitations but *organs* of reality, since it is solely by their agency that anything real becomes an object for intellectual apprehension, and as such is made visible to us.... For the mind, only that can be visible which has some definite form; but every form of existence has its source in some peculiar way of seeing, some intellectual formulation and intuition of meaning.[10]

This manifesto of Cassirer's lays the foundation for a symbolic-phenomenological approach to man's world. Man's experience, the content of human consciousness, is not to be described only with the reference to "things out there" of naive realism, but also with reference to the symbolic order.

At this point we must digress in order to situate our understanding of the symbolic order in the broadest possible terms, for symbolic regression psychology begins with the notion that the mind is grounded in mind-transcending reality. The ultimate reality by which psychic functioning is to be known is Being. Three thinkers give us background for understanding this reality. Martin Heidegger has brought Being back into the realm of serious thought in the twentieth century, most significantly through his book, *Being and Time*.[11] Paul Tillich has made the concept of Being the key to his *Systematic Theology* and thus has made it the singular reference point for coherence in discourse which is focused on cosmic speculation.[12] Thirdly, Abraham Maslow has introduced the notion of Being into the discussion of human experience and human behavior, most notably in his book, *Toward a Psychology of Being*.[13]

Abstractly defined, Being is the total field of energy which is the ultimate and absolute condition for any and all phenomena, whether these phenomena take on a psychic or a material mode. In the present use of the term, the emphasis is on the qualities of unity and totality which make the reality to which it refers the most comprehensive one conceivable. Our usage is decidedly non-dualistic. This fact must be kept in mind even where traditionally dualistic concepts have been replaced by the concept of polarity, which will be invoked from time to time for the sake of clarity.

Being may be directly intuited, but it can only be indirectly expressed as a concept. Thus an abstract definition is not adequate to convey this reality to which one can only indirectly refer. Yet, as a symbolizing animal, man can and must suggest it indirectly through his symbols. A developed understanding of the nature of the symbolic will sharpen our sense of this reality. In order to grasp it adequately, we must wisely interpret the words of Chuang Tzu: "The fishing net is used to catch fish. Let us take the fish and forget the net."[14] Here, the symbol, like the net, is only a means to apprehending Being which, like the fish, is elusive although, once apprehended, it makes the net superfluous. From this juxtaposition we realize that it is often the creative expressions of the poets that most adequately hint at or convey a small sense of this reality through their indirect but pregnant use of language. Boethius, for example, the late Latin poet-philosopher, writes of Being as the love that unites all things.[15] Dylan Thomas expresses it as "the force that through the green fuse drives the flower."[16] And William Wordsworth describes his sense of it as:

> A presence that disturbs me with the joy
> Of elevated thoughts; a sense sublime
> Of something far more deeply interfused,
> Whose dwelling is the light of setting suns,
> And the round ocean and the living air,
> And the blue sky, and in the mind of man:
> A motion and a spirit, that impels
> All thinking things, all objects of all thought,
> And rolls through all things.[17]

Being, the ultimate reality, is related to immediate experience or awareness through a doubly mediating reality which consists, objectively, of the symbolic order, and, subjectively, of images or consciousness. If all of these elements were schematized together in a series of four concentric circles, the largest circle would be Being. It is this essentially invisible backdrop of experience which Heidegger writes about. Second, within Being is the symbolic order. The symbolic order is the structure of Being which is at once psychic and physical, coherent and substantial, because it underlies both consciousness and matter. It is the "roughing in" of the house of Being which mediates between Being and man. It is substance becoming consciousness; it is cosmic reality being made personal. This is the dimension focused on by Tillich in his essays on the symbolic. Third, within the symbolic order is its subjective counterpart, image consciousness, the realm of the human psyche. An image as distinguished from a symbol is any given human energy constellation which is both the subject and the object of awareness at any given moment. It is experience itself, the aspect of the symbol which is the experience of the individual and which becomes a constituent part of the individual memory. Finally, within this sphere, as figure in relation to ground, is the immediacy of the individual's present awareness. Maslow focuses on the last two of these circles, the phenomenological dimension of our analysis.

Being itself as the largest sphere can be ranged according to the dimensions which we are here developing in the analysis of consciousness and the symbolic order. These dimensions are: the organic, the personal, and the cosmic. They correspond roughly to the biological conscious, the sociocultural conscious, and the supra conscious in the analysis of Pitirim A. Sorokin, the integral social theorist, in his book, The Ways and Power of Love.[18] A cultural and metaphysical exposition of this same threefold analysis can also be found in C. S. Lewis, The Abolition of Man.[19] Being at the cosmic level is known through mystical insight, through the vision of cosmic unity. Being at the personal level manifests itself in utopian thought and the ideal of community with regard to society, and in self-esteem with regard to the individual. Being at the organic level is manifest as the life force, the elan vital, and is humanly expressed as the affirmation of life.

This same range of Being is again set forth at the most immediate or phenomenological level in the hierarchy of needs developed by Maslow. Maslow gives most urgent priority to

CONSCIOUSNESS

the needs at the organic level, which he calls physiological and safety needs. Second come the needs at the personal level, affiliative and self-esteem needs. Where these prior needs have been relatively met, man can direct his energies to fulfilling his cosmic or self-actualization needs, which include the drive toward individuation, the search for meaning, and the urge to create. We invert Maslow's analysis of the iterrelations of these priorities, in a sense, for the cosmic dimension is the spiritually revitalizing frame of reference which transforms the individual's whole hierarchical need system from the top down.

At any rate, man lives, in Rilke's phrase, in an "interpreted world."[20] Our consideration of man as a symbolic being helps to focus on the problems of ordering and integrating the various levels of human experience. It helps us to face directly the "task of consciousness" as the decisively human task. With this broadest frame of reference firmly in mind, we now return to our consideration of the symbolic order for a closer examination of what we will call the three dimensions of the symbolic order and of their corresponding structure at the subjective level, the three levels of consciousness.

While taking Cassirer's suggestive starting point as our own, we diverge from him for the purpose of ranging the symbolic order which underlies human experience along the lines suggested by Paul Ricoeur. Ricoeur distinguishes among three levels of consciousness, which he calls bios, thumos, and logos.[21] These are what we have called the organic, the personal, and the cosmic levels of consciousness. They correspond more or less to the commonplace Medieval categories, the vegetable soul (or sensation), the animal soul (or imagination), and the spiritual soul (or intellect).[22] These levels are interrelated modalities of man's capacity for symbolic representation. Our distinguishing among them allows us a heuristic perspective which at once accounts for the broad range of human experience and provides a means for the positive reintegration of experience which is the task of consciousness.

Bios, man's organic consciousness, is the first level of consciousness. It consists of his mental energy at the vital level of bodily instincts and physical needs. With this level of consciousness we are able to see man as symbolizing the life of the body, particularly his sexuality. It is this realm to which Freud refers in his doctrine of the unconscious and in his theories of the economics of of instinct and repression. The behaviorists too see man from this perspective—as an animal whose actions can be empirically charted. Symbolizing at this level constitutes consciousness of <u>things</u> in the natural world. The telos or end of this level of consciousness is bodily satiation and pleasure.

<u>Thumos</u>, the second level of consciousness, is man's personal consciousness. This is his mental activity at the level of his social existence. At this level the individual symbolizes himself as an "I" involved with other "I's" who also have the attributes of personal identity. Here the individual defines and understands himself in relation to his passionate strivings toward selfhood in his possessions, his powers, and his self-esteem. This level of consciousness corresponds to Freud's ego, the reality principle, and it is best understood in phenomenological terms as that intentionality which relates every thing or person to a finite, personal self. Symbolizing at this level constitutes the individual's self-consciousness, and his subjectivity and sense of otherness in the intersubjective realm of human society. At this level the individual is aware of the existenial dimension, both in his family relationships and in his having a social and an historical role. He is also aware of his self-identity as this is projected in the manifestations of his culture. The telos of this consciousness is not reducible to terms of means and ends. Rather, this telos is a process, the open-ended quest to substantiate the self and ultimately to affirm one's sense of self-worth.

<u>Logos</u>, or cosmic consciousness, the third level, is man's mental energy as he participates in the total order of energy and flux. At this level of consciousness man symbolizes the life of the spirit, his ultimate intuition of the meaning of Being. This level no longer concerns the individual relating to entities as a finite "I." Rather, intentionality is here directed to Being rather than to entities, if we might apply Heidegger's fundamental distinction. This is, as it were, intentionality toward the "whole." Symbolizing at this level constitutes transpersonal consciousness of Being. The telos of this consciousness is an ultimate sense of peace and harmony, the enduring repose which has been called "the peace of God which passes all understanding."

We began with the correlation between symbolic representation and human consciousness which is a primary assumption in Cassirer's philosophy. From this it is natural to expect that there is a "dimension" or modality of symbolism which

CONSCIOUSNESS   13

corresponds to each of the levels of consciousness which we
have described. This expectation is more or less fulfilled
if we follow Ricoeur's analysis in Freud and Philosophy and
The Symbolism of Evil. Ricoeur begins his analysis of the
modalities of symbolism with the observation that all three
of the dimensions of consciousness are made present in every
authentic symbol.[23] And much of Freud and Philosophy is
devoted to discussing how the three dimensions of symbolism
interplay (pp. 506-51).[24] Yet Ricoeur does not hesitate to
distinguish these as three distinct dimensions. They are:
the oneiric, the poetic, and the hierophanic dimensions of
symbolism.

The oneiric dimension of symbolism is related to the
cosmic dimension:

> Cosmos and psyche are the two poles of the same
> "expressivity": I express myself in expressing the
> world; I explore my own sacrality in deciphering
> that of the world. (The Symbolism of Evil, p. 13)

Yet this dimension, the dimension of dream symbols, primarily expresses the biological level of consciousness if
we read dreams in Freudian terms. The archaic quality of
dream symbolism, when it is interpreted from the perspective
of a Freudian economics, is such that these symbols are

> sedimented symbolism, various stereotyped and
> fragmented remains of symbols, symbols so common-
> place and worn with use that they have nothing
> but a past . . . here the work of creative symboli-
> zation is no longer operative. [Dream symbols are
> mere] vestiges on the plane of sedimented
> expressions. (Freud and Philosophy, pp. 504-05)

The poetic dimension of symbolism is the cultural
dimension of imagination and it is expressed in the diver-
sity of the arts, particularly the verbal arts. At this
level symbols are expressions of creativity and are commonly
taken as objects. As opposed to the archaic sedimented
symbols of dreams, poetic symbols are "prospective symbols":
they are creations of meaning that take up the traditional
symbols with their multiple significations and transform
them to serve as the vehicles of new meanings. The process
of creating meaning reflects the vitality of the symbol as
it becomes a vehicle for cosmic energy to manifest itself
at the personal level. Such creative symbolization is the
means of man's self-consciousness, for the individual knows

himself as a self indirectly through the cultural objects which explore his human possibilities and provide him with an image of man's ultimate dignity:

> When Van Gogh sketches a chair, he at the same time portrays man; he projects a figure of man, namely the man who "has" this represented world. Thus, the various modes of cultural expression give these "images" the density of "thingness"; they make these images exist between men and among men, by embodying them in "works." It is through the medium of these works and monuments that a human dignity and self-regard are formed. Finally, this is the level at which man can become alienated from himself, degrade himself, make a fool of himself, destroy himself. (p. 510)

Thus self-consciousness is symbolically represented to a large extent through man's cultural objects. Yet the potential of this creative symbolic dimension is ambiguous, as Ricoeur warns. Self-consciousness, or reflection, uses the symbolic in this sense.

> Reflection is not so much a justification of science and duty as a reappropriation of our effort to exist; . . . I am lost, "led astray" among objects and separated from the center of my existence. [This condition] signifies that I do not at first possess what I am. . . . That is why reflection is a task—the task of making my concrete experience equal to the positing of "I am." The positing of self is not given, it is a task. (Freud and Philosophy, p. 45)

It is the third dimension, the dimension of cosmic symbolism, to which we must have recourse in order to find the key to man's wholeness as a conscious being.

The hierophanic or cosmic dimension of symbolism is expressed in myths, rituals, and the language of the sacred. Ricoeur treats this dimension extensively in his book, The Symbolism of Evil:

> First of all it is the sun, the moon, the waters—that is to say, cosmic realities—that are symbols. For these realities to become a symbol is to gather together at one point a mass of significations which, before giving rise to thought, give rise to speech . . . Thus, the symbol-thing

is the potentiality of innumerable spoken symbols
which are knotted together in a single cosmic
manifestation. . . . Spoken symbols and symbols
of the self are already on the way to cutting
themselves loose from the cosmic roots of symbolism. The progress in the development of these
cosmic symbols in the evolution of human consciousness is from cosmic to narrative to historical to
fully interiorized reference. [Yet,] the richness
of this symbolism, even when it is fully interiorized, is the corollary of its cosmic roots.
(pp. 11-12)

According to the phenomenology of religion, the
myth-narration is only the verbal envelope of a
form of life, felt and lived before being formulated; this form of life expresses itself first
in an inclusive mode of behavior relative to the
whole of things; it is in the rite rather than
in the narration that this behavior is expressed
most completely, and the language of the myth is
only the verbal segment of this total action.
. . . Thus, the phenomenology of religion
seems to dissolve the myth-narration in an undi-
vided consciousness that consists less in telling
stories, making myths, than in relating itself
affectively and practically to the whole of things.
(p. 166)

Paradoxically, this dimension of cosmic symbolism is ultimately creative by virtue of its being ultimately regressive.
Opposites meet, and man finds himself as a cosmic being.
Theodore Roethke expresses this conjunction of regressive
and cosmic elements in the concluding lines to his major
poem, "North American Sequence":

Near this rose, in this grove of sun-parched,
    wind-warped madronas,
Among the half-dead trees,
    I came upon the true ease of myself,
As if another man appeared
    out of the depths of my being,
And I stood outside myself,
Beyond becoming and perishing,
A something wholly other,
As if I swayed out on the wildest wave alive,
And yet was still.
And I rejoiced in being what I was:

In the lilac change, the white reptilian calm,
In the bird beyond the bough, the single one
With all the air to greet him as he flies . . .[25]

A symbol is a unit of expression or experience, whether language, gesture, or natural entity, which functions as a basic component of the act of consciousness. Symbols may be used as signs, as referential, non-emotive units of language. When they are so used, they are transparent, pointing to things, and the individual is able to manipulate his environment through them. Symbols may also be used with an emphasis not on their reference but rather on their sense. In this case, the symbol indicates some element of man's sense of his meaning as an end in itself rather than merely designating an object for the sake of some instrumental purpose. With such a use, the symbol functions in terms of its opacity. It suggests or points to the reality or plenitude of intention rather than to mere things.[26]

The task which Socrates made central for his life and for philosophy when he said that "the unexamined life is not worth living" is summed up in the oracular command, "Know thyself."[27] This task, when based on the reality of the individual's birthright, is the task of consciousness. Yet the goal of self-knowledge is not an achievement to be attained once for all as a result of simply applying a given method, for the self is by its very nature hidden and changing. The self must be approached by continuing effort and by indirect methods. It can only be known indirectly, by the symbol as Ricoeur defines it. Man is a symbolic being and his self-knowledge, as all of his knowledge, is constituted by his symbols. Thus, the more a man understands about the nature and function of symbols as symbols and the more he understands of his own particular uses of symbols, the more he understands his own nature. Because of the evolution of consciousness, the split between the existential and the visionary poles of experience which comes with forgetting one's birthright now enables us to recover the nature of symbol as symbol in a way that was not possible up to this time. As a result, we are now in a better position to understand ourselves as conscious, symbolic beings than every before in man's history.

Man must learn to see himself as a symbolic being. He must learn to use all three dimensions of symbols—the oneiric, the poetic, and the cosmic—in order to express and to understand his being. Man must use words as necessary but limited representations of himself. He must see the kind of insight that orients his relationship to all of

Being. He must learn to listen with the kind of hearing that responds to all three of the dimensions of his nature as well.

At the root of western tradition we find words of Jesus which seem to push man towards this kind of symbolic self-understanding. Jesus' use of symbolic language in his teaching is exemplary for man's cosmic self-understanding. In fact, he stresses the importance of using the symbolic as a means of self and cosmic-relatedness when he explains why he teaches in parables in Matthew 13. First, he speaks of seeing and hearing to distinguish between mere understanding at the level of referential signs and understanding through attunement to the depth meaning of symbols: "While seeing they do not see, and while hearing they do not hear, nor do they understand" (Matthew 13:13). That is, symbolic understanding or cosmic-relatedness is not something everyone experiences. Yet, by his exhortation, Jesus teaches that this kind of perception can be learned; "He who has ears to hear, let him hear" (V. 9). This kind of perception is a matter of the will according to the passage from Isaiah which is used to support his point: "they will not hear" (v. 15). Yet this symbolic understanding has a positive effect.

>They will see with their eyes,
>And hear with their ears
>And understand with their heart, and turn again,
>And I will heal them.[28]

The seeing and hearing which are more than mere sensory perception result in a depth understanding which leads to healing which is both wholeness and health. Once the nature and effects of symbolic understanding are clearly set forth, Jesus then explains the parable of the sower which was given before (vv. 3-8). The parable itself is about this very principle of symbolic understanding: "The one on whom seed was sown on the good ground, this is the man who hears the word and understands it . . ." (v. 23).

The principle of symbolic understanding is applied throughout the teaching of Jesus. He consistently uses natural symbols—light, the agricultural cycle, water—and stories to teach his message of man's cosmic-relatedness. The primary symbol in all of the teaching of Jesus is the father. In the Sermon on the Mount, for example, this image is used eighteen times with reference to cosmic-relatedness, no doubt because it so effectively integrates both personal and cosmic dimensions of consciousness into one experienced symbol. This double usage of father is again reflected in the epistle to the Ephesians: ". . . I bow before the Father from whom all fatherhood, earthly or heavenly, derives its name" (3:14f).

Man as a spiritual being, as a being having a cosmic level of consciousness, is part of a reality which is not knowable by the usual perceptual processes, by signs referring to objects in his day to day experience. Man's spiritual consciousness consists of an intuitive kind of perception which understands the self in relation to cosmic meaning through his depth symbols. Man's reality ultimately lies in the cosmic level of consciousness which transcends his own finite self-awareness and of which this awareness is only a part. This cosmic level of consciousness feeds his awareness and actually grounds it so that self-awareness is possible within a cosmic context. Man's perception of his reality as a spiritual being, his awareness of his relationship to a universe of meaning which corresponds to his personal existence, is the foundation of all mental and emotional wholeness. This cosmic perception is a kind of faith--not a cognitive assent to propositional statements. Rather, it is the intuitive apperception which is characterized by a child's sense of trust and it is the sense of cosmic fidelity characterized as "faithfulness" in Martin Buber's distinction between faith and belief in Two Types of Faith.[29] It is this kind of spiritual responsiveness to the ultimate nature of things to which Jesus refers when he talks about healing faith:

> As thou hast believed, so be it done unto thee. . . .
> According to your faith be it unto you. . . .
> Thy faith hath made thee whole.
> (Matthew 8:13; 9:29; 9:22)

Each time Jesus makes a person whole in this healing ministry he thus specifically refers the healing event to the individual's awareness of the cosmic dimensions of his being. This awareness is the starting point for consciousness and for psychotherapy. The individual's consciousness must be affirmed as an integral part of universal or cosmic consciousness. The purpose of the theory of symbolic regression psychology is to explain how and why it is absolutely necessary for psychology to start with this point.

THE CHALLENGE TO CONSCIOUSNESS:
THE DAWN OF THE COSMIC AGE

When we go back far enough in our anthropological theorizing to start with the idea that man is a symbolizing being, we range ourselves with the most broadly speculative of thinkers. With this scope of thought we find ourselves in the tradition of those who incisively combine their creative analytical awareness of human experience with far-ranging metaphysical intuitions, thinkers such as William James, Karl Jaspers, C. G. Jung, and Teilhard de Chardin. Such men are speculative philosophers as well as sharply intuitive psychologists. The anthropological and cosmic speculations of two in particular are helpful for our explorations at this point. Pierre Teilhard de Chardin, the Jesuit paleontologist, highlights the biological and cosmic aspects of the evolution of human consciousness in his book, The Phenomenon of Man.[30] And Karl Jaspers sketches the historical dimensions of this evolution in The Origin and Goal of History.[31] The combined free speculation and creative thinking in these writers provides a comprehensive scope for understanding man's evolving struggle for consciousness, and thereby allows for a new and more adequate integration of the cosmic, personal, and organic dimensions of human experience.

Man's struggle for consciousness has always been his struggle to relate his self-reflective processes to the ground of his being. A consideration of this struggle in terms of its historical development helps us to situate the task of consciousness and thereby to understand the uniqueness of this task as it now confronts us.

Chardin's schematic description of the evolution of consciousness provides a history of consciousness of the broadest possible scope. He describes this evolution as a process of developing complexity and intensifying organization which consists of four stages. At the outset, matter gains complexity by its own inherent organizing principles. Then there is the evolution of life and animal sentience. This is followed by the emergence of human self-consciousness. The final stage, towards which we are now evolving, is the state in which transpersonal consciousness becomes universal and man finds his fulfillment as a cosmic being. The last three of these stages correspond to the development of the organic, the personal, and the cosmic dimensions of consciousness in man.

Chardin's vision presents the cosmic dimensions of man's existence. Keeping this cosmic frame of reference in mind, we can now narrow our scope to human history for a more intensive analysis. Karl Jaspers posits four major turning points in the total history of human consciousness, and a fifth one which is about to emerge. First is the threshold of the prehistoric Promethean Age in which speech, tools, and fire came about, and through which man became man, the symbolizing being. The second phase is the period of ancient civilizations (5000-3000 B.C.). This period served as a basis for and a transition to the third phase, which Jaspers sees as "the axis of world history," the period from 800 to 200 B.C. At this point, the development of human consciousness took its most decisive turn: self-reflection became central in man's psychic functioning. As a result, the spiritual foundations of humanity were laid, and man began to unfold his full human potentialities. Jaspers tells the meaning of this transformation:

> Man becomes conscious of Being as a whole, of himself and his limitations. He experiences the terror of the world and his own powerlessness. He asks radical questions. Face to face with the world he strives for liberation and redemption. By consciously recognizing his limits he sets himself the highest goals. He experiences absoluteness in the depths of selfhood and in the lucidity of transcendence. (p. 2)

For Jaspers, this "Axial Period" is the basis upon which mankind still lives. Yet, out of the last several centuries of European development there has emerged a fourth period, the scientific-technological age which is characterized by the consciousness of universal history and of the global unity of man. This fourth period is now radically transforming the style and quality of human life throughout the world. Jaspers compares this period with the first one, also a threshold of technological advancement, calling it "the new Promethean Age" (p. 24). He speculates that, just as the Promethean Age of prehistory led up to the transformation of consciousness in the Axial Period, so it is possible that the modern scientific-technological age, by its current transformations of man's possibilities, may be ushering in a further turning point, "a new, second Axial Period, the final process of becoming-human" (p. 24). He gives ideal characteristics to this future phase. It will be

the world of humanity dominating the globe, when it
has entered into the unity of its legally ordered
existence, whose spiritual and material horizons
are infinite. (p. 26)

Jaspers thus thinks that man's radical technological
advances have created a kind of tension in human existence
which is the necessary condition to evoke a corresponding
breakthrough or revolution in the development of consciousness.

With the hopeful anticipations about man's future
development posited by both Chardin and Jaspers before us,
let us consider the evolution of human consciousness along
the lines they have suggested. John Cobb, a contemporary
Protestant theologian, distinguishes three psychic functions
in his analysis of the development of consciousness.[32]
First, there is receptive consciousness, or animal sentience, the psychic activity which is a general responsiveness
to the field of energy within which the individual exists.
Second, there is reflective consciousness, or imagination,
the power to relate external stimuli to the symbolic order.
This consciousness emerges as the origin of man at the
opening of the Promethean Age. It is originally determined
by mythical thinking, the psychic activity characterized by
direct symbolization. It gradually emerges in its autonomy
as this is expressed in rational thinking, the kind of
psychic activity which elementary logic attempts to bring
to self-consciousness. The centrality of reflective
consciousness in the development of the human psyche is
emphasized in Cobb's analysis:

Reflective consciousness is necessarily symbolic,
primordially mythical, but incipiently rational.
It is necessarily symbolic, because reflection is
possible only in symbols. It is primordially
mythical, because the process of symbolization
was originally unconscious and determined by the
laws of psychic satisfaction as such. It is
incipiently rational, because its attention is
directed to data supplied by the receptive consciousness. (p. 49)

If the emergence of symbolization marks the emergence of
man, then the moment reflective consciousness becomes autonomous it becomes a new center for psychic life. This is
the moment when man begins to be an active participant in
the process of his own evolution. This moment is the Axial

Period. As Chardin's theory suggests, this is the moment of greater complexification and greater concentration of man's functioning, and it is thus the moment which calls forth a greater integration of man's total powers.

Man's attainment of autonomous reflective consciousness means that he can now choose to move toward or away from the other elements of consciousness which Cobb analyzes. The stylized description of the evolution of man's response to cosmic symbolism given by the history of religions school may not be totally accurate historically. But it does provide a continuous path which man can retrace if he determines to attain the kind of integration which his present state of evolved consciousness now calls forth. An overview of this description will thus help us to see this path. On the basis of the work of Mircea Eliade in The Myth of the Eternal Return, and of Ricoeur in The Symbolism of Evil (pp. 6-12), we derive three cumulative stages in the development of man's cosmic symbolizing.[33]

The first stage is the stage of hierophanic symbols. In this stage, cosmic realities--sun, moon, waters--are taken as symbols. At this stage the given symbol is a hierophany, a naked representation of the totality of meaning. At this stage biological and cosmic consciousness seem to be one, and personal consciousness is not yet differentiated. Here consciousness represents itself in the conjunction of nature (bios) and meaning (logos). This stage marks the power of the symbol in its nascence. It is by nature prehistoric and thus a part of the Promethean Age, because it is atemporal.

The second stage might be called the stage of mythical consciousness. It begins with the dawn of history in the rise of ancient civilizations and is characterized by rites and narrated symbolizing which represent the self within the cosmic order. At this stage man's symbolizing activity is on its way towards cutting itself off from the cosmic grounds of symbolism. The world is known as a cosmic drama, an ideal history, and it is represented in myths, rites, and dramatic productions. At this level, narratives represent the hierophany as the object of human longing in the pattern of loss and desire, for mythical and narrative modes of symbolizing move man a step away from the cosmic roots of his consciousness towards historical and personal dimensions of his existence.

The third stage is that of autonomous rational consciousness. This stage was inaugurated in the Axial Period when reason began its autonomous course. Autonomous reason has now reached its apotheosis in the development of empiricism in the modern scientific-technological period. In this stage of autonomy, man no longer relates in traditional ways to the cosmic dimension of symbols. Self-reflective consciousness is abstracted from other levels of man's being. The individual finds himself isolated, cut off from nature and from other persons. His symbols represent only his interior states as they appear to exist apart from society and the cosmos outside of himself. He exists as a fragment of consciousness in a disjointed world. But by the same process, he has also become open to new, higher possibilities of individuality and freedom. Man has become an existential being, the being who must choose how he is to fulfill himself and his destiny.

The second stage includes developments that lead to the third. These developments merit some consideration. Two elements of autonomous consciousness came about through the rise of Christianity. First, the sacred history which Christianity adapted from the Old Testament replaced the mythic consciousness of ancient man with historical consciousness. This historical consciousness developed away from cosmic awareness to the point where it became a major characteristic of secular, historicized, modern man. Along with this shift from cosmos to history came a second change: the intensification of self-consciousness. Both of these changes can be seen in St. Augustine, a person who bridges gentile and Christian moments in the development of man's consciousness. First, Augustine is shocked to find St. Ambrose reading silently when he meets him in Milan.[34] Ambrose did not need to vocalize, as man had done until his time, because the new intensity of self-awareness which came about in the Christian era allowed the person to recognize his inner self, not his body, as the recipient of written symbols. Second, Augustine is the first among many persons to write a comprehensive philosophy of history, the City of God.

This shift toward self- and historical consciousness at the beginning of the Christian era was further intensified at the Enlightenment, when the hierophanic element of the Christian myth itself was itself set aside for the reign of empirical reason. Mind and world, however, were dissociated in this process. Rene Descartes is at the center of this shift, for he theorized an absolute separation between experience or consciousness (the res cogitans) and the world or matter (the res extensa). At once this Cartesian division made it possible for man to represent the world in ways that gave him power over it and led to the rise of modern science and technology. But this gain was a costly one, for in it man furthered his neglect of his capacity to represent himself as a direct participant in the cosmos. Cut off by Cartesian doubt, he no longer sought recourse to the older uses of symbols which were the life blood of traditional mythical consciousness.

T. S. Eliot expresses the nature of this shift at the level of man's cultural imagination in his analysis of what happened to poetry in the seventeenth century. At that time, he says, a "dissociation of sensibility" set in so that poets since then may be "masters of diction," but they are no longer "explorers of the soul." Until that time poets were able to

> feel their thought as immediately as the odour of a rose. A thought was an experience; it modified [the poet's] sensibility.[35]

Since that time, Eliot maintains, poets express a fundamental disjunction between thought and feeling, and between self-representation and the cosmic order.

Thus in recent times, technology has developed along with an intensifying problem of fractured consciousness. Man has extended his powers to the point where he now has almost unlimited control of things. Computer and electronic technologies have put massive human populations at the disposal of a few individuals. Rocket technology, as the ultimate step in this process, has finally made it possible for man to transcend his terrestial limits. Man has ushered himself into the Space Age. But space travel, this last extension of his technological achievements, has once again confronted man with the cosmic dimension of his being, his ultimate part in the cosmos as a whole. Thus the exploration of technological frontiers is finally pushing us back to the cosmic/psychic frontier and to the discovery that the complete interiorization of man's self representations is at bottom "the corollary of his cosmic roots" (Symbolism of Evil, p. 12).

The shift from mythical consciousness to rational consciousness is indeed a very long process, one that has occupied the whole history of man. The fact is, however, that as much as modern man has become a rational being he is also still completely involved in mythical consciousness, for each stage in the development of consciousness

builds on the ones which have preceded it. This whole
evolutionary process leads to the unprecedented position of
modern man. Now man must participate in directing his own
evolution by choosing how to use and develop his various
powers. The second Axial Period, which Jaspers envisions
and which man can choose to bring about, will be the age of
transpersonal consciousness. This higher level of consciousness, already previewed in widespread experiences of diverse
individuals over the last several centuries and now being
studied by humanistic psychology, will be characterized by
an integration of all of man's hitherto developed levels of
consciousness and of symbolization. This integration is to
be a recapitulation of the mythicizing consciousness which
was predominant in the earlier parts of man's history and of
the receptive awareness which is the psychological substratum
common to all sentient beings. The new element in this
recapitulation is that it is to be done from within the
latest element of human consciousness: autonomous reflective
consciousness. That is, man can now choose to gain access
to, to activate, and to develop these older, deeper layers in
the evolution of his consciousness.

As Ricoeur puts it, man's very loss of contact with the
cosmic dimension of his being is precisely the condition
which opens up a new possibility: for the first time in the
development of human consciousness we are now in a position
to use symbols as symbols and myths as myths. Only now can
we recover the mythical dimension as such for our self-understanding:

> In every way, something has been lost, irremediably
> lost: immediacy of belief. But if we can no
> longer live the great symbolism of the sacred in
> accordance with the original belief in them, we can,
> we modern men, aim at a second naivete in and through
> criticism. In short, it is by interpreting that we
> can hear again. (Symbolism of Evil, p. 351)

Indeed, it is this hearing of cosmic relatedness to which
Ricoeur at the dawning of the Space Age summons us. With
T. S. Eliot we must now resolve to take up this new dimension in our explorations:

> We shall not cease from exploration
> And the end of all our exploring
> Will be to arrive where we started
> And know the place for the first time.
> ("Little Gidding," V)

Man's ascent into space is the realization of a dream that man has had since ancient times. Cosmic flight is an integral part of Plato's imagining in his myth of the transmigration of souls. According to Socrates, the soul after death joins the gods in coursing through the Zodiac of the heavens:

> Amidst that happy company we beheld with our eyes
> that blessed vision, ourselves in the train of Zeus,
> others following some other god . . . free from all
> alloy, steadfast and blissful were the spectacles
> on which we gazed in the moment of final revelation;
> pure was the light that shone around us, and pure
> were we . . . .
> (Phaedrus 250b-c) [36]

St. Paul, too, remembers a cosmic flight: "fourteen years ago [I] was caught up to the third heaven . . . into Paradise, and heard inexpressible words, which a man is not permitted to speak" (II Corinthians 12:2-4). Likewise, in Cicero's account of Scipio's dream, Scipio receives political wisdom from his father and grandfather from the extraterrestrial perspective of the fixed stars.[37] Extraterrestrial experience is also a major theme in writings of Dante, Rabelais, Cervantes, Ariosto, Milton, Kepler, Fontenelle, and Swedenborg.[38] With these recurring symbolic associations preceding it, man's actual entry into the Space Age means that we now need to rediscover the cosmic dimension of our being. This new mode of relating to our cosmic dimensions rekindles the need to explore our inner life with the excitement which the new symbols from actual experience in space provide.

Any technology as mere control obliterates man's oneness with the universe. Such an obliteration inevitably results in the disruption of man's contact with the biological, personal, and cosmic levels of his being. For man to acknowledge and express his essential nature as a spiritual being, it is necessary for him to go beyond the material dimensions of his existence. For the development of consciousness to take place, man must make use of all of the resources which his mind and his culture can provide. As he works to integrate the various disciplines and the diverse modes of discourse which are at his disposal, man will find that together they yield potential for an integration that man has hardly dared to dream of.

The significance of the cosmic dimension for psychotherapy cannot be stressed enough. For without integrating all of the disciplines into an understanding of man in his cosmic context, nothing but the denigration of consciousness can result, even in the healing frame of reference of psychotherapy. The cosmic dimension of consciousness is absolutely indispensible for every phase of human development.

When the Apollo rocket blasts off from its launching pad, the area is flooded with humans watching the ascent of the craft through the sound and space barriers. In the experience of this accelerating lift-off, man envisions himself as a microcosm of meaning within the immensity of the universe. What a man perceives in the launching of the Apollo rocket, however, is analogous to a far greater psychic reality. In a sense, man himself, during his evolutionary development, has blasted off and launched himself into an equally awesome inner universe of self-consciousness. He has blasted himself beyond the limits of instinctive consciousness into the realm of cosmic consciousness. His very substance as a conscious being now enables him to will to participate in cosmic change. Man must once again become aware of and begin to actualize his potential harmony with his psychic space. This psychic space, to which he has gained access by becoming a being with autonomous reflective consciousness and into which he has thrust himself, is the very means by which he is becoming transformed. We must therefore learn to interpret ourselves through creatively integrating the diverse powers of our consciousness. These powers can only be provided by a psychology which acknowledges man's potential consciousness in the cosmic dimension. Such a psychology will help man to discover the dynamics of his relationship to Being, and thereby continually alter his nature as he travels through the expanding galaxies of his own inner space. On this symbolic journey man will discover his own cosmic self with the same sense of wonder which Plato said was the beginning of philosophy and which Keats expressed at discovering the symbolic realm of Homer's poetry:

> Then felt I like some watcher of the skies
> When a new planet swims into his ken;
> Or like stout Cortez when with eagle eyes
> He star'd at the Pacific—and all his men
> Look'd at each other with a wild surmise—
> Silent, upon a peak in Darien.[39]

As a person who has probed and explored these frontiers for quite some time now, I have come to the point where I can now express my understanding of conscious living as the ability to turn myself over to those deeper dimensions of my inner self which make it possible to decide just what it is that I want. I have come to the state of feeling that what I want _is_ what I am—at the same time that what I am is harmonious with all of Being. Moreover, what is harmonious with Being is harmonious with my being. My life has become harmonious with Being. I feel, as a result, that for me there is very little difference between what it means to be alive and what it might mean for me to be dead. Because my life harmonizes with the energies which are propelling me into consciousness, I am not afraid of what life brings to me. I can decide to accept and to relate to those energies in ways that harmonize my self-reflective processes, and that cause me intuitively to understand the essential nature of Being as it relates to my day to day existence. I can think about the nature of the tasks which I perform in my role as a scientist with an awareness of the larger cosmic meaning of these tasks. Neither I nor anyone else must allow himself to become degraded in his being by the depersonalizing pressures of the age of technology. We must find ourselves as persons by relating more completely than ever to the ground of our being.

Not long ago, I had a dream which seems to represent my growing sense of cosmic integration and harmony in symbolic language, the only means possible for man to understand himself as a cosmic being:

> On a plane flight for what seemed like many days, we had long since passed what I considered my destination. I questioned the hostess about our being so long overdue and she said, "Oh, you are one of those who believe our destination is earth. Well, our destination is not earth—it is outer space."
> I said, "Well, I did not sign up for this trip."
> She said, "This is not a flight that anyone signs up for. You are either on it or you are not." I was resigning myself to my fate when she continued, "We will soon be docking with the outer space ship, and of course there is no return."
> We docked and entered the outer space ship. Then I could feel the ship hurtling through space at millions of miles per hour. Disoriented, I half floated and half stood in this craft which seemed to be moving without gravity. When I saw the darkened

skies and the stars passing outside I realized that
whatever it was that I was heading for, I was not to
return to where I came from.
 I said that this was more than I could take.
The pitching and rolling made me nauseous; I did not
believe that I could complete the journey. Someone
answered that this was merely a transitional phase
and that soon we would be docking with the "spaceless
spacecraft." Then I felt the shuddering of the ship
as the two craft joined.
 As we left the spaceship I was told, "We have now
reached the boundaries of the universe. We are
passing beyond into spaceless space." I looked back
and saw the darkness of the universe and all its
millions of lights, its stars, its suns and moons.
Then as I looked ahead I noticed that we were entering gray-blue soft light. Here was total freedom of
movement and we were floating through infinity. I
was told we were in formless form, timeless time,
and spaceless space.
 A young woman passed down the line, taking
passengers' names in gold symbols on her blue pad.
She tried to pass me by, but I stopped her. She
said my name was too long for space symbols. I took
her tablet and wrote my name across it in pencil. I
told her the important thing was to have my name,
whether or not she could reduce it to symbols. Then
I was told that there were no beds or food, because
the time for eating and sleeping would never come.

This dream has had a profound effect on me. It deepened my
sense of the eternal dimension of my being. The dream itself
was a very relaxing experience and as a result of this dream
I gained a feeling of immense tranquillity and of oneness
with all of life. I felt as if I had gained access to a
realm which at once went beyond yet also included the problems, pressures, and demands of my personal and professional
life. It was as if the promise of life had come true for me.

 This dream, constituted by the imagery of travel in
outer space, actually represents the discovery and exploration of that inner space which is man's because man is a
cosmic being. It dramatizes a profound integration of the
self with its cosmic roots, for consciousness significantly
develops in the course of the dream: my unwilling and
involuntary participation in an unknown journey at the outset
changes to my resignation and wonder as the journey becomes a
cosmic one; finally, it changes to my active self-inscribing

as the experience begins to transcend the dimensions of
space and time. The developing symbols of the self-
transforming flight and of the question of "signing up"
represent the cosmic and the personal dimensions of the process of man's becoming conscious of himself as a cosmic
being. This becoming conscious is the ultimate scope of
human development, and the dynamics of this process are the
dynamics of symbolic regression. The development of consciousness thus points to and is built upon symbolic
regression. The principle of symbolic regression is the key
to consciousness.

THE TASK OF CONSCIOUSNESS:
THE PATH BEYOND FREUD

Behavioristic and Freudian psychological theories both
take the biological dimension of man as their starting point
and generalize from the study of those aspects of human
existence which are pre-reflective and instinctual. The
importance of man's biological dimension cannot be denied.
But we begin with the assumption that an entirely different
approach to man's psyche is necessary, one which will incorporate this dimension along with the personal and cosmic
dimensions into a larger perspective, for approaches to the
human psyche limited to man's biological dimension are inadequate to cope with the total range of human consciousness.

Human consciousness is not merely a specific and complex
organization of chemical entities which have come together
by chance in the randomness of galactic space. The evolution
of physical organisms to the point where they have become man
as he is recognized today has taken place along with a second
kind of evolutionary process, one that has placed man in
another sphere altogether. That second process is the
development of human consciousness, man's symbolizing
behavior. Chardin begins with the assumption that the complexifying development of consciousness along with the
organic aspect of man is a fundamental principle in man's
evolution:

> The vitalization of matter has been involved with
> the growth of psychism within more and more
> interiorized organic systems, that is, living super
> molecules. (The Phenomenon of Man, p. 171)

In the long process of the evolution of his consciousness,

man has thus arrived at the point where he is aware that he knows himself as a reflective being. Having arrived at this point in his autonomous self-awareness, man's basic substance has been altered. He has become a different being than he had been until this point in his development. He has turned certain of his psychic energies back upon themselves and has entered into a new phase of his existence.

As a result, the psychology of man today cannot aid man in his self-understanding and personal integration unless it approaches him as a cosmic being, a being whose qualities make him absolutely and fundamentally different in both kind and degree from non-reflective sentient beings. Such a psychology of man cannot treat man's relationship to time, to space, to nature, to his capacity to innovate, and to his social experience as mere elaborations of pre-reflective animal existence. In the development of his psychic structure, man has gone beyond this plane of mere sentient existence. Yet at the same time he is continuous with it. His distinctness from and his continuity with animal sentience, taken together, is the principle which makes it possible for him to continue to develop into consciousness. Actually, it is dangerous to think of man merely in terms of animal instincts because instinct is merely the expression of man's lower, organic needs; it is other levels of consciousness which actually direct man's psychic energies. To attempt to explain these other levels of man's being as nothing more than elaborations or extensions of instinct is to deny the dimension of man's consciousness which opens him up to fully exploring his inner universe.

Animal sentience is of a different cosmic substance than reflective intelligence. This fact does not denigrate the results of scientific research on animal instincts. Rather, it should serve as a challenge for man to reflect critically on the limits of his present scientific knowledge so that he may discover realities which lie beyond the scope of scientific method as it is now practiced. Thomas S. Kuhn's description of the revolutions in man's scientific knowledge suggests what is now needed in psychological theory. He describes several of the major innovators in the history of science:

> Each of them necessitated the community's rejection of one time-honored scientific theory in favor of another incompatible with it. Each produced a consequent shift in the problems available for scientific scrutiny and in the standards by which

the profession determined what should count as an admissible problem or as a legitimate problem-solution. And each transformed the scientific imagination in ways that we shall ultimately need to describe as a transformation of the world within which scientific work was done.40

It is now time for man to begin to understand himself with a new conceptual model, a paradigm of man based on his existence as a cosmic-symbolic being. It is now time for man to incorporate a different method into his researches. The kind of theorizing which I am calling for on the frontiers of human consciousness must be abductive and dialectical rather than inductive and empirical or deductive and rational. Only from a phenomenological starting point based on clinical and practical experience is it possible to determine what issues evoked by consciousness are most important to deal with at inductive and deductive levels. The breakthrough in consciousness now re-symbolized by the launching of superterrestial space travel has once again put man in critical need of developing his self-reflective capacities. As a result, abduction or dialectical thought, reasoning leading from conscious experience to the discovery of its hidden ground, is now the kind of thinking man needs in order to determine what kinds of issues he must confront in his pursuit of psychological understanding.

Human faith, human hope, and human love are not on the same level of existence as instinct. As a consequence, they cannot be understood on the same basis. Human consciousness as a distinct and relatively new reality must be taken into account. Man's self-reflectiveness must become the new frame of reference within which psychological theory is developed. The disciplines of philosophy, theology, and anthropology must be taken together for an adequate psychology of the human being. The psychologist must be an artist in the sphere of human consciousness in the ancient sense of the Greek word for artist, tekton. At the root of this word is techne, "art," "craft," or "skill." Tekton thus refers to the "builder" or "carpenter," the one who applies these powers. The psychologist is a tekton in this sense. He has both the creative intuition to discern the elements of experience in relation to the symbolic order, and the practical skill to apply this discernment in developing an understanding of consciousness. He brings self-consciousness into relation with its ground.

CONSCIOUSNESS

The problem of scientific knowledge in psychology is not whether man learns by conditioning, or to what extent he learns in this manner. It is obvious that man is instinctual and that he learns in this way. It is also obvious that experimentation in animal psychology provides much helpful understanding of human behavior. The real problem is this: how does the element of conditioning in human behavior relate to man's nature as a self-reflective being? How can trust, love, and optimism be taught? In other words, has man developed a unique learning apparatus in his development of self-reflective consciousness? If man has indeed made this fundamental step in the evolution of consciousness, then what will enable him to keep himself rooted in the primal ground of his being and thus to live in relation to his cosmic meaning?

In answer to these questions I now believe that within each person's inner being there is a point of natural harmony with all of Being. I now believe man's adventure as a cosmic being means that each person can begin to experience the attitude of consciousness expressed in Walt Whitman's "Song of Myself":

All goes onward and outward—nothing collapses;
And to die is different from what any one supposed,
    and luckier.

Has any one supposed it lucky to be born?
I hasten to inform him or her, it is just as lucky to
    die, and I know it.

And I know I am solid and sound;
To me the converging objects of the universe perpetually
    flow;
All are written to me, and I must get what the writing
    means.

I know I am deathless;
I know this orbit of mine cannot be swept by the
    carpenter's compass;
I know I shall not pass like a child's curlycue cut
    with a burnt stick at night.

I know I am august;
I do not trouble my spirit to vindicate itself or be
    understood;
I see that the elementary laws never apologize;

.   .   .   .   .

I exist as I am—that is enough;
If no other in the world be aware, I sit content;
And if each and all be aware, I sit content.

One world is aware, and by far the largest to me, and
    that is myself;
And whether I come to my own to-day, or in ten thousand
    or ten million years,
I can cheerfully take it now, or with equal cheerfulness
    I can wait.

My foothold is tenon'd and mortis'd in granite;
I laugh at what you call dissolution;
And I know the amplitude of time.[41]

Each person's life is an unending quest to discover and to realize the promise given to him in embryo at his birth. Each person seeks this birthright in the midst of the conflicts of life which seem to convince him that such harmony and fullness are in reality a ridiculous fantasy, and that all of his ideals about life are some great hoax. Indeed, even when a person's life is not spent directly in the attempt to recover his original birthright, the person spends much effort interpreting his life in ways that keep his quest for the birthright alive in the face of personal and organic disharmony with Being. The overall structure of this quest for Being as the essence of man's spirituality, and the various possible strategies by which the individual attempts to realize this quest are the foundations for understanding the meaning of consciousness.

Freud as the founder of psychoanalysis produced a theory which bases the motivation of human behavior on unconscious processes. Both in his clinical experiences and in his theoretical assumptions Freud found that man is in the power of strange, sexually perverse, and criminal fantasies. Every man is activated by these forces so that none can deny that the dark depths of his personality have a profound effect on his behavior. Through Freud and others, such as Nietzsche, Sartre, and Derrida, we have learned that man cannot afford to deny these deep, dark forces in his psychic nature and that some of these forces are very destructive.

It is necessary that we see man's entanglement in his inner destructive forces along with his striving for higher consciousness in order for us to understand the skepticism which is a symptom of modernity. The higher dimensions of consciousness towards which man aspires are those dimensions

of himself which deliver him into the promise of his being.
They are the means of access to his birthright. Thus modern
man's skepticism can serve as a dialectical element in this
quest by throwing man back upon himself. As his energies
move towards their ultimate source, towards his sense of his
original birthright, they also bring to the surface the
content of the hidden depths—a part of his reality which has
always been there but which can also lie indefinitely below
the level of consciousness. Much of the evil in the world is
directly related to the obliteration of these lower, hidden
forces by which man is driven when he lacks contact with the
higher dimensions of consciousness. Ultimately, it is just
as easy to use cynicism as it is to use religion as a mask
for true consciousness. Both can deny consciousness by denying the reality of man's nature as a symbolizing being. Jung
stresses the dangers of relating only to the lower material
of the psyche to the neglect of man's spiritual energies:

> Freud himself, the founder of psychoanalysis, has
> thrown a glaring light upon the dirt, darkness, and
> evil of the psychic hinterland, and has presented
> these things as so much refuse and slag; he has thus
> taken the utmost pains to discourage people from
> seeking anything behind them. He did not succeed
> and his warning has even brought about the very
> thing he wished to prevent: it has awakened in many
> people an admiration for all this filth. We are
> tempted to call this sheer perversity, and we can
> hardly explain it save on the ground that it is not
> a love of dirt, but the fascination of the psyche
> which draws these people.[42]

The development of man's consciousness changes his very
substance. If the psyche were not altered in the development
of consciousness to enhance psychic life-processes, and if
the unconscious were basically filled with realities that
only threaten man, nothing in life could make any normal man
find it at all tolerable. Man would not progress into consciousness. But we must remember that Freud's theoretical
formulations represent an embryonic period in the study of
the psyche. For his early exploration provides background
from which more transcendent and more cosmic approaches to
human life can emerge in the further development of psychology. Through Freud and others, consciousness has become an
area of human inquiry. Too, the growth of consciousness is a
given. And the need for the individual to maintain his unity
with the cosmos through relating to the symbolic has also

become a given. Jung expresses the dynamic nature of our situation as a result of Freud's original work:

> The psychic depths are nature and nature is creative life. It is true that nature tears down what she herself built up—yet she builds it once again. Whatever values in the visible world are destroyed by modern relativism, the psyche will reproduce their equivalents. At first we cannot see beyond the path that leads downward to the dark and hateful things—but no light or beauty will ever come from the man who cannot bear this sight. Light is always born of darkness, and the sun never yet stood still in heaven to satisfy man's longing or to still his fears. (p. 215)

Our task now is to sort among these various powers, integrative and destructive, with the discernment of the tekton. As a consequence we can also build with the tekton's skills.

Since the beginning of the nineteenth century man has given an increasingly important place to the exploration of the psyche. This is because, with the rise of individualism and the decline of traditional values, man is more and more aware of his need for consciousness and for recovering meaning in life for himself. Freud's work shows how modern man is unaware of those kinds of reality within him which are preventing him from attaining cosmic relatedness. Furthermore, Freud's contribution serves as an impetus to man to determine why he is cut off and how he might recover access to his birthright. The astronauts of the Apollo space craft as it circled the moon were led by their own inner spirit and by their awareness of the harmony of Being in the beauty of outer space to give voice to one of the most ancient of symbolic expressions: "In the beginning, God created the heavens and the earth . . ." The beginning of modern space exploration and travel has thus rekindled an awareness of primordial cosmic symbolizing. But for mankind who is thereby now confronted by the enigma of consciousness, the question of his inchoate role in the cosmos, this moment can also symbolize a new beginning of man's exploration of his inner cosmos. The unknown vastness of interstellar space reflects the unknown vastness of man's inner being. Man must become continually more aware of this inner reality if he is to be genuine with himself and his fellow man, and to be at home in his world. He must become familiar with the ground of his being if he is to be able to liberate himself so that he can enjoy the new freedoms which the space age brings into possibility.

NOTES

1. Georg Simmel, "On the Concept of the Tragedy of Culture," in The Conflict in Modern Culture, (New York: Teachers College Press, 1968), p. 28.

2. William Wordsworth, "Ode: Intimations of Immortality from Recollections of Early Childhood," in The Poetical Works of William Wordsworth, ed. Ernest de Selincourt and Helen Darbishire (Oxford: Clarendon Press, 1947; rpt. 1966), vol. 4, p. 281.

3. William Blake, "Songs of Innocence and of Experience," in The Poetry and Prose of William Blake, ed. David V. Erdman (Garden City, New York: Doubleday and Company, 1965), pp. 7-32.

4. Virgil, The Aeneid, trans. W. F. Jackson Knight (Harmondsworth, England: Penguin Books, 1956; rpt. 1972), book VI, pp. 166-69.

5. John Milton, Paradise Lost XII, 11. 585-87, in John Milton: Complete Poems and Major Prose, ed. Merritt Y. Hughes (New York: Odyssey Press, 1957), p. 467.

6. Thomas Stearns Eliot, "The Wasteland," in The Complete Poems and Plays 1909-1950, (New York: Harcourt, Brace and World, 1952; rpt. 1971), p. 47.

7. Wystan Hugh Auden, "For the Time Being," in The Collected Poetry of W. H. Auden, (New York: Random House, 1945; rpt. 1967), p. 412.

8. Poetical Works, vol. 5, pp. 4-5.

9. Ernst Cassirer, An Essay on Man: An Introduction to a Philosophy of Human Culture, (New Haven and London: Yale Univ. Press. 1944; rpt. 1973), p. 26.

10. Ernst Cassirer, Language and Myth, trans. Susan K. Langer (New York: Dover Publications, 1946; rpt. 1953), pp. 8-9.

11. Martin Heidegger, Being and Time, trans. John Macquarrie and Edward Robinson (New York: Harper and Row, 1962).

12. Paul Tillich, Systematic Theology, vol. 1 (Chicago: Univ. of Chicago Press, 1951).

13. Abraham Maslow, Toward a Psychology of Being. 2nd ed. (Princeton: D. van Nostrand, 1968).

14. Cited in Chang Chung-yuan, Creativity and Taoism: A Study of Chinese Philosophy, Art, and Poetry, (New York: Harper and Row, 1970), p. 26.

15. Boethius, The Consolation of Philosophy, trans. Richard Green (Indianapolis: Bobbs-Merrill, 1962; rpt. 1975), book II, poem 8, p. 41.

16. Dylan Thomas, "The force that through the green fuse drives the flower," in The Poems of Dylan Thomas, (New York: New Directions, 1957), p. 10.

17. "Lines composed a few miles above Tintern Abbey," ll. 94-111, in Poetical Works, vol. 2, pp. 261-62.

18. Pitrim A. Sorokin, The Ways and Power of Love, (Boston: Beacon Press, 1954), pp. 88-114.

19. Clive Staples Lewis, The Abolition of Man, (New York: Macmillan, 1962), pp. 11-17.

20. Rainier Maria Rilke, "The First Elegy," in Duino Elegies, ed. and trans. J. B. Leishman and Stephen Spender (New York: Norton, 1939), p. 21.

21. Paul Ricoeur, "The Antinomy of Human Reality and the Problem of Philosophical Anthropology," trans. Daniel O'Connor, in Readings in Existential Phenomenology, ed. Daniel O'Connor (Englewood Cliffs, New Jersey: Prentice-Hall, 1967), pp. 400-02.

22. Murray Wright Bundy, The Theory of Imagination in Classical and Medieval Thought, (Urbana: Univ. of Illinois Press, 1927).

23. Paul Ricoeur, The Symbolism of Evil, trans. Emerson Buchanan (Boston: Beacon Press, 1967; rpt. 1970), p. 10.

24. Paul Ricoeur, Freud and Philosophy: An Essay in Interpretation, trans. Denis Savage (New Haven and London: Yale Univ. Press, 1970), pp. 506-51.

25. Theodore Roethke, "The Rose," in The Far Field, (Garden City, New York: Doubleday, 1964).

26. Paul Ricoeur, "The Hermeneutics of Symbols and Philosophical Reflection," *International Philosophical Quarterly*, II, no. 2 (May 1962), p. 192.

27. Plato, "Apology," trans. Hugh Tredennick, in *Plato: The Collected Dialogues*, ed Edith Hamilton and Huntington Cairns (Princeton: Princeton Univ. Press, 1961; rpt. 1973), S. 38a, p. 23.

28. *The Holy Bible*. Revised Standard Version (New York: Thomas Nelson & Sons, 1952), Matthew 13:16, emphasis added.

29. Martin Buber, *Two Types of Faith: The Interpretation of Judaism and Christianity*, (New York: Harper and Row, 1961).

30. Pierre Teilhard de Chardin, *The Phenomenon of Man*, trans. Bernard Wall (New York: Harper and Row, 1959; rpt. 1965).

31. Karl Jaspers, *The Origin and Goal of History*, trans. Michael Bullock (New Haven: Yale Univ. Press, 1953).

32. John B. Cobb, Jr., *The Structure of Christian Existence*, (Philadelphia: Westminster Press, 1969).

33. Mircea Eliade, *The Myth of the Eternal Return: Cosmos and History*, trans. Willard R. Trask (Princeton: Princeton Univ. Press, 1954).

34. Aurelius Augustinus, *The Confessions of St. Augustine*, trans. John K. Ryan (Garden City, New York: Image Books, Doubleday, 1960), book VI, chapter 3, p. 136.

35. Thomas Stearns Eliot, "The Metaphysical Poets," in *Selected Essays*. New ed. (New York: Harcourt, Brace, 1932; rpt. 1950), p. 219.

36. "Phaedrus," trans. R. Hackforth, in *Plato*, S. 250 b-c, pp. 496-97.

37. Marcus Tullius Cicero, *Basic Works*, ed. Moses Hadas (New York: Modern Library, 1951).

38. Marjorie Hope Nicolson, *Voyages to the Moon*, (New York: Macmillan, 1970).

39. John Keats, "On First Looking into Chapman's Homer," in *John Keats: Selected Poems and Letters*, ed. Douglas Bush (Boston: Houghton Mifflin, 1959), p. 18.

40. Thomas S. Kuhn, The Structure of Scientific Revolutions. 2nd ed. Foundations of the Unity of Sciences Series, Vol. 2, No. 2 (Chicago: Univ. of Chicago Press, 1970), p. 6, emphasis added.

41. Walt Whitman, "Song of Myself," in Leaves of Grass. 1st ed., ed. Malcolm Cowley (New York: Viking Press, 1855; rpt. 1959), parts 6,7,28.

42. Carl Gustav Jung, Modern Man in Search of a Soul, trans. W. S. Dell and Cary F. Baynes (New York: Harvest Books, Harcourt, Brace and World, 1933; rpt. 1955), pp. 208-09.

Chapter II
Symbolic Regression

THE CONCEPT OF SYMBOLIC REGRESSION

> . . . the end of all our exploring
> Will be to arrive where we started
> And know the place for the first time.[1]

The concept of symbolic regression is the basis of symbolic regression psychology. This concept is best understood in relation to Freud's notion of regression. The comparison between symbolic regression and Freud's notion will make clear both the continuity of this concept with Freud's original formulation and the radical development beyond it which characterizes symbolic regression psychology.

Originally there were no positive or negative values associated with the notion of regression. To regress meant simply, "to walk back," "to retrace one's steps." Thus regression was originally understood "as readily in a logical or spatial sense as in a temporal one."[2] Freud sees the foundation for this process in human nature itself:

> The infantile past—of the individual or even of humanity as a whole—remains forever within us: 'The primitive stages can always be reestablished; the primitive mind is, in the fullest meaning of the word, imperishable.'[3]

In Freud's system, however, the term usually has negative significance. It refers to a reversal of the normative pattern of individual psychosexual development which Freud had charted into a series of stages of life. Freud explains this reversal in an individual's development by the concept of fixation. When an individual has a traumatic experience at some point in his development, he goes back to the safety and security of an earlier mode of functioning. He does this to protect himself from the threat to his existence which he has experienced in the trauma. He interprets continued development as threatening at that point and prefers the "tried and true" modes of earlier functioning to the unknown and contingent aspects of experience which he senses will come with continued organic development. Regression is thus a conservative and defensive reaction to suffering. Regression in this system is negative. It is nothing more than a behavioral symptom of fixation, or arrested growth.

The originality and truth in Freud's concept of regression are not to be denied. The pattern of trauma, fixation, and regressive behavior is a universally recognizable phenomenon. Freud's articulation of this pattern is a major step toward understanding the psyche. Freud has opened the door to understanding a major principle underlying the life of the psyche. But the pattern which he describes must itself be seen as merely a small element of a much larger process, the process of symbolic regression. Moreover, this pattern must be given a context very different from the context of Freudian pathology in order for its ultimate positive significance to emerge.

Freud's concept of regression is essentially a pathological term. It refers to symptomatic behavior. But if we use the original definition of regression, "to walk back," "to retrace one's steps," "to return to an earlier level of functioning," then we can see it beyond the limits of Freud's psychopathological frame of reference. We term Freud's concept <u>regressive behavior</u> and link it to the symptomatic acting out which is the expression of an individual's attempt to deal with a traumatic break which he experiences with his own past and primal needs. On the other hand, we term the concept developed here <u>symbolic regression</u> and define it as an aspect of the symbolizing activity which we have described as the primary characteristic of man as man. It is absolutely fundamental to make a distinction between regressive behavior and symbolic regression, for this distinction is the basis of the psychology of symbolic regression.

Symbolic regression is the process of bringing one's personal and primordial history directly to bear upon his present experience. This is the process by which the individual relates himself to the promise of his birth by gaining access to the enduring cosmic and organic dimensions of his being. Symbolic regression is not for the most part a conscious psychic function. However, it can work at the level of dream, myth, meditation, or certain imaginative states. It is the act of creating and investing symbols with psychic energy so that they mediate and express the full range of the relationship between self and Being. This process takes place within all three dimensions of consciousness: the organic, the personal, and the cosmic.

Symbolic regression makes it possible for the individual continually to reorganize the self material according to emerging consciousness. It thus resolves the problems of change and permanence, time and timelessness in psychic functioning. It does this by actualizing the self as at once a temporal and a trans-temporal entity. Symbolic regression is the psychic function by which the self gives expression to the ground of its being in a unique and individualized way. In Heidegger's terms, it indicates Being through symbols.[4]

The experience of symbolic regression heals the discrepancy between self and Being which characterizes much of human consciousness. The concept of symbolic regression will further the development of personality theory by giving new focus to the personal dimension of the self. It will become a new basis for synthesizing the individual and the universal aspects of the self, both of which are indispensible in Western thought. It will bring about a perspective by which Western man can experience the Eastern personalism expressed by Haridas Chaudhuri: modern man's development now enables him to express his uniqueness at the same time that he incarnates the imperishable—he can now actualize the creative urge of Being in which he is grounded.[5]

If one's capacity for symbolic regression were complete, he would be a healthy, happy, totally integrated, cosmic, personal, and organic self. He would live in a state of continually relating himself consciously and unconsciously to his uniqueness to Being so that he feels continuous with all that is natural. He would possess consciousness. He would live in relation to his roots. He would have recovered his birthright. To the extent that an individual is removed from this continually integrative state, he is disordered, distorted, a disrupted and divided individual. To the degree that the individual develops this capacity, he can live in a state of inner peace, because he symbolizes and relates to those dimensions of Being which ultimately stabilize him. Symbolic regression transcends the disruptive hiatus between his personal and his primordial existence. It harmonizes his cosmic and organic foundations with his personal self. The task of psychotherapy is the task of expanding this capacity in the life of the person who has to some degree lost touch with his own powers of symbolic regression.

With the distinctiveness and centrality of symbolic regression in mind, we now go back to Freud's focus on regressive behavior as a symptom of disruption in the psychic economy of the individual. Using the abductive method in psychological theorizing, we discern that symptomatic behavior is more than a mere object for diagnosis and therapeutic prescription. Regressive behavior is an abortive attempt of the individual to relate self to the ground of Being. That is, it not only shows the problem; it is also the unsuccessful attempt to resolve the problem. It is an individual's way of saying, "Stop the world and make a place for me that is harmonious with my being, for if you do not, I cannot go on." Thus symptomatic behavior is a sign that the individual needs to discover his powers of symbolic regression. It points to the need for symbolic regression.

Erik Erikson recognizes the abductive significance of regressive behavior. He says:

> While the depth of regression and the danger of acting out must of course guide our diagnostic decisions, it is important to recognize from the start a mechanism present in such a turn for the worse . . . This consists of a quasi-deliberate giving in on the part of the patient to the pull of regression, a radical search for the rock-bottom—i.e., both the ultimate limit of regression and the only firm foundation for a renewed progression.[6]

Regression is thus part of the life process of a person whose consciousness has been disrupted. It is a desperate search for the primordial basis of personality. In the regressive attempt the personality is stabilized by ego at some more primitive level. Thus, even regressive behavior has significance for the stabilization and integration of the person.

Jung also identifies regression as part of this more positive frame of reference. Regression is a response to ego's failure of adaptation which goes back to recover a broader base and hitherto untapped powers in the psyche which will allow ego a greater range of possibilities in the struggle for adaptation.[7] Regression for Jung is the turn inward to the symbolizing function in the individual's search for a coherent way of relating self to Being.

We have now shifted from Freud's concept of regressive behavior as symtomatic behavior to the larger realm of regression itself. Freud himself sees regression from a larger perspective in a few passages, but he is not willing to concede much positive power to it. Two of the most notable reference points for this concession are Freud's essays, "Creative Writers and Daydreaming," and Civilization and its Discontents.

Freud's essay, "Creative Writers and Daydreaming," interprets creative work as a kind of regression.[8] But this particular case of regression is given some sanction. It is understood as "regression in the service of the ego." Freud's notion at this point is closely tied to the theories of regression in both Erikson and Jung.

We have seen the positive potential in regression in its more general meaning in Freud, Jung, and Erikson, and we have seen how this potential is actualized in the concept of symbolic regression. Freud talks about regression in Civilization and its Discontents in ways which touch upon the concept of symbolic regression.[9] However, his use of these common areas is for the most part from a frame of refernce which is totally opposed to that of the psychology of symbolic regression.

Freud links the child self of regression to cosmic awareness in his rejection of the sense of dependency as the basis of religion. Yet he rejects the child self as a valid adult experience. The psychology of symbolic regression is based on the opposite viewpoint: the gateway to the symbolic regressive state is through the child self. Fixation upon a certain developmental level will persist until the symbolic regressive capacity is restored to the point where it is adequate to free the child self into the experience of the present. Once this has occurred, the individual is able to relate expressively to his organic and cosmic dimensions.

One fundamental difference with Freud here lies in our ability to affirm ultimate confidence in the unity of meaning and Being where he was only able to express skepticism concerning meaning, and stoicism in relation to the cosmos. His ultimate statement in Civilization and its Discontents sums up his own tragic vision:

I have not the courage to rise up before my
fellow-men as a prophet, and I bow to their
reproach that I can offer them no consolation.
(p. 92, emphasis added)

Freud does not let himself imagine a cosmic frame of reference within which human needs can legitimately and adequately be expressed and met.

A closer look at Civilization and its Discontents will show the centrality of the issues of symbolic regression and also the radicalness of the difference between Freud and what is here set forth. In his discussion of the "oceanic feeling," which he understands to be the essence of religion, Freud defines it as "a feeling of indissoluble bond, of being one with the external world as a whole" (p. 12). He then attempts to explain this feeling genetically and traces the development of the individual from his experience as an infant at the breast who "does not as yet distinguish his ego from the external world" to modern adult self-relatedness:

> Originally the ego includes everything, later it
> separates off an external world from itself. Our
> present ego-feeling is, therefore, only a shrunken
> residue of a much more inclusive—indeed, an all-
> embracing—feeling which corresponded to a more
> intimate bond between the ego and the world about
> it. (p. 15)

The psychology of symbolic regression would make an almost identical analysis of the development of the individual. In fact, Freud follows this analysis with a description of what seems to be the state of symbolic regression:

> If we may assume that there are many people in
> whose mental life this primary ego-feeling has
> persisted to a greater or lesser degree, it would
> exist in them side by side with the narrower and
> more sharply demarcated ego-feeling of maturity,
> like a kind of counterpart to it. In that case,
> the ideational contents appropriate to it would
> be precisely those of limitlessness and of a bond
> with the universe. (p. 15)

We define this state, as Freud describes it, as the condition necessary for psychic health. Freud's valuation, however, is exactly the opposite of ours:

The whole thing is so patently infantile, so
foreign to reality, that to anyone with a friendly
attitude to humanity it is painful to think that
the great majority of mortals will never be able
to rise above this view of life. (p. 21)

These passages serve to show at once both the penetrating
truth of Freud's insights into the essentials of human
experience and the inveterate falsehood of his judgement
concerning the ultimate meaning of these essentials. With
this in mind, we are ready to consider the three major
moments in the process of symbolic regression.

SYMBOLIC REGRESSION AND THE CHILD SELF

. . . blest the Babe,
Nursed in his Mother's arms, the Babe who sleeps
Upon his Mother's breast; who, when his soul
Claims manifest kindred with an earthly soul,
Doth gather passion from his Mother's eye!
. . . . .
No outcast he, bewildered and depressed:
Along his infant veins are interfused
The gravitation and the filial bond
Of Nature that connect him with the world.
[He], as an agent of the one great Mind,
Creates, creator and receiver both,
Working but in alliance with the works
Which he beholds. . . .[10]

Each person has an inner child or child self. This child
self is an inherited field of awareness which has been in
part informed by our early experience. Yet in each person
this inner child has been thwarted by oppression: restraints
and confinements have been imposed upon our child's existence
by the socially mediated experiences which have become
decisive moments in our development. Thus each person has the
constant task to rediscover the primal child self and to enjoy
the play of its spontaneous energies within his existence as
an adult person. The maimed condition of the child self in
the adult makes it impossible for persons fully to experience
their rightful participation in the energies inherent in the
natural child self. By having been taught to act in imitation of self-depriving adults, we have lost contact with our
right to regress into the true primitive needs and the spontaneous responsiveness which were originally natural to us as
children.

Because we have been taught that primal feelings are emotionally immature at best, that the simplicity of the child's disposition is actually meaningless or to be humored, and that simple, child-like experiences are illusions inappropriate for life in the "real" adult world—most people completely give up the reality that can be experienced through the child self. People have been taught that wonder and hope and the magic of potent childhood fantasy are worthless and illusory. Having succumbed to such negating beliefs, which are imposed on each individual to some degree or other, each person has abandoned his ties with these energies and in their place has accepted the encroachments of self-deprivation to the point where such child energies have become virtually inaccessible to him. The resulting loss of hope makes the constantly occurring attempt at symbolic regression into a symptomatic strategy: the individual manipulates images which are no longer really believed in. He has insulated himself from the primary levels of experience. Persons can actually degenerate to the point where they become defensive against the child self's orientation toward its primary needs. Frequently husbands and wives will act toward each other as if they did not really need each other and as if the comforting which any child would instinctively enjoy did not exist for them. Spouses often cannot express their needs for this kind of personal comfort because they are protecting a precariously instilled sense of "adult" dignity and autonomy. They do not understand that dignity and autonomy themselves must be redefined in terms of a more basic reality, which is the nature of the child self.

If we take the child self as the true locus of orientation, then the adult who is able to be childlike, who is able symbolically to regress, and who is able to admit the simpler and more natural needs of his being becomes in reality the mature human being. It is this person who is truly autonomous, for he is living not out of a symbiotic relationship, but rather out of genuine contact with his own basic needs. From this orientation, he is able to adapt to and to arrange the conditions within which he finds himself. This deeper, organic autonomy strongly contrasts with the appearance of maturity which belies an unintegrated person whose symbolic processes are split off from Being while functioning to disguise this loss.

Earl Biddle has shown that the symptomatic behavior of the adult which is the expression of the fixated consciousness of the inner child is based on the underlying need for spiritual union with others. Through the use of hypnotic regression,

Biddle discovered that the inner child was not fixated on an irrational attempt to maintain an Oedipal relationship with the mother. Rather, the evidence pointed away from the Freudian hypothesis. In the experience of hypnotic regression, the child self was actually attempting a symbolic and spiritual rather than a sexual union with the parent. When the parents became impossible to cope with, the child self necessarily interpreted the parents in terms of good, nurturing qualities. The child self did this costly act of symbolically maintaining its integrity through the intensified exercise of fantastic imaginative activity.

In an unpublished presentation, Biddle gave a case history in support of these findings:

> The adult male was regressed to the age of two, and he said he wished to be close to mother, so I asked, "How will you get inside mother's body?"
> He said, "I will just walk into her."
> "How will you do that?"
> "I will walk up to her and keep on walking inside of her."
> "Would this be like walking through a wall?"
> "Yes, I would be like a ghost."
> "Then you could walk through her skin?"
> "Yes."
> "Could you get in in any other way?"
> "I could go through her nose, or her eyes, or into her mouth—like a ghost goes through a keyhole."[11]

The desire expressed in this dialogue is what Freud misinterpreted as an Oedipal desire. Biddle's interpretation of such repeated findings is that the child fantasizes getting inside of the mother, getting into the most intimate of all unions. But the child enters into this union in totality, he goes into the mother as a total body, not merely sexually, as Freud understood. When the subjects were asked in the state of regression whether they would like to have relations with mother like father does, their response was relatively consistent: "Oh, no! Only grown-up people can do that, but children can't do things like that."

This kind of symbolic activity, consistently discovered in Biddle's researches in hypnotics over a period of many years, suggests that the innate capacity for symbolic regression is universal in human nature. The spiritual union with the parent which Biddle found the child self repeatedly attempting is a major symbolic manifestation of the universal human quest for union between the self and the energies of Being.

In contrast to Freud, the regressive experiences in Biddle's work point primarily toward a spiritual and not toward a sexual fulfillment for human desire. This element of regressive experience suggests the essential meaning of symbolic regression psychology. In symbolic regression, the person is constantly attempting to unite spiritually with the energies of Being through the vehicle of the inner child, for the good inner child implicitly exists as the beneficiary of the goodness of the natural, nourishing parent and as the being who participates in the cosmic dimensions of this goodness. In other words, the inner child and the inner parent find their unity in a correspondence to one another which is the essence of symbolic regressive activity. Out of the state of symbolic regression arise the individual's images of the authentic fullness of meaning and Being.

The whole line of thought involved in the concept of symbolic regression completely transcends the economy of sexual desire, for the child self is most fundamentally the aperture through which the energies of the transpersonal self become accessible to the personal self. One of the most naive assumptions about the needs of the child is that the child self is primarily oriented to the tasks of physical survival. This is simply not true. The child is mostly concerned with the spiritual, affectional, and love energies which must be present to him in order for his environment to be a sustaining one. It is less destructive to the child to miss having his material needs satisfied for a time than it is for him to miss being loved. The child self withers and dies if it is not loved. Infants who are well nourished and yet do not receive warm maternal comforting actually atrophy and die. By extension, the adult who is cut off from the presence of his emotionally nourished inner child cannot be a mature, loving person. Symbolic regression psychotherapy is the process that enables the individual to recover contact with this inner child.

The state of the child self is the most natural one, one not necessarily calling for any particular attention in the "normal" functioning of the human person. It is only when symbolic regression is in some way cut off from the individual and from constantly renewing the self that a state of alarm arises. When consciousness functions through the child self, it unites the transpersonal energies of the self into an integrated continuum with the personal self so that the individual can live an integrated, non-polarized life. Through his child self the individual accepts the masculine-feminine aspects of his personality and identifies his energies with his socially defined gender specific role, for the energies of the transpersonal self and the energies of the body originate together at the level of the child self. Contact with the child self is the key to all the levels of being brought into play in personal integration.

In the healthy person symbolic regression is a constant process. Such a person is able to relate directly to his needs for nourishment, for creative expression, and for spiritual union with his environment and with his cosmos at large. The body, as a result, is able to function without the impediments of psychosomatic symptomizing, for such stress is a signal that symbolic regression is blocked and that the individual is not able comfortably to adapt to the body's spontaneous nurturing processes. Moreover, the healthy psyche, through the process of symbolic regression, reaches down deep into the primordial mother and draws upon those resources of nourishment and inner rhythm which give the person a sense of harmony and of oneness with the cosmos. The healthy psyche is also able to maintain open access to the universal father and to the energies of decisiveness and action which the universal father symbolizes. It maintains this openness to Being without becoming overbearing and therefore disharmonious with the true nature of Being.

The concept of the inner child underlying this theory of integration is based on an ontological assumption: that it is of the nature of the universe to produce energies in the human being that from the inception of the individual life flow in harmony with it. These energies are what can be called love energies. Tillich says that love is the anticipation of the reunion of self and Being which at once confirms the individuality of both the lover and the beloved and also actualizes their reunion as a state of being: "The normal drive for self-fulfillment . . . strives toward union with that which is a bearer of values because of the values it embodies."[12] Here the drive toward fulfillment becomes expressed as love. It is ontological, for it is the drive toward Being, or ultimate value. While Being/value is the object of this drive, it is embodied or symbolized in the image of the nurturing and sustaining parents and in the world as a field of consciousness. Thus the child loves the parent and desires union with him or her as the bearer of ontological significance. This union with the parent and the world is actually a harmonious integration of distinct energies, an integration within the psyche of the child which is actually constituted by his very act of desiring it. Love so defined is innate in all human beings. In fact, this primal love energy is the essence of the child: <u>the child self is ontologically rooted in its loving the parent.</u> To take this ultimate starting-point seriously is to transform one's conception of the meaning and nature of the therapeutic task. Properly understood, this reality becomes a new basis for all discipline, for all parental interaction with the child, and for all of the certainty which man can have regarding human life. It becomes the foundation for understanding man's essence, his quest for the harmony of Being, and his realization of his ultimate destiny.

There are many misunderstandings about the true nature of the child self and about its inherent dimensions in the human imagination. It is completely natural for the parent to love the child. It is also just as natural for the child to love the parent. It is easy for parents to believe that they love their children. The converse is perhaps the most overlooked fact in psychology: often the child is not aware that he naturally loves the parents. In fact, the being of the child is grounded in this love for the parent. When a child is taught that he does not love the parent or when the child's love for the parent is discounted or not acknowledged—and we are all taught this to some extent—then the child grows up to become an adult who doubts that his child loves him. This spiritual state of negative expectations creates a pattern of rejection which the child in his openness and vulnerable receptivity introjects. Thus the child is forced to interpret and to relate to a vitiating message: "If you do this, you love me. If you do not do this, you do not love me." In actuality the true message motivating all behavior ought to be the opposite of this: "Since you love me, then I expect this. Since you love me, then I can be firm with you about what is good for you. Since you love me, and I know you love me, and I love you, then there can be differences between us. Each of us can have his own autonomy."

Jesus emphasized the goodness of the child to his disciples:

> Then some children were brought to Jesus so that he might lay his hands on them and bless them; and the disciples rebuked them. But Jesus said, "Let the children alone, and do not hinder them from coming to me, for the kingdom of heaven belongs to

such as these." . . . and he said, "Truly I
say to you, unless you are changed and become
like children, you shall not enter the kingdom
of heaven." (Matthew 19:13-14; 18:3)

Jesus rebuked his disciples when they attempted to come between him and the children, for he taught that the simplicity of the child's love, faith, and hope is the spiritual essence of his gospel. The child naturally loves, is open and trusting, is ready for creative discovery, and hopes for ultimately good things. It is these qualities that relate the person who has access to his child self to the transcendent dimensions of Being in which he experiences the nourishing and sustaining qualities of life and by which he understands himself as blessed. When such nourishing levels of experience have been made accessible within the individual, he has developed his capacity for symbolic regression. But when the innate state of primitive love energies embodied in the child self becomes vitiated or inaccessible, then this state must be recovered in its pristine purity in order for consciousness to continue to develop. This recovery and development is the activity of symbolic regression. It is the purpose of symbolic regression psychotherapy to set this process once again in motion.

Regressive behavior must be respected for what it truly is. It is an abortive attempt of the individual to relate symbolically to the child self, and through it to the cosmic levels of Being. Thus regressive behavior is a symptom, for it symbolizes a disruption between the individual's awareness and the reality of the child self. The childish behavior called "symptomatic acting out" must be validated as messages calling for the integration of the multiple levels of consciousness in the individual. Thus regressive behavior shows the need for the symbolic regressive state, the state of all non-fixated behavior.

Regressive behavior indicates that the inner child is becoming expressive and that the energies embodied as the inner child are demanding to be integrated into the total function of the person. The struggle and difficulty represented in this acting out is the sign of the health and vitality of the child self struggling to realize itself. In this behavior, primitive energies are pushing to be recognized and resymbolized as part of the whole psychic economy. Indeed, regressive behavior and its symptomatology are a fundamental part of the healing process, for it is this very activity which, like the throes of labor at childbirth, can lead through the sense of ultimate struggle and impasse to the birth of meaning and greater integration. The "bad child" of regressive behavior is thus the push toward the rebirth of the good inner child of symbolic regression into the "economy" of the adult personality.

Man's tragedy is that the child self is locked away in the psyche and made inaccessible by negative social introjects, the demands which others make upon it to fulfill prescribed social roles. That is, parents often ask their children to keep them feeling safe and secure with their own learned social masks. This problem of introjects requires a look at the function of the child self in the integrating of the personality.

There is an altogether valid natural child self in every human being. That is, each person has within him a child self which is directly and specifically related to his individual imaginative powers, and yet is universal or archetypal in scope. However, there is also an introjected child self which has been received from the child's social environment and which is at odds with the natural child self. The natural child self and the introjected child self can become locked in conflict in the individual's imagination, producing great disruption and upheaval in the personality. However, the individual can learn to redirect his energies so that the introjected child self is disarmed and the natural child self is set free. Thereby, the individual has successfully gone beyond the transfixing power of the introjected, bad child self and the configuration of his energies comes to correspond to the energies of the true or natural child self and through it to the energies of Being.

People are often unaware that they are to some extent afraid of becoming conscious. This fear, characteristic of the introjected child, masks itself with unconsciousness and with the state of non-related existence. Such unconsciousness is a blindness to two realities: first, it is blindness to the meaning of what happened to the individual when he was a child; second, it is blindness to the continuing presence of the person's original inner child energies. As long as a person doubts the validity of the inner child, he cannot risk a loving relationship, for he doubts the reality of his love and of the energies associated with it. This doubt throws one's inner family as well as his inner child into jeopardy. And the continuity of being and consciousness is attacked by frightening negative images which make the process of becoming conscious appear to be dangerous. These frightening images arise out of the false images of the negative, non-parenting inner family which have been introjected through the individual's actual early experiences. The path back to consciousness lies in the task of resymbolizing the self in relation to Being through experiences of more nourishing, life-oriented cosmic energies. The recovery of these positive energies enables the inner child to feel safe and relaxed to the point where the person is freed to become more conscious. In other words, when the inner child feels abandoned, trapped, ignored, or punished for having its own innate consciousness, the person must learn to relate to the self through experiencing a realm of images more congenial to the development of consciousness.

Regression is the attempt of the psyche to symbolize the person as validly participating in positive affective states. As long as barriers to the primitive aspects of consciousness exist in the adult, a therapist's work is limited to conjectures about what is truly going on in him. The barriers to consciousness which analysis as such merely manipulates must be replaced by a real, conscious relationship between the therapist and the client. This relationship must first of all be genuinely offered to the client by the therapist. When the therapist is intellectually sophisticated but unconscious, the client can manipulate himself out of integration by merely shifting the self-depriving patterns which he learned from his parents at an early age and repeating them at a new level. Thus the client simply relates to both the therapist's unconsciousness and his own unconsciousness by betraying his own most basic needs, those of the child itself. He takes up the role of "parenting" the therapist just as he began to do early in life when his parents somehow denigrated him as a spontaneous child. This strategy can be called "idealization." Through it, the person becomes "mature" while at the deepest level he remains alienated from his innate childlikeness. Such "maturity" is actually a symptom of insulated self-deception. When a person is in such a state, insight as a mental activity does not produce change. Insight may be considered to be "mature," but it is not the result of higher consciousness, for such consciousness immediately acknowledges the validity of the innate, incipient child self which resides deep within both therapist and client.

Psychotherapy is often the means which enables the individual to recover contact with his inner child, for when he experiences the collaboration provided in a therapeutic encounter, he receives the emotional and spiritual support necessary for him to ground his sense of self in the validity

and reality of his child self. In this process, the person
must have a primal sense of the therapist's identification
with and support for his attempt to recover access to the
energies of the child self, the energies which lie closest to
the root of the individual's intuitive powers.

The therapist helps the individual to hope by reinterpreting his regressive symptoms as genuine attempts to find himself real and to rediscover the foundations of his identity. As the person develops the capacity for symbolic regression, the child self comes into ascendency in the personality. Such recovery of the energies of the child self lays the ground for the appropriation and integration of experiences at the transpersonal level, for these primal energies are intimately related to nature and to the ultimate energies of the cosmos as well.

Janov says that insight is the mental result of pain.[13] Pain is a person's awareness that he has lived with himself and his parents as if the ontologically necessary bond between the self and the self of the parent did not exist. Too often pain is seen merely as a symptomatic manifestation of unconsciousness. Thus the gap between introjects and Being which it indicates is given scant consideration. Actually, the capacity for symbolic regression is closely related to the capacity for feeling, experiencing, and interpreting pain, for admitting the reality of pain is the fundamental means of affirming and recovering the reality of the child's power to love. Thus man, if he is to recover his consciousness in this complex cosmic age, must learn deliberately to remain close to the meaning of his pain. This is done through symbolic regression into the meaning of the child self. The child self knows that pain is meaningful, because it is the index of his distance from his rightful experience of the good, nurturing parents.

Negative social introjects oppress the inner child in every person through five major image elements: inattention, abandonment, deprivation, punishment, and imprisonment. Each person has within him an altogether bad child who is victimized by these elements. At the same time, each person has within him an altogether good child who is at home in the world, who is the beneficiary of cosmic energy, and whose characteristics are inherent in the nature of the imagination. The bad child state, the inner child that is constituted by the bad social introjects, is absolutely distinct from and ultimately inferior to the good child state in the psyche. However, in his attempt to relate to himself, each person must confront and pass through the introjected bad child self in order to come home to the good child self implicit in his being. Each human being has three capacities which are activated in this process: first, he can redirect his energies by his regressive efforts; second, he can shift away from relating to the self through the images of abandonment, imprisonment, punishment, and deprivation; and third, he can reorient himself through participation in the inner good child's energies in himself. To realize these capacities, each individual must recognize the ontological distance between the positive natural and the negative introjected child selves within him. The recognition of this distinction becomes the foundation upon which the individual can reorganize himself in relation to the symbolic material of the psyche. In other words, each person must learn to trust in the reality of the inner good child in himself. Similarly, he must discover and understand the nature of the social introjects that he encounters in his experience so that their power can be neutralized and so that the strategies formerly established to perpetuate that power can be abandoned.

In the process of the growth of consciousness, one's contact with the child self becomes a deeper dimension of every decision a person makes. Consequently, an adequate understanding of the nature of symbolic regression turns every decision into a possible step in the recovery and realization of the child self. The therapist's major task is to provide a context in which the child self is given free expression in the personality in every decision-making process. Through the therapist's provision of this freedom and through his support, the individual learns to stay simple and primitive with himself in the most complex and demanding moments of his life. As the capacity for symbolic regression is expanded, the processes of consciousness become routed through the child self, and the potential for contact with the energies of the transpersonal self is opened up. Primary needs, because they belong to the essential nature of the emerging child self, are then experienced as authentic and serve as the informing perspective for all of the person's choices.

The child self is the seed point of consciousness. When this child self is recovered through symbolic regression, the "I" is experienced as conscious. In this state, the person, rather than relating to his feelings and emotions as if they were mere objects, experiences a oneness within himself as he participates in the reality of his feelings and emotions. This state of participation transcends objectivity. It is trans-objectivity, or true subjectivity. It is objectivity which comes from within the experience of participation itself, so that there is no split between subject and object, between consciousness and meaning and Being. The person has entered into the simplicity of the child state: the primary processes of his being, and the polar elements of his being have become poised in a natural, balanced relationship. When the individual speaks from within this experience, he does not speak as if he were an adult who is simply remembering what he once was as a child. He speaks out of the continuity between what he is and what he was. Thre is no bifurcation of past and present. To address my parents as parents becomes in reality a way to address myself—to affirm the reality of my inner child.

This experience of the child self puts the individual within the good, nourishing and sustaining world which corresponds to the image of the divine child as this image comes to widespread expression in diverse myth material. Apocalyptic myth expresses the image of the child as the subject of a full future realization of man's ultimate longings. In Hebrew terms, the Messianic Age will be characterized by a harmony, the focal point of which is the child:

> The wolf also shall dwell with the lamb, and the leopard shall lie down with the kid; and the calf and the young lion and the fatling together and a little child shall lead them. . . . for the earth shall be full of the knowledge of the Lord, as the waters cover the sea.
> (Isaiah 11:6,9)

Similarly, the Roman, Virgil, uses the image of the child to give focus to his myth of the Augustan Age:

> Only do thou, at the boy's birth in whom
> The iron shall cease, the golden age arise,
> Befriend him, chaste Lucina; 'tis thine own
> Apollo reigns. . . .
> He shall receive the life of gods, and see
> Heroes with gods commingling, and himself
> Be seen of them, and with his father's worth
> Reign o'er a world at peace. For thee, o boy,
> First shall the earth, untilled, pour freely forth
> Her floral gifts . . .   (Eclogue IV)[14]

Our urgent need to recover the inner child today is based on the fact that human beings are essentially rational creatures, each of whom must grow into increasingly more developed states of consciousness for his psychic survival. Cosmic consciousness and the rationality necessary for survival are both aspects of man's essence as man. Relationships between one form or level of consciousness and another require the development of a comprehensive continuity of consciousness which extends from the primitive state of the child self to the most developed orders of transpersonal consciousness. A break in this continuity suspends the expansion of conscious experience, brings about states of insulated islands of energy and unconsciousness within the person, and isolates the dimensions of consciousness from one another. The image of the child arises within this situation, bearing with it the promise of man's wholeness:

> The Lord himself shall give you a sign:
> Behold, a woman shall conceive, and bear a son,
> And shall call his name Immanuel, God with us.
> (Isaiah 7:14)

SYMBOLIC REGRESSION AND THE ORGANIC SELF

The most fundamental image state in symbolic regression is the child self, for the child self is at once complete and accessible to image consciousness through memory and experience. Furthermore, because the child self is complete, it is also the seed out of which emerge all of the other symbolic dimensions of the self in the total personality. We have already seen that the child self is the aperture through which the person becomes at home with the self in its cosmic relatedness. But it is equally true that the child self also contains the potential for us to be aware of ourselves as organic selves, for human consciousness emerges within an original organic matrix, the womb. We now turn to consider this organic self and its vicissitudes as these relate to the quest for full consciousness and the recovery of man's primal birthright.

When the continuity between consciousness and organic being as this is experienced in the natural child state is disrupted, the body suffers. The mental and emotional stress of this disruption finds expression in physical tension. When the capacity for symbolic regression is not developed in an individual, body symptoms arise as distress signals coming from the deeper levels of the organic self to indicate that the body is at odds with its true nature.

All physical symptoms have a psychic dimension. Physical symptoms indicate the denial of consciousness. They mean that the person is blocking out of awareness the powerful grounding of his body in primal being. On behalf of the organic self, these symptoms are saying, "I have been taught not to nourish myself, not to feed myself. I am in pain."

The means of alleviating these symptoms is always the same simple process: the self and the reality of bodily being must be reconciled through the resymbolizing of the personality. Images which express the organic meaning of the self must be discovered and integrated into the experience of the self. A state of relaxation harmonizes body states with the emotional and spiritual levels of conscious experience. There are several areas of imagery which can be focused on to foster this kind of integration: incorporation of food, sexual expression, revisiting the primal scene, touching and otherness, parts of the body, and modes of bodily interiorization.

As an example of how this imagery works, the person may be asked to imagine that he has been invited to an aborigine village. He is presented with the symbolism of initiation: he is carried by the tribe to a jungle clearing where he is buried head up so that he might be transformed into an adult member of the tribe in the course of the night. During the night he discovers his latent aboriginal powers as a member of this primitive tribe. At first he experiences his helplessness, the helplessness of his own nature as he has customarily experienced it. Then he regresses to participate in deeper levels of his own nature. Soon he experiences a sense of his oneness with all of nature. Finally, his sense of oneness with the natives functions as a symbolic regressive image of his oneness with all of mankind at the level of man's most primitive essence. Step by step he is asked to participate in earth, in the night or dark side of his being, in his own atavistic urges in the form of animals, and finally in living substance as such. The symbolism of the dark in relation to the light unites lower and higher dimensions of his nature, the cosmic self with the organic self. This symbolic transformation shows the individual that any dimension of his nature always stands to be transcended by another. That is, he experiences the fact that consciousness requires that man always stand in a symbolic regressive stance with himself.

SYMBOLIC REGRESSION

Persons are often fearful of the primitive nature of their emotions. In particular, many persons are deeply afraid of their potential for anger. For example, Pat's experience with the nocturnal initiation scene illustrates how release and integration are made possible through the process of symbolic regression. Pat produced the image of an attacking tiger with which he could not symbolically cope in his first effort at visualizing it. He began to regress, to identify with the tiger, to let it become his friend, to let it lick his face, and finally to have it stand guard over him through the deep of the night. In imagination he was enacting the fact that man must symbolically relate to primal emotion so that anger and agressiveness can become his friends. This enabled him to go beyond using such emotional states for mere survival or merely in response to negative introjects. He came to the point where he could spontaneously use his anger and aggression as vehicles for creative self-expression. The sublimation of primitive emotional states is necessary only to the degree that a person is alienated from his own nature. Recovery of the process of symbolic regression transcends the need for this sublimation.

Theory in clinical psychology is just beginning to acknowledge the problem of organic deprivation and its interrelationship with psychic deprivation. In clinical practice as well, it is extremely difficult to help individuals understand that their willingness to poison themselves with tobacco, alcohol, drugs, and sugar-ridden foods is inextricably tied with states of psychic self-deprivation, for the underlying problem is the need to symbolize and to enjoy nourishing modes of relating to Being through the body. In symbolic regression the individual learns to resymbolize the self and its relationship to organic being. This integrative resymbolizing results in the relaxation of bodily functioning. When the individual experiences states of relaxation through exercises that expand the powers of imagination, the relationship between consciousness and organic being begins to shift and his experience of life changes. He is then able to begin to listen to his pain and to deal with it more realistically than he has in the past.

Ernest Hilgard writes that heart aberrations and high blood pressure are the body's reactions to the individual's strategy of displacing and disguising pain.[15] According to Hilgard, stress in the cardio-vascular system is nothing less than an oblique message that the person as a total system is in pain. Here the abductive method points beyond the presenting symptoms to a more comprehensive problem. In the case of cardio-vascular stress, the underlying cause lies in the presence of social introjects which are antithetical to the true nature of the self. These introjects hold the person in unconsciousness, making him powerless to discover that they are forcing the body to work overtime in order to defend itself against relating naturally to the self.

Franz Alexander is another psychological theorist who links somatic ailments and psychological symbolism.[16] He indicates that the individual's psychological integration is intimately related to the language of the total organism. According to Alexander, the presence of tension in the personality is often difficult to relate to any specific, immediate psychological cause. The lack of a specified and localized cause points beyond the symptom to a broader problem: the disruption between consciousness and organic being. Thus, such diffuse somatic tension is a most significant sign. It shows the need for symbolic regression and for developing the capacity for healing through imagination. This analysis opens the way to treatment of somatic stress through symbolic regression psychotherapy.

According to Alexander Lowen, a third theorist of the relationships between mind and body, the body image introject is the field within which the individual understands his sensory experiences.[17] This field is constituted by the nature of the physical contact between the child and its parents in the first years of life. If this introject is constituted by the experience of strong, positive early experiences of warm, comforting body contact, the person will spontaneously enjoy himself as an organic being. He will be comfortable and at home with his organic self. But if this introject takes shape through disruptive, affectless, or hostile bodily contact, the individual's consciousness will be contaminated and distorted by the introject, and he will experience himself as unrelated to the organic dimension of his being.

The experience of separation between consciousness and organic being is the cause of symptomatic behavior. Where the disturbance is great, the individual relates to his body in distorted ways, ways which seem to symbolize the attitude that the body is nothing or of no account, or that the body is a hindrance to the self. In this state of detachment, the body loses its vitality. It acts as if it belonged to a person who is neither child nor adult, neither actively masculine nor actively feminine. In this state of vagueness and withdrawal from his concrete existence, the individual idealizes his experience of being deprived of bodily comfort. He protects his innate sense of a nourishing world by detaching his consciousness from his pained body and involving himself solely with the introject as be both denies it and becomes absorbed by it. Then, emotionally dying to his body, he finds himself living in a world of images made frightening by his introjects. He begins to feel that he must separate himself from these images as they intrude into one level of his idealized consciousness after another. His stepwise process of withdrawal becomes symptomatized in the further loss of bodily vitality, and the aura of indifference and futility begins to settle down over all of his physical actions. This individual no longer expects to experience meaningful exchange in bodily contact, and the process of withdrawal is confirmed and accelerated by growing ranks of self-confirming negative expectations. Underlying this process is the futile attempt to regress to a simpler state in which the individual can be allowed to experience the body at the same time that the conscious self is "protected" by unconsciously allowing itself to be cut off from the meaning of this regressive strategy.

This growing estrangement between consciousness and organic being is movingly presented in Franz Kafka's story, The Metamorphosis.[18] Gregor, the main character, awakens from uneasy dreams one morning to find himself transformed into a giant insect. This literal realization confirms the negative body image produced out of a family experience characterized by the lack of bodily warmth and physical contact. Gregor's parents respond to his transformed body with disgust. They lock him in his room, so that he is imprisoned within the dwelling place of his parents as well as within the body which has become a cold mockery of the mood of the family.

Gregor withdraws by degrees in his self-conscious, obedient response to his family's disgust at his body. First, he hides himself when someone enters his room so that he might protect them—and himself—from their disgust. Then he gives up human speech in order to fulfill the family's expectations: they don't want to communicate with him. Instead, they talk about him as if he were not present and a person. He duly eats the garbage his sister feeds him in spite of its putrefaction and lack of nourishing substance. Finally, his last ditch attempt to approach his sister for even a small token of warmth many months after his metamorphosis provokes her to an outbreak of final rejection. She can no longer recognize her brother in this body that has become monstrous to the family, and she therefore refuses to use his name to refer to him. At this loss of even her residual warmth, which is his last hope of human contact, Gregor stops eating and dies. The next morning, the maid finds the body and sweeps it out. This story, often regarded as a bizarre existentialist parable, radically dramatizes the individual's experience of bodily deprivation in a body-denying family. It traces how the disruption between consciousness and organic being evolves into a process of ultimate disintegration.

But there is hope in the face of this process. For the psychic disintegration which bodily stress symptomatizes can be turned into a process of reintegration through psychotherapy. The task of symbolic regression therapy uncovers the meaning of such regressive symptoms and interprets this meaning from the perspective of a larger organic and cosmic frame of reference. The ultimate starting point for therapy is the assumption that the natural positive image of the body is available to each individual because human nature itself is grounded in organic being and is furthermore a part of all Being. The method of approach, accordingly, consists of two processes. First, the person is helped to uncover the illusions of idealization and his strategies of deprivation and dissociation. Second, he is helped to discover various means of access to the deeper, more positive levels of his own being and of all Being.

A person can be made to know that he is unconsciously deadening his body in order that he may avoid feeling the pain of not having a continuing experience of bodily comfort. He can be taught that this strategy of avoiding the pain of deprivation is based on the deep-seated fear that nobody really cares for his body and the corresponding expectation that body comfort will never become part of his experience. He can be taught to recognize that he has a negative image of his body as a body alienated from all other bodies, one that is inexorably trapped or jailed in a state of cold isolation. The body is withdrawn, and the individual is filled with fear that he is in imminent peril of being destroyed. Such negative body images often lie latent in the human psyche. However, the natural positive image of the body is also available to each individual, at least to some degree of realization, because human nature is grounded in organic being. Each person alive experiences some degree of disruption between his organic being and the field of body-self images available to consciousness. The distance between Being and consciousness in the organic dimension produces conflicts in the entire person. The individual can learn to stop fighting his own reality and to overcome this hiatus only by expanding his body awareness through symbolic regression.

This education in awareness, in interpreting the structure of deprivation and deprived unconsciousness, is supplemented by direct work with imagery in dream interpretation and in the guided visualization experience. Work in a therapeutic group adds a social-existential dimension to these modes of the therapeutic work.

The two phases of resymbolizing the organic self are the two parts of a dialectical process. In the first or negative phase the individual learns to desensitize the self-defeating social introjects which have entered his imaginative life, such as the images of oppressive and rejecting parents. In the second or positive phase, he learns to integrate his organic functions with his cosmic and personal energies. These phases are the systole and diastole of the therapeutic process. They express the good parental qualities of Being. Within this dialectic, the increase of differentiation between negative and positive images must always be followed up by a further degree of integration of the energies of consciousness. The presenting symptoms only subside when all three energy levels—the organic, the personal, and the cosmic—begin to come into play with one another. Until this integration is achieved, the negative introjects will continually reappear in devious ways as they channel and rechannel their modes of expression and continue to give off warning messages.

Through the development of the capacity for symbolic regression, the individual is able to expand the functions of imagination. When organic being and consciousness are at odds with each other, the body is so to speak frozen; it cannot relate to its cosmic energies. In this state, the body is unconscious and houses symbolic processes which are alienating to the self. This condition must be overcome. The desires for bodily closeness and sexual fulfillment which are part of each person's birthright must be realized through bodily interaction with others in close and continuing contact. Bodily pleasure must be learned as a valid and stable social experience. The individual's right to closeness to and warmth with his mother must be validated through a relaxed acceptance of this need within a validating social context. For this reason, therapeutic groups often use exercises to relax muscular tensions. This relaxation in such a social context permits the individual to resymbolize his body and thus to become more aware of his true bodily needs.

The early experience of bodily deprivation causes a disruption between consciousness and organic being. Lowen presents the typical family context for this schizoid syndrome in his description of the seductive, rejecting parent who forces the child to act as an ersatz parent by validating the actual, rejecting parent. The child forced into this situation feels trapped, impotent, and angry all at the same time (p. 86). It is most difficult to impart the healthy meaning of touch to someone whose life has been shaped by this kind of double bind. As a matter of fact, this is the key task upon which the success of therapeutic intervention in such cases depends. The dynamics of this intervention can be seen at work in the following example.

A mother came for the treatment of her almost catatonic son. When she and her son became involved in the therapeutic process, the son began to uncover his anger at his mother. At this point the mother withdrew and attempted to have the son committed to a mental institution. As the son became more aggressive and independent as well as more loving, the mother attempted to seduce him from therapy, telling him that the therapy was not helping him and that the therapist was mistaken. As the son continued to gain his autonomy and as he began to trust the therapist and his group, the mother turned to his sisters to support her judgment and to help her have him committed. When the son finally panicked and fled from his mother because her rejection became intolerable, the therapy group became a place of acceptance and identity affirmation, even a place of survival for him. Whenever he doubted his autonomy as a person and faltered, it was because the mother told him that she loved him greatly, that he should leave therapy and return home, and that if he did so all would be well.

One thing was obvious in this family story: the body contact between mother and son was seductive. The mother was afraid to touch and to physically comfort her son. At the same time, the mother was asking the son to act as if he were a strong father who would correspond to her sense of herself as an infantile daughter. In response to this situation, the group required the son to face his needs as a faltering son who was uncomforted and frightened. The group helped him to see that whenever he began to assert his independence, his mother became theoretical, diagnostic, and frightening to him. He began to understand that his mother was unable to let him need her physically because she feared comforting him would turn him into the emotional invalid which she felt herself to be.

Through symbolic regression therapy, this young man began to uncover the strategy that he had been using in response to his mother's symbiotic demands. He learned to see how he had controlled his mother's reactions by acting as if he were a problem. This strategy had been his means of combatting his fear of seduction, but it was one which could only be carried out at the expense of his own need for body reassurance and body consciousness. As he abandoned this futile strategy of trying to have his body identity validated by his rejecting mother, he learned to seek bodily reassurance and fulfillment from persons within his group and in his life whose warmth was more genuine.

We have seen how bodily stress is a symptom of the disruption between consciousness and organic being, and how this disruption is overcome through imagination and through social experience, two possible modes of symbolic regression. Sexuality as a major mode of bodily experience provides a focus which will help us to understand how resymbolization transforms the meaning of a person's actions.

Alexander Lowen relates the disruption between the individual's organic being and his consciousness to compulsive sexual behavior (p. 84). In Lowen's terms, this disruption consists of a poor body image, one that is not based on an alive and responsive body surface. This condition produces a general genital excitation which must be discharged. As a result, sexual behavior becomes compulsive and devoid of true affection. The disruption of self and being finds expression in sexual experience in this way: sexual intercourse releases genital excitation, but the body is at some level or other withheld from total abandonment to the experience. As a result, the truly satisfying pleasure of sex is missing from sexual activity. This condition makes sex one of the great paradoxes of human experience, for the same act can be either an act of ultimate union or an act of ultimate alienation. It is important to realize that sexual behavior itself is not the issue at stake here. The problem is rather the fear that the sex act itself is the only meaning of intimate human contact.

When the body is resymbolized so that its powers correspond to positive image states, then sexual behavior is experienced as the completing of body-Being unity. The body comes alive. In this experience of unity, sex has taken on a new meaning for the participant, and the compulsive syndrome has fallen to the wayside. The meaning of sex has shifted away from sex as an act to discharge a sexual tension which is related to unpleasant introjects. Instead, it has become an ultimate expression of the unity of one's own body with its ground in Being. The sexual act has become transformed into an expression of human love and affection. Sexual release is integrated with encompassing personal emotions. As a result, it is experienced as comforting and fulfilling and having cosmic significance. In this integrative context, the choice to have sex is a personal one in which the individual is affirming his unity with nature. This free choice which is constituted by the positive image state does not become a means of "proving" closeness where closeness may be in doubt. Rather, it is a choice within the context of bodily comfort, bodily affection, bodily acceptance, and bodily love. It is the conscious affirmation of organic being.

When the organic self is related to the symbolic regressive process, the body comes to life. It takes on a mobility characterized by spontaneity. It seems to glow and is filled with feeling. Therapy must begin by confronting persons with the fact that their bodies are in many ways deadened and lack the responsiveness of vital energy. Most people are far too habituated to the introjected lie that their bodies are mere projections of the intellect. Such introjects require them to accept the deadness of their bodies as normal. Persons in our society tend to idealize this state of bodily deprivation by turning to external means to interpret the meaning of their physical wellbeing: they measure height and weight, compare physiognomies, order cosmetic surgery, and undergo long-term orthodontic work. A concern for the depths of organic being must accompany and extend this care for the body's surface appearance. People must learn to feel their bodies, to interpret their bodies, and to listen to what their bodies are saying to them. Only through this deeper attention will they be able more fully to enjoy the original promise of life for the body.

SYMBOLIC REGRESSION AND THE COSMIC SELF

> . . . man dissevered from the earth
> and stars and his history . . .
> for contemplation or in fact . . .
> Often appears atrociously ugly. Integrity is wholeness,
> the greatest beauty is
> Organic wholeness, the wholeness of life and things, the
> divine beauty of the universe. Love that, not man
> Apart from that, or else you will share man's pitiful
> confusions, or drown in despair when his days
> darken.[19]

In the recovery of the birthright towards which all men strive, the organic self finds itself at home with the cosmic self as well as with the personal self, the most ultimate and yet the most immediate dimension of consciousness. A person experiences himself as a cosmic self when he simultaneously feels both his uniqueness and his oneness with all of Being. That is, in such an experience, he intuitively senses his ultimate harmony with Being from the perspective of his own unique individuality. Such discovery of the cosmic self can be aided in part by the symbolic regression technique of guided visualization.

For an example of how this technique can bring about such awareness, I refer to the visualization experience of Peter, an eighteen-year-old youth. After being given exercises which helped him to enter a deeply relaxed state, Peter was instructed to imagine that he had reversed the time process and that he was going continuously backward in time. He went back to the point where he became a fetus in his mother's womb. Once a fetus, he continued backwards in time by becoming smaller and smaller. He became a zygote. Then the sperm withdrew from the egg. He was asked to regress even further, to continue imagining this process of reversed time. Continuing as an egg, he experienced the maternal body around him become younger until it too became an egg. This process continued until a transfer of images took place in his experience of being an egg. Peter then remarked: "I have become a thought in the mind of God." What happened at this point is to be explained in terms of psychic energy. According to our metaphor of Being as energy, the psychic energies of this person shifted from one dimension to another and there was a corresponding shift of consciousness from the awareness of the self as a personal entity to awareness of the self as a transpersonal reality. When he reached this cosmic awareness, Peter was for a time permitted to experience being "a thought in the mind of God."

The experience of this imaginative state through a symbolic regression technique allowed this person to experience the totality of his meaning by symbolizing it. When Peter returned to waking reality, he had a new understanding of himself as a transpersonal being who transcends his individual conscious experiences. He remarked that he now knew that he had somehow existed before his mother, and that he was no longer as dependent on his mother as he had once felt himself to be. Likewise, he somehow had existed before his father, and was no longer as dependent on him as he had once imagined.

Peter has a father and a mother, and they are important personal realities to him. But above and beyond this and all of the disruptions and difficulties of his daily life, he understands that he is a being who is more than all such discordant moments. He has begun to see that he himself is and has a distinct part in the ultimate order of the cosmos. With the quality of objectivity which this experience of regression brought to him, he is now able to have a much more relaxed attitude toward himself, for he has experienced himself as a being whose dimensions go beyond the usual parameters of time and space. As a consequence, he now feels more at home with himself at the organic and personal levels as well as at the cosmic level of consciousness. This kind of experience of the cosmic self integrates the personality from an ultimate perspective and gives one a sense of his coherence as a cosmic being, as a being who is more than the sum of the distinct and individual parts of his experience.

"No man is an island, entire of itself; every man is a piece of the continent, a part of the main."[20] John Donne's metaphor of the continent expresses the kind of knowledge that the cosmic self has. Man is able to perceive that he is tied to the universe and to other human beings by a transcendent consciousness, of which his own consciousness is only a small part. This awareness is expressed variously as "participation mystique" in anthropology, as "corporate personality" in Hebrew religion, and as "illumination" in the language of the mystics. Psychological writers have begun seriously to explore this aspect of human experience only in the last decade or so. It is important for any psychological theory to take this kind of experience seriously. In fact, an integrative therapy such as this one cannot be constructed without it.

Abraham Maslow is one psychological theorist who takes this cosmic dimension of experience into account in his

discussion of personality.[21] He talks of values based on
meta-needs and meta-pathologies which have profound implications for the process of self-actualization. His fundamental
distinction between deficiency needs and being needs is based
on the assumption that spiritual values as such are of an
entirely different yet ultimately homogeneous order in human
consciousness than are man's physical needs. Maslow, on the
basis of this distinction, calls for a new kind of counselor,
the "meta-counselor."

The "meta-counselor" is to help the individual learn to
meet what Maslow calls "meta-needs." Maslow says that it is
as necessary for man's survival to meet these needs as it is
to meet his needs for food and the other physical constituents of life, for the values upon which these needs are based
are the meaning of life. Yet, in spite of their primary
importance, many people do not know that they have these
needs. Thus, part of the "meta-counselor's" task is to make
the individual aware of these fundamental needs in himself.
One day, he suggests, counselors will think of themselves as
philosophical or religious counselors. Maslow describes
human life as a search for value and for love. This view of
life is what is meant here by cosmic consciousness. From
this perspective, man devotes himself to nothing less than
what is ultimate in his search for meaning. When a person
is relating to himself as such a cosmic being, he expresses
his energies in wonder, in communion, and in transparent
love.

Teilhard de Chardin, too, looks at man as a cosmic being,
although from a much different perspective than Maslow's.[22]
Chardin places man within the framework of cosmic time. He
describes cosmic evolution as a process of diversification
and complexification which took place over the eons until a
significantly new stage was reached: man appeared on the
scene. Man's appearance is marked by the emergence of human
consciousness, a unique substance which is characterized by
its powers of self-reflection. This, according to Chardin,
is a heightened and widening consciousness which emerged from
an ever rising center of reflection, and which is now the
dominant element in the further evolution of the earth. The
attainment of a distinctly human consciousness is based on
the emergence of the self, that which is symbolized as an
observing eye in the act of consciousness.

Roberto Assagioli takes this concept of the self as the
observing eye from the context of Chardin's cosmic evolutionary theory and applies it to the unfolding of

consciousness in the development of the individual. This principle becomes the theoretical basis for Assagioli's use of the "technique of dis-identification," the goal of which is "self-identification."[23] The technique of dis-identification consists of four stages. The person realizes one step at a time that he is not his body, that he is not his emotions, and that he is not his intellect. He reflects on these phenomena, affirming that he is more than any one of them. This process, similar to the negative way in the progress of the mystic, leads to the fourth step, which is its goal: the individual recognizes and affirms that he is a center of pure consciousness. The self or observing eye becomes experienced as the center of "affirmative transcendence" (pp. 116-25).

St. Augustine describes a nearly identical process as a spontaneous development in his own experience:

> I entered into the depths of my soul . . . and with the eye of my soul, I saw the Light that never changes casting its rays over the same eye of my soul, over my mind. It was not the common light of day that is seen by the eye of every living thing of flesh and blood, nor was it some more spacious light of the same sort, as if the light of day were to shine far, far brighter than it does and fill all space with a vast brilliance. What I saw was something quite, quite different from any light we know on earth. It shone above my mind . . . because it was itself the Light that made me, and I was below because I was made by it. All who know the truth know this Light, and all who know this Light know eternity. It is the Light that love knows.[24]

Here the act of self-reflection includes acts of dis-identification. Augustine sees light, the most central symbol for cosmic consciousness, and dis-identifies it from animal sensation and from ordinary mental experience. With the eye of the soul he experiences cosmic light, a sense of eternity, and all-encompassing love.

It is extremely important that the experience of self-identification described here not be seen as a rejection of the body. Rather, this experience affirms one's body and one's thoughts from a new perspective. This experience is an effort to realize intuitively that the center of consciousness, of willing, and of being lies beyond the limitations of any individual experience, including itself. The experience of self-identification in this technique points beyond itself to pure subjectivity. The prevalent Greek ideal, which was formulated numerous times by Plato (for example, in Phaedo (82e-83e) and is still widespread today, is that the soul as light and the body as a dark, heavy prison-house are irreconcilable states of being:

> Pure was the light that shone around us, and pure were we, without taint of that prison house by which now we are encompassed withal, and call a body, fast bound therein as an oyster in its shell.
> (Phaedrus 250c) [25]

In this view, the intellect is a superior function and to be affirmed to the exclusion of emotions and sensations because it is closer to pure consciousness, while the emotions are inferior to the intellect and to be spurned because they are governed by the appetites of the body. Such concepts center consciousness in man's thinking functions and ultimately cut him off from the human realities of emotion and sensation. In contrast to Plato's hierarchical division of human experience, the view of self in Assagioli and in symbolic regression psychology integrates action, emotion, will, and reason all under the overarching transcendence of pure consciousness.

Lying beyond the personal conscious self, the center or core of pure self-awareness, is what Assagioli postulates as a prior or transcendent self (p. 19). This higher, or cosmic self is unaffected by the flow of the mind stream or by the concrete conditions of bodily existence. This overarching self is the source of the personal self, and the personal self is its reflection. Little is known about this transcendent or cosmic self, but this self can be inferred from the experience of transpersonal states of consciousness. The essential difference between the personal self and the cosmic self is that the personal self is self-reflexive. That is, it is an awareness of itself as a distinct individual. This sense of individuality at the level of the personal self brings with it the concomitant experiences of solitude and of separateness from the not-self. It is this experience of the limits of the self in reflexive awareness which becomes irrelevant in the transpersonal experiences of the cosmic self. This transpersonal state of awareness is characterized by a sense of expansiveness, of freedom, and of oneness with all selves and with the reality of Being. A sense grounded in universality rather than in individuality, the experience of this state of consciousness resolves the polarity of individual and universal at a level so profound that it redirects the whole orientation of the person described above. The transpersonal self is more than the sum of the functions involved with it, just as the whole is greater than the sum of its parts.

The cosmic self is the center of pure spiritual being. The individual who raises his center of consciousness up to the level of transpersonal consciousness opens himself up to the realm where symbolizing energy is being activated beyond consciousness at all levels of the transpersonal self at all times. As a result, the individual experiences his participation in the universal. This state commonly occurs among creative persons such as artists, mystics, and lovers. For some who experience this transpersonal consciousness, however, there is no experienced continuity between their experience of the undifferentiated cosmic self and their experience of the personal self. Such persons have a difficult time integrating transpersonal experiences into the personal dimension of their lives, for they lack the broad basis and developed conceptualization by which they might move smoothly from the one level to the other. They do not have the necessary integrative frame of reference for such experiences. That is, they have not developed their symbolic regressive capacity. Again, St. Augustine's story illustrates that this experience can be disruptive for those who lack the integrative frame of reference for it:

> Reason withdrew my thoughts from their normal course and drew back from the confusion of images which pressed upon it. . . . And so, in an instant of awe, my mind attained to the sight of the God who IS. Then, at last, "I caught sight of your invisible nature, as it is known through your creatures." But I had no strength to fix my gaze upon them. In my weakness I recoiled and fell back into my old ways, carrying with me nothing but the memory of something that I loved and longed for, as though I had sensed the fragrance of the fare but was not yet able to eat it. (Confessions Book VII, Chapter 17, pp. 151-52)

This conceptualization expressed here in the images of seeing and falling back to habitual self helps to understand the sometime baffling juxtaposition of intuition and frustrated existence found in the lives of many artists.

A psychology of the transpersonal self, such as this one, is founded on the ultimate reality of subjectivity. Such a starting point becomes the basis for understanding both the personal and the transpersonal dimensions of the self. At the level of the personal self, consciousness has the capacity

to objectify much of experience. Western man's empirical
approach to knowledge is a program based on the illusion that
this capacity is the only means to ultimate knowledge and
that it in itself is limitless. But, as we have already
seen, the reality of limits is part of the ontological
structure of the personal self. Moreover, it is this process
of empirical objectification which has led to modern man's
rejection of metaphysical symbols such as "the soul."
However, what is offered here is a third way of looking at
man which is limited to neither empirical nor metaphysical
categories of thought: man is a conscious or symbolizing
being and what was once called the soul is nothing other than
the focal point of pure consciousness.

Jung tries to accommodate himself to the empirical attitude in a way that is not attempted here.[26] He postulates
the self as the totality of forces which constitute the psyche
as a system. As such it makes possible both the experience of
oneness and the experience of individuality. But ultimately
Jung in his capacity as a scientist must disavow any transcendent meaning for this system. In contrast to Jung, the
theory of symbolic regression rejects out of hand any
reasons to conform to empirical dicta or empirically sanctioned modes of verification. Jung's limits in this regard
did nothing to gain him any credibility. The casting off of
this kind of restraint enables us to develop a radical view
of the self: the self is conscious substance, awareness of
which is latent as man's unique capacity for self-reflexive
consciousness. It is the center of conscious and unconscious
functioning. It is actual living substance which is constantly arranging and rearranging itself, with its conscious
and unconscious dimensions, around Being. It is the point of
true consciousness.

According to Jung, the self is a psychological entity.
According to the definition we here set forth, it is a
reality alive, a living entity. The self is the subject.
It is not merely a process of becoming, not merely some sort
of object of phenomenological investigation. Rather it is
true being. The important fact is that the transpersonal
self is reality, it is a conscious substance. It is not
simply a thing being constituted out of nothing. Rather, it
is substance which is constantly being reorganized. It
partakes of the nature of cosmic substance through which it
constantly reconstitutes itself in the act of symbolizing.

This concept of the transpersonal self corresponds to
the superconscious elements of experience which Maslow has

articulated in his studies of "peak experiences."[27] Along similar lines, Churchill points out that the experience of superconsciousness is an important means for harmonizing and resolving both intrapsychic and interpersonal conflicts.[28] In this context, symbolic regression becomes a crucial means for contacting the higher and more integrative cosmic dimension of experience, for symbolic regression resymbolizes the self from the perspective of cosmic consciousness.

Cosmic symbols which correspond to consciousness include light, height, and states of weightlessness and timelessness. When such symbols are focused on and intensively experienced through symbolic regressive techniques, they bring into awareness the true nature of primitive energies, and disidentify the self from the destructive social introjects which have entered the imaginative life through interpersonal experience. When a person imaginatively experiences cosmic consciousness, integrating energies of broad scope and high intensity are transmuted to the personal self and thus released to become ultimately expressed in the quality and style of the individual's behavior. A person is ready for this dimension of symbolic regressive experience when it becomes apparent that these energies are actually accessible to the personal self, based on the strength of the person's identity as an individual being. At this point the person is introduced to cosmic dimensions of his being so that gradually the energies of the transpersonal self are transmuted through the experience of imagery and they become realities which the personal self finds to be accessible. The transpersonal self consists of all of the energies which motivate, release, and activate the personal self in its concrete existence.

Energies have their source in both the personal and the transpersonal dimensions of being. Personal energies can be transmuted into transpersonal energies, just as transpersonal energies can be transmuted into personal energies. Imagination is the link which enables the person to harmonize these levels of energy so that the mode of body function and behavior is an integral expression of the experience of pure consciousness. The integration made possible by this process synthesizes the aesthetic-ethical pole of experience with the sexual-sensual pole. This synthesis is the basis of the most satisfying forms of human conduct. The diverse vibrational frequencies of these vastly different energies are transmuted and harmonized in the imaginative process so that the personal self expresses them in ways that are cosmically useful. As a result, the polarities within the

SYMBOLIC REGRESSION

personality flow together with the universe of Being as well as with the individual's concrete and particular social and physical environments.[29]

As we have seen in chapter one, the drastic break with myth which man underwent in his entry into self-reflective consciousness at the beginning of axial civilization was one of man's major steps away from the cosmic self. Man made a radical shift toward a conscious, reflective attitude towards his archetypes and cosmic symbols. These contents were then repressed from awareness, but they have remained as the hidden constituents of the cosmic dimension of human consciousness. Thus man gained civilization, but in the process lost myth. Now, thousands of years later, man is faced with the need to rediscover the true meaning and power of myth, to rediscover the true nature of consciousness as it is related to Being. Man's involvement in myth is his involvement with the symbolic regressive dimensions of his person. Symbolic regression is the means of once again relating man's personal self to man's essential nature as a cosmic being.

Myth relates man to all of Being while abstract reason is a focusing of his consciousness at merely one of its levels. Images evoke aspects of imaginative experience which unite the transpersonal world with the individual's environment in ways that language as mere signs cannot. When myth enters human experience, it enters through the sluice gates of imagination. It unites man's transpersonal and his personal selves in a spiritual union. Myth is a mode of symbolic regression which unites man to himself and to his cosmic and transrational being. The integration of mythic and rational modes of consciousness into a harmoniously functioning totality within the experience of the individual enables the individual to find himself at once a personal and cosmic being. This awakening of consciousness is the goal towards which William Blake would direct us:

> If the doors of perception were cleansed every
>   thing would appear to man as it is, infinite.
> For man has closed himself up, till he sees all things
>   thro' narrow chinks of his cavern.
> . . . .
> Man has no Body distinct from his Soul for that
>   calld Body is the portion of Soul discernd
>   by the five Senses, the chief inlets of Soul
>   in this age
> Energy is the only life and is from the Body, and
>   Reason is the bound or outward circumference
>   of Energy.
> Energy is Eternal Delight [30]

NOTES

1. Thomas Stearns Eliot, "Little Gidding," in The Complete Poems and Plays 1909-1950, (New York: Harcourt, Brace and World, 1952; rpt. 1971), p. 145.

2. "Regression," in The Language of Psychoanalysis, ed. J. LaPlanche and J. B. Pontalis (London: Hogarth Press, 1973), p. 386.

3. "Regression," in The Language of Psychoanalysis, p. 387.

4. Martin Heidegger, Being and Time, trans. John Macquarrie and Edward Robinson, (New York: Harper and Row, 1962), p. 205.

5. Haridas Chaudhuri, Being, Evolution and Immortality: An Outline of Integral Philosophy, (Wheaton, Ill.: Theosophical Publishing House, 1974), p. 7.

6. Erik H. Erikson, "The Problem of Ego Identity," in "Identity and the Life Cycle: Selected Papers," Psychological Issues, 1959, 1(1, Serial No. 1), p. 133.

7. Carl Gustav Jung, "On Psychic Energy," in The Collected Works of C. G. Jung, trans. R. F. C. Hull, ed. Herbert Read, Michael Fordham, and Gerhard Adler, (Bollingen Series XX, New York: Pantheon Books, 1954), vol. 8, pp. 39-40.

8. Sigmund Freud, "Creative Writers and Daydreaming," in The Complete Psychological Works of Sigmund Freud, ed. James Strachey, (1908; rpt. London: Hogarth Press, 1959), vol. 9, pp. 143-53.

9. Sigmund Freud, Civilization and its Discontents, trans. James Strachey, (New York: W. W. Norton, 1961), pp. 11-20.

10. William Wordsworth, The Prelude (1905), II, 239-43, 272-75, pp. 56, 58.

11. W. Earl Biddle, unpublished talk, Los Angeles, California, June 1966.

12. Paul Tillich, Love, Power, and Justice: Ontological Analyses and Ethical Applications, (New York: Oxford Univ. Press, 1960), p. 30.

13. Arthur Janov, The Primal Scream. Primal Therapy: The Cure for Neurosis, (New York: G. P. Putnam's Sons, 1970), p. 242.

14. Virgil, Eclogues IV, in The New Testament Background: Selected Documents, ed. Charles Kingsley Barrett, (London: Society for the Propagation of Christian Knowledge, 1958).

15. Ernest R. Hilgard, Introduction to Psychology, 3rd ed., (New York: Harcourt, Brace and World, 1962).

16. Franz Alexander, Psychosomatic Medicine: Its Principles and Applications, (New York: Norton, 1950).

17. Alexander Lowen, Physical Dynamics of Character Structure: Bodily Form and Movement in Analytical Therapy, (New York: Grune and Stratton, 1958).

18. Franz Kafka, The Metamorphosis: Die Verwandlung, trans. Willa and Edwin Muir, (New York: Schocken Books, 1948; rpt. 1968).

19. Robinson Jeffers, "The Answer," in Such Counsels You Gave to Me and Other Poems, (New York: Random House, 1937).

20. John Donne, "17 Meditation," in Devotions Upon Emergent Occasions, ed. Anthony Raspa, (Montreal and London: McGill-Green's Univ. Press, 1975), pp. 86-87.

21. Abraham H. Maslow, "The Farther Reaches of Human Nature," Journal of Transpersonal Psychology, 1969, 1(1), 1-9.

22. Pierre Teilhard de Chardin, The Phenomenon of Man, trans. Bernard Wall, (New York: Harper and Row, 1959; rpt. 1965).

23. Roberto Assagioli, Psychosynthesis: A Manual of Principles and Techniques, (New York: Viking Press, 1965; rpt. 1973), p. 119.

24. St. Augustine, Confessions, trans. R. S. Pine-Caffin, (Harmondsworth, England: Penguin Books, 1961), Book VII, Chapter 10, pp. 146-47.

25. Plato, "Phaedrus" 250c, trans. R. Hackforth, in Plato: The Collected Dialogues, ed. Edith Hamilton and Huntington Cairns, (Princeton, New Jersey: Princeton Univ. Press, Bollingen Series LXXI, 1961; rpt. 1973), p. 497.

26. Carl Gustav Jung, "Psychological Aspects of the Mother Archetype," in The Collected Works of C. G. Jung, vol. 9, part 1.

27. Abraham H. Maslow, "A Theory of Metamotivation: The Biological Rooting of the Value-Life," Journal of Humanistic Psychology, 1967, 7, 93-127.

28. Gregg Churchill, Contributions of Psychosynthesis Toward a Growth Oriented Model for Pastoral Counseling, unpublished Doctoral Dissertation, Claremont Univ., 1973.

29. For a thorough description of the transmutation of these various energies through imagination, see Robert Gerard, Psychosynthesis: The Psychotherapy for the Whole Man, (New York: Psychosynthesis Research Foundation, 1964).

30. William Blake, "The Marriage of Heaven and Hell," Plates 14, 4 in The Poetry and Prose of William Blake, ed. David V. Erdman, (Garden City, New York: Doubleday and Company, 1965; rpt. 1970), pp. 39, 34.

IMAGINATION

Chapter III: Imagination

INTRODUCTION: THE CONCEPT OF IMAGINATION

Imagination is most simply defined as the symbolizing function, the function of forming mental images. Mental images are the elements of awareness which are present to the person in a different way than are sensory stimuli. In the history of thought this image making power has been given various roles as a means of human knowledge. To the Medieval schoolmen, it was a means of knowledge secondary to rational intuition and it was subject to illusion. To empiricists such as Hume, it became synonymous with illusion. To idealists such as Kant and the Romantics, it became the organ of all human knowledge. The respective positions of the empiricists and the idealists are foreshadowed in the dialogue of Theseus and Hippolyta in Shakespeare's A Midsummer-Night's Dream.[1] Theseus describes imagination as illusory, as mere invention, the act of creating something out of nothing:

> THESEUS: The lunatic, the lover, and the poet
> Are of imagination all compact:
> One sees more devils than vast hell can hold
> That is, the madman; the lover, all as frantic,
> Sees Helen's beauty in a brow of Egypt:
> The poet's eye, in a fine frenzy rolling,
> Doth glance from heaven to earth,
>   from earth to heaven;
> And, as imagination bodies forth
> The forms of things unknown, the poet's pen
> Turns them to shapes, and gives to airy nothing
> A local habitation and a name. (v,i,7-17)

In this negative description imagination is characterized as being primarily visual, as the kind of experience in which the person imagining "sees" what he expects rather than what can be consensually validated, and therefore as illusion because it lacks verification. Hippolyta responds to this characterization by pointing out the reality of imagination's effects, even if the thing itself is a bit awesome and difficult to delimit:

> HIPPOLYTA: But all the story of the night told over,
> And all their minds transfigur'd so together,
> More witnesseth than fancy's images,
> And grows to something of great constancy,
> But, howsoever, strange and admirable.
> (11. 23-27)

The exaltation of imagination as a means of knowledge comes in the Romantic period. This exaltation is made possible by an expanded conception of the function of imagination. To the empiricists and to man in general up to the Romantic period, imagination was seen to function as the means of illusory fantasies. This limited definition of imagination is the one applied when someone says, "He did not see that—he only imagined it." The idealists broadened the scope of imagination beyond the "as if" quality in this statement to include the whole realm of human knowledge as the function of imagination. Coleridge as a representative Romantic defines imagination in this comprehensive, epistemological sense:

> The imagination I consider either as primary, or secondary. The primary imagination I hold to be the living power and prime agent of all human perception, and as a repetition in the finite mind of the eternal act of creation in the infinite I AM. The secondary imagination I consider as an echo of the former, co-existing with the conscious will, yet still as identical with the primary in the kind of its agency, and differing only in degree, and in the mode of its operation. It dissolves, diffuses, dissipates, in order to recreate; or where this process is rendered impossible, yet still at all events it struggles to idealize and to unify. It is essentially vital, even as all objects (as objects) are essentially fixed and dead.[2]

Here Coleridge's famous distinction makes imagination both the power of apperception and the power of perception, at once the constituting ground of awareness and the specific act which unifies sensation into awareness.

The fortunes of the concept of imagination, the extremes of which we have suggested, are recapitulated in the history of twentieth century psychology. Psychological theories built more or less on empirical assumptions, such as psychoanalysis and behaviorism, give little attention to imagination as a topic of psychological concern. On the other hand, psychological theories built on or sympathetic to idealistic assumptions, such as phenomenological and humanistic psychology, provide language and values which acknowledge the central role of imagination in human behavior. The time has now come for a synthesis of the methods of these two approaches to man's mental life.

Leslie Farber indicates that psychology in the twentieth century has not given imagination a central place in man's mental life.[3] He shows that Freud's influence has to some extent limited the concept of imagination for modern psychological thought. Freud's approach to imagination was tangential rather than explicit and direct: he touched on it in such concepts as "object," "super-ego," "introjection," and "projection." He interpreted fantasy behavior primarily as a defensive and reactive behavior, an intrapsychic substituting for reality. And he did not focus on imagination as the creative, central power of perception. Nevertheless, he did discover the influence of parents upon personality through the process of socialization, the individual's internalization of images through childhood experience. Moreover, Freud emphasized the imagery of dreams as "the royal road to the unconscious." In spite of these contributions, however, he overlooked the central role of imagination as a mental function because he refused to acknowledge the cosmic dimension of human consciousness.

Freud's denial of the cosmic dimension of human consciousness is linked with his commitment to empiricism. According to that commitment, he distrusted everything which the psychologist could not reduce to empirical truth. As a consequence, he dismissed religion, art, and philosophy as merely comforting illusions. He even felt it necessary to warn against "the black tide of mud . . . of occultism."[4] Thus Freud found it necessary to interpret both the empirical and the fantastical aspects of subjectivity within the frame of reference of natural science. But as a result, the meaning of subjectivity was constricted and all psychic processes were reduced to Theoretical explanations in terms of instincts. This reduction makes intellectual and aesthetic values nothing other than pre-intellectual organic conditions and non-symbolic drives. On this basis, philosophy can be dismissed as the childish and illusory attempt to invent coherent images of the universe.

This reductive interpretation of man's reflective powers denies his reality as a self-reflecting being who orients himself to cosmic meaning through creating and experiencing images of a coherent universe. At the heart of Freud's perspective lies a deep distrust of subjective reality and the fear of any mode of knowledge which dares to claim a validity equal to that of empirical knowledge. The consequence of this blindness has been the failure to distinguish between the use of art and philosophy as pathological and illusory strategies on the one hand, and the ultimate meaning which these modes of experience can have for man as a symbolizing being on the other. When man is not viewed as primarily a symbolizing being, his existence can only be debased.

Some of Freud's followers in the field of psychoanalysis moved closer toward acknowledging the centrality of imagination, but they did not go so far as to attribute ontological significance to it. Melanie Klein, with her extensive attention to the thinking of children, was one of these.[5] She emphasized the imagination and the early formation of personality in relation to parental images. Nevertheless, she stopped short of seeing imagination as the function which relates man to Being.

Eric Berne's phenomenological position is somewhat more open.[6] He indicated that a person acts and feels, not according to what things are really like, but according to that person's mental image of what things are like. Berne even admitted that some images took on universality. He said that their power is so great that if the reality challenges these images, the individual becomes sad and anxious or mentally ill. However, Berne's general statements do not go far enough. He does not develop his theorizing to the point where it accounts for the ultimate meaning of man's images.

Ernest Becker links the reluctance of empirical psychologists to deal with symbolism to the difficulty they find in deriving means to approach it or to conceptualize it empirically.[7] But the difficulties which the symbolic element of mental life poses for empirical methods do not justify the reductionistic conclusions which often result from these methods. Rather, the difficulties indicate the need for other kinds of approach and verification so that man can be adequately understood as a symbolizing being, for imagination relates the individual to the total field within which he emerges. For Becker and a growing number of others, imagination is a priority: it must be rediscovered and restored to its rightful place as a subject of inquiry in the human sciences.

Phenomenological description is one approach which provides more adequate possibilities for the study of imagination. According to Combs and Snygg, the phenomenological method sets aside the task of explaining the mechanism of imagination in order to focus on the actual experience that the person has in the act of imagining. The way that a person perceives himself becomes more important than the explanations of how or why this perception is constituted. Consistency of self image is the enduring element in the description of self-experience. Every act is committed and interpreted in accordance with this principle:

> All behavior, without exception, is completely determined by, and pertinent to, the perceptual field of the behaving organism. [This perceptual field is] the entire universe, including himself, as it is experienced by the individual at the moment of action.[8]

Both self and world are posited within the perceptual field. At each moment of awareness, the individual acts as a part of his perceptual field: he is taking a role and composing an impromptu drama for his part in this perceived world. When he reflects on his actions or experiences, the individual's phenomenal field becomes an inner world of images and meanings among which his intentions make their way. Such phenomenological descriptions of experience conceptually augment the otherwise limited observations of the empirical approach.

C. G. Jung has adapted phenomenological description for his own purposes, and in this he and his followers have perhaps come closest to attributing ontological significance to the imagination. Jung developed a symbolic psychology based on the principle of psychic polarity between the conscious ego and the personal and collective unconscious. Jung taught that the collective unconscious was a primordial fund of symbols of which all men partake. Jung believed that elements of man's imaginative life evoked by the common archetypes of these collective depths produce disruptive experience

unless they are carefully integrated into the totality of
the individual's psychic life. Jung does not speak explicitly of imagination. Yet his theory leaves little room for
it to be treated otherwise than as the central mental
function. Thus Jung's speculations are a point of departure
for any psychology in which imagination is given a central
place.

Imagination is the central mental function according to
the theory of symbolic regression psychology. We begin with
the axiom that imagination is rooted in cosmic energies.
This assumption has far-reaching implications for personality
theory as well as for psychotherapeutic practice. This
assumption is also a timely one at this moment in the history
of psychology, for according to Ernest Becker's assessment,
the concept of imagination has been receiving ever increasing
attention over the past several years. Furthermore, mental
imagery is also now reappearing as a subject for psychological investigation in fields as diverse as parapsychology,
brain research, and dream analysis.

Clemens Benda points out that an understanding of imagery
as the realm within which a person lives leads to a comprehensive understanding of his being, for the way that he configures his images is his world.[9] Jacques Maritain illustrates this principle from the realm of art:

> Oscar Wilde's saying, "Nature imitates art," is but an
> obvious truism, as far as our perception of the
> beauty of Nature is concerned. For man's art and
> vision too are one of the ways through which mankind
> invades Nature, so as to be reflected and meant by her.
> Without the mirrors worked out by generations of
> painters and poets, what would our aesthetic penetration of Nature be? Only after Giotto had replaced the
> gold backgrounds of early medieval art with peaks and
> mountains did we become aware of the beauty of mountains. When you are walking in Rome, part of your
> joy depends on Piranesi . . . .[10]

The image produced by imagination is the object that stands
out in awareness at any given moment, and the inner order of
one's images determines the significance of any individual
entity in that person's phenomenal field.

At the experiential level, Wolgang Kretschmer shows how
relaxation exercises bring deeply felt imagery to a person's
mind and he argues that this kind of imagery awareness is

the basis of psychological integration.[11] When a person focuses on deeply felt inner symbols, he has entered into a state of symbolic regression, and he returns to the creative foundations of his life. Kretschmer describes two practical applications of this process. First, he says that concentration on a chapel as a symbol will lead the subject into the innermost sanctum of the mind, which contains the possibility of psychic transformation. Secondly, he uses mandala images (geometrical drawings symbolizing cosmic harmony and used in conjunction with Eastern meditation practices) not to produce extensive fantasy contents as one would do with a Rorschach design, but rather to evoke an experience of the cosmic meaning of the design.

Hypnosis is a phenomenon which has received increasing attention in the past several years. In fact William Kroger's standard textbook of hypnosis (1963) has had to be considerably revised for the 1977 edition. Kroger claims that the therapeutic process amounts to "hypnosis in slow motion."[12] That is, through his relationship with the therapist, the person's recovery of a symbolic regressive orientation amounts to the gradual, integrative rediscovery of his own latent inner powers and their actualization in the person's lived experience. Hypnosis is a particular type of focusing of the process of imagination. There are two types of hypnoid state that are particularly significant for the psychology of symbolic regression.

First is the state of hypnotic regression which has been used with great success by W. Earl Biddle in his pioneering work in symbolic regressive theory and phenomena, a precursor of symbolic regression psychology.[13] Biddle's work brings into focus the relationship between the regressive phenomenon and man as a symbolic being. He has explored the nature of imagination through experimentaion with hypnotic age regression. Biddle concludes his study with the notion that images are psychic entities which have a kind of ultimate meaning for the person, and that the person's behavior takes shape according to this image. On the basis of such findings, he calls for a comprehensive reappraisal of all the factors of mental life which relate to mental images.

Biddle believes that imagination is the function of forming, conserving, and reproducing images, and that the primary thing which psychotherapy treats is the mental image. Accordingly, the purpose of clinical psychology is to change these images which interfere with personal and social adjustment. Therefore, Biddle has based his theory

of therapy on the idea that imagination is the ultimate
element of mental life and on the notion that each individual has the capacity to orient himself in relation to his
imaginative life, to change the stance by which he relates
to his inner images. It follows from this that the
individual who is oppressively fixated on destructive images
which constitute for him a bad and undesirable world can be
taught to shift his orientation so that he experiences a
good world of more profound order. Through imaginative
refixation, man can discover covered-over or forgotten
images of the restorative and good parent, and of the good,
well-ordered cosmos. This reorientation toward good images
is concomitant with the restoration of the individual's
dignity and self-esteem. The person is thus enabled to
reenter the sphere of man's ultimate hope.

Second is the hypnagogic state, the therapeutic method
known as the guided daydream, which is a tool for the conscious reorientation of the person to the symbolic regressive
dimensions of imagination. The guided daydream used as a
clinical technique in symbolic regression therapy is a collaboration between therapist and client which evokes the
conscious experience of the symbolic regressive imagery which
Biddle discusses through refocusing the process of imagination. The conscious focusing of imagination on basic cosmic-regressive images facilitates the integration of the total
psyche with the state of symbolic regression.

Use of the guided daydream, which was referred to in the
discussion of the birthright of consciousness at the outset,
is relatively simple. Once the therapist has guided the
person through muscle and breathing relaxation, he asks him
to imagine himself in a setting representing the symbolic
regressive process, such as a meadow, a mountain, the womb,
or reversed personal time, and then to describe to the
therapist what he sees and feels from within this imaginative
experience. For the person in this hypnagogic state, his
focus is on his own images while he plays the role of
narrating them to the therapist. This narrating is extremely
important, for it enables the person to mediate the lived
images representing his inner psychic energies to a significant other person in a safe, accepting social context which
encourages the symbolic regression necessary to the awareness of the person's natural inner imagery. This in itself
gives integrative order and continuity to the dimensions of
social fact and inner fantasy in the person's experience.
The therapist acts as a gentle guide for the daydreamer by
first providing or suggesting an initial image or setting and

then supporting positive images in the symbolic regressive encounter. In this encounter, the therapist encourages exploration and provides "principles of management," tools so that the person can overcome barriers to ongoing symbolic regressive events.[14]

The writers we have discussed in this chapter manifest a growing trend away from strictly empirical methods in psychological inquiry. Such writers open up the possibility for a kind of psychology which is at once intuitive and speculative, experiential and practical. This new openness leads to the recovery of imagination and imagery as the essence of mental life. In all of the various psychologies which are the heirs of Romanticism, imagination is increasingly coming into its own: Gestalt psychology, Jungian psychology, Psychosynthesis, and transpersonal psychology are but a few of these. It is now time to synthesize the various psychologies of consciousness and of the human potential movement into a psychological theory which is founded on the central place of imagination in the life of man. We now begin to do this, and our point of departure will be a deeper discussion of the function of imagination.

THEORY OF IMAGINATION:
NATURAL VS. INTROJECTED SYMBOLIC ORDERS

The language most adequate for discussing mind, according to symbolic regression psychology, is the language of process and experience. It refers to realities that are best characterized as dynamic and existential rather than to empirical objects and measurable behavioral phenomena. Thus, the word "imagination" is often used without the definite article to emphasize that this concept does not refer to a faculty or to any kind of mental entity. "Imagination" is a term used to characterize a psychic function or process. It is to be distinguished from any entities connected with a faculty psychology. It is a function, not an entity, a process, not a faculty. Sometimes the limits of language will force us to treat imagination as a thing, a manifold or nexus of experiencing, but this use of language should not be construed as implying that imagination is anything other than a dynamic function. With this emphasis in mind, we now consider the nature of imagination.

According to its simplest definition, imagination is the function of forming mental images. These images are the elements of awareness which are present to the person in a different way than are sensory stimuli. Sylvan Tomkins helps to clarify the distinction between sensory apperception and imagery.[15] He says that sensory stimulus is not itself directly transformed into awareness because sensory input is immediately matched by an energized feedback mechanism, an image pattern produced by the mind. Thus the object of conscious perception is the imagery which is created by the organism itself and not the sensory stimulus given by the thing outside of the organism: "the world we perceive is a dream we learn to have from a script which we did not write" (p. 114). This formulation of the nature of human experience makes imagination central, for the act of dreaming in Tomkins' metaphor is the act of imagining which fuses sensory input and inner images into the experienced moment.

The image which comprises a moment of experience is not produced out of nothing; rather, it is an embodiment of psychic energy. We can best understand the nature of the image if we relate it to a continuum which ranges from the abstract conception of Being to the concreteness of a moment of experience as it is experienced. We have defined Being as the total field of energy as such, the absolute and ultimate condition for any and all material and psychic phenomena. Out of this total field of energy emerges the symbolic order, the "rough frame" of the house of Being, manifesting itself as cosmic substance as it transforms itself into human consciousness. This symbolic order impinges upon the individual psyche as images. An image is a unit of experience, a moment of consciousness or nexus in which the individual and the cosmos come to be manifest together. The image is the experience of the act in which both self-relatedness and cosmic-relatedness occur at once. In this moment of experience, imagination is the action, the mediating between the organic needs and the cosmic substance of the self. This action manifests itself in the form of an energy which is both psychic and cosmic—the image. By definition, this conception of imagination as a mediating function makes fantasy awareness and "thing" awareness two aspects of a single psychic process.

Considered phenomenologically, there are three constitutive elements which imagination mediates in any given moment of experience. They are: the image, which constitutes the experience as an experience; the implicit field of meaning or "world" within which the experience takes place and which we call "the order of images"; and the self which

IMAGINATION   91

is implicitly constituted within this field, the element
which "has" the experience. In other words, in the act of
imagining, the image appears as awareness in a "world" or
ultimate realm of all possible images, and an implicit self
is presented with this image. Normally, the symbolic order
is the ground of meaning on the basis of which persons act,
for meaning is the intuition of the correlations between
self and Being, and the desire for Being assures the con-
gruency of a person's acts to this end. This symbolic
order, within which man lives and by which man functions, is
Being as it is made into experience by the continual
symbolizing process, imagination.

   Man's imagination is at once the most mysterious and the
most important of his powers. A person's sphere of meaning,
the way he relates to or interprets symbols through imagination, is inseparable from the ultimate scope and direction
which his life will take for him. Imagination is the focal
point for the energies of the self and the nexus of the
symbolizing processes which are the ego. Imagination both
constitutes any given act of perception and contextualizes
it by relating it to Being. It is in this latter function
that imagination is self-transcending. Thus, imagination as
a fusing action ultimately grounds self in Being. It
transposes Being into the subjective reality of the individual. At the same time, it transposes subjectivity into
Being. The energies at play in any one moment of symbolizing
are always cosmic and organic as well as personal. Imagination as this continual fusing function is the process of
symbolic regression, and is the foundation for the integration and growth of the person.

   Imagination constantly reconstellates the personality
through reworking self, things, consciousness, and cosmos in
a free-ranging play of images. It fuses, focuses, directs,
and disperses all of the various energies of the individual
in relation to Being. It ceaselessly constitutes the self
in relation to Being, and it orients and re-orients both the
style and the strength of the relating of self and Being.
The scope of the self is constituted by the symbolic
dimension--whether organic, personal, or cosmic--which
happens to be the focus of consciousness at any given
moment of experience. As the means of self-reflection,
imagination is the personal ego function. As such, it mediates the finite and the infinite elements of experience, the
intuition of the finite self and the sense of ultimate
meaning, the intuition of the correlation of self and Being.
This unique function in man sets him apart from other forms

of sentient life and is the basis of his essentially cosmic nature. Through imagination, the individual and the cosmos become symbolically ordered and related to each other.

Man's psychic energies are constellated by unfolding networks of meanings, more or less idiosyncratic structural systems or topographical ranges of symbols. Intentionality is the flow of psychic energy which in any given instant of experience pulsates through the network of a man's symbols, striking reverberations and forming a Gestalt. A given intention embodies itself in an image or in a cluster of images. Imagination is the function of embodying these images as expressions of the energies of the individual. Imagination fuses the immediate reference of the intentional act with its ultimate context for the individual. That context is the structure of meanings which he has built up through his lifetime of uniquely relating to Being. Thus, meaning is the intuition of the fusing of the individual's order of images with the apprehension of the unique immediacy of a new situation, the moment of experience. This fusing is awareness. Awareness is constituted by the transfer of energy to the constellation of symbols which relates the self to the total order of symbols, and thus to Being.

In other words, imagination as the activating of certain given symbols within a particular existential field implies a self, a perspective-giving agent who stands out in relation to the order of symbols. Thus imagination, as the act of symbolizing, constellates self and Being by bringing self and consciousness into play. The unique way in which these elements are brought into play out of the order of images constitutes the character of a given person's imagination. The order of images can be regarded as a sphere or collective "world" of a given individual's experiences. This sphere corresponds more or less to the order of Being. This correspondence is a dynamic one because imagination both initiates and completes a dialectic of expectation and fulfillment which runs according to the person's natural organic-psychic rhythms of desire and satiation. The sphere as a whole is a person's consciousness, the psychic energy field within which imagination relates self and Being through symbols. For a growing, healthy person, consciousness is built on the symbolic order, the structural nexus of Being and consciousness which each person's conscious experience touches through symbolization. The resulting order of meaning corresponds to the structure of Being, and this structure of Being, in turn, corresponds to the substance of the human psyche.

IMAGINATION

The psyche as an energy system is driven by its relating to Being. Its telos is to substantialize itself as a participant in cosmic process. Directly or indirectly all intentionality expresses this end. Energy is discharged toward this end by the formation of symbols, by consciousness. The psyche substantializes the self through the activity of symbolizing. Thus the symbol mediates self-Being by implicitly re-presenting the self in the act of presenting "world." "World" is the self-Being relationship as this is constituted in the individual's experience. The activity of mediating self and Being naturally takes place at each of the three levels of consciousness simultaneously.

Man's experience would be constantly integrated with itself and harmonious with Being if he were only to symbolize, that is, be conscious according to this natural symbolic order. But portions of the spectrum of consciousness to which each person is open in infancy (on the basis of the natural correspondence between the underlying structures of consciousness and the underlying structures of matter in Being) become blocked out of awareness for the individual through learned unconsciousness, or introjects. Introjects are formed in two ways. First, there is the introject formed because the child imitates the parents when they act as if there were areas of unconsciousness. This is the learned introject, the material of awareness gained through social transmission or the imprinting of the subjectivity of the parent. In this, one applies the subjective perception of another person as this is articulated ad hoc to his own experience without re-thinking it in relation to himself. An example of this kind of introjection is the parent who imposes his sense of developmental psychology on the child by talking baby-talk, robbing the child of his natural autonomy, not expecting the child to love him, or not allowing himself to receive from the child. The second mode of introjection is tied to trauma: the person fixates his consciousness in response to traumatic experience. He personally develops strategies of pain avoidance, such as avoiding risks to prevent possible pain or denying injury to the sense of self by idealizing his situation. Such strategies detract from the natural flow of energy that takes place in the symbolizing of self in relation to Being. This shift severely restricts the scope of the individual's natural intuitive relating to Being. Too, it takes away from the natural growth of the individual's consciousness: it actually militates against it by absorbing more and more energy into a vortex of self-destruction. Like a nova, such a complex of introjected material burns brighter on its self-extinguishing course.

Turning back to the nature of introjects themselves, they are perhaps best described as areas in the psychic spectrum blanketed from consciousness like a palimpsest. A palimpsest is a document which has two messages. There is an original message content which the document was originally intended to express. This message has been painted over and a new, different message has been written on top of it which completely hides the old message, the one which served the document's original purpose. The new message, on the surface, seems to constitute a different document altogether. Through the work of the curator, however, the original message is rediscovered and restored. The original purpose of the document is recognized and its restored meaning yields a larger, more coherent awareness of the field of concern within which it originally appeared. Similarly, the introject is a painting over or a superscribing of foreign and inferior images (contents of awareness) over a part of the original full and freely playing spectrum of the individual's psychic energies.

In summation, introjection is a part of every person's social development which interferes with his natural psychic functioning. It puts the individual in an inauthentic stance in relation to the symbolic order, and thus to Being. It also forces the individual to create an implcit counterfeit symbolic order out of the images emerging in the distorted symbolizing activity which is his psychic process. The person thus lives in a deformed, emaciated, and oppressed "world" or sphere of consciousness. The project of developing an individual's consciousness is the project of enlarging his sphere of consciousness where it has become deformed or oppressed through the destructive influence of introjected images on the world of his experience.

Man's problems and his unhappiness stem from the phenomenon of introjection, for this means that there are two states of consciousness, natural consciousness and introjected consciousness. Corresponding to these two states are two orders of symbols, the natural, authentic order of symbols which can be mediated into man's experience from beyond it, and the counterfeit, introjected order of symbols which is projected out of man's social experience. The first order constitutes the field of meaning by virtue of its emerging directly out of Being. But this order gets overlaid by the second order, which is built through the process of

IMAGINATION   95

socialization. This invasion of alien material into consciousness thwarts the person's spontaneous growth and natural vitality. Consciousness becomes blocked and divided. The person finds himself and his energies deterred from their natural expressiveness and restricted in growth. Nevertheless, there is hope in the midst of this marring and confusion, for the crux of the problem lies in the orientation of the imaginative process towards the counterfeit, alienating order of symbols, and its solution lies in the recovery of a positive orientation toward the vital and authentic order of symbols which is grounded in Being. A consideration of the nature of these orders of symbolism will help to clarify the theoretical basis of symbolic regression psychology.

If we were to make a topography of "grammar" of the natural order of symbols, we might arrange them vertically, as Northrop Frye suggests in Anatomy of Criticism.[16] In such a scheme the highest sphere is the cosmic sphere, the realm of supernatural light. The second level is the realm of earthly paradise above the mundane world. The third is the realm of man's everyday existence. And the fourth is the realm of subterranean being. Frye's topography moves down from light and spirit to darkness and matter. This scheme is a helpful ordering of symbols into a spectrum that is roughly analogous to the cosmic, the personal, and the organic symbolic dimensions described in chapter one above.

It is necesssary at this point in charting a topography of symbols to differentiate between our understanding of symbols as ranged into two fundamentally different orders, the natural and the counterfeit order, and the Platonizing understanding which underlies almost every systematic approach to symbols. In most systems there is an ultimate division between "higher" and "lower" symbols, with the more positive value being given to the "higher" symbols. "Higher" is taken to correspond with "more significant" or "better." This is emphatically not the case in symbolic regression psychology, for we start with the fundamental axiom that all registers on any scale of natural symbols are equally valuable and equally to be affirmed.

Frye is one among many students of symbolism who organizes symbols on the basis of traditional Christian motifs and values which were influenced by dualistic thinking, the source of the idea of the supremacy of mind over matter, of light over darkness, and of height over depth. Thus, in Frye's Secular Scripture, the highest realm becomes Heaven, the place of the presence of God.[17] The second realm becomes Paradise, the place of blissful pre-lapsarian existence. The third realm becomes earth, a place of obscurity which nevertheless offers the potential of ascent to the higher and better realism. And the fourth realm becomes Hell, the realm of tyranny, deprivation, torture, and entrapment.

The notion of two orders of symbols presented here, however, provides a different way of interpreting this spectrum, one affirming the values inherent in human experience. The ultimate division between the natural, authentic symbolic order and the introjected symbolic order which counterfeits it becomes the basis for a completely different interpretation of symbol systems. Starting with the nature of man as an embodied being, we find it impossible to range this scale of symbols according to the traditionally construed hierarchy of values. Thus, we find that the qualities of height, light, and weightlessness at one end of the scale, and the qualities of depth, darkness, and density at the other are all equally good and positive when they are part of the natural symbolic order. It follows from this perspective that the highest realm is that of cosmic spirit in which man naturally participates as a conscious being, that the second realm is the realm of fraternal society within which emanate natural human love and concord, that the third realm is the realm of practical work within which arises the material aspect of man's well being, and that the fourth realm is the realm of organic processes and physical passions, the depths which ground man ultimately in the earth itself.

The contrast with the natural goodness of these levels of symbols when it becomes superscribed by interpreted material is striking. Each level becomes perverted and oppressive when it becomes taken up and reflected in the alien, introjected order. Dogmatic Christianity can often function as just such an introjected system of symbols. When this is the case, even the Christian God, the inhabitant of the highest realm, is seen as a harsh and oppressive ruler. Similarly, Paradise becomes an inaccessible or illusory realm. Earth becomes a dreary exile. And of course, the subterranean realm functions as Hell, the place of ultimate and irrevocable enslavement.

Now Christian tradition is the ultimate set of motifs informing western man's imagination. The purpose here is not to evaluate this fact in terms of its ultimate

beneficence or destructiveness. Rather, it is to see how
the material of this tradition can be ordered and used for
good or for ill for any given person. This way of looking
at it will enable each person to determine how he can best
relate to what is given to him in the tradition and how it
ought to move him.

The Faust story, along with Tristan and Iseult, is one
of the two major legends of Europe. Marlowe's <u>Doctor
Faustus</u>, written in 1593, is a compelling example of the
destructive power of introjected symbols. Doctor Faustus is
unable to interpret the symbols of Christian tradition in
terms of their natural power to console man. Instead, he
interprets scripture with an inexorable logic which sees
only condemnation and death:

> The reward of sin is death. That's hard.
> If we say that we have no sin,
> We deceive ourselves, and there's no truth in us.
> Why then belike we must sin,
> And so consequently die.
> Aye, we must die, an everlasting death.
> What doctrine call you this? Che sera, sera:
> What will be, shall be! Divinity, adieu![18]

Faustus is reading these words as if they were part of an
order of destructive, introjected symbols. This reading at
the outset is consistent with the orientation of his
behavior throughout the play. This behavior is characterized
by isolation, illusionary strategies, and the gratuitous use
of dangerous powers. At the highest level, the level of
spiritual authority, he dupes the pope. He also impresses
political leaders with his illusions, although he cannot
really relate to them as persons. He fools a peasant by
selling him an illusionary horse. He avenges his peers by
making them foolish. And at the end he resolutely interprets himself to be beyond hope as he is carried off to
destruction by unrelenting demons.

Similarly, introjected symbols have their oppressive
influence at all levels of modern thinking. Nietzsche and
Kafka both find the traditional Judaeo-Christian God
oppressive.[19] Even Pascal feels horror at the vastness
of cosmic space.[20] In Sartre's <u>Nausea</u>, earth becomes a
terror which threatens to engulf Roquentin.[21] And in
Dostoevsky, subterranean existence is characterized as
misery and living death for the narrator of <u>Notes from
Underground</u>.[22]

If we turn to the natural order of symbols for contrast, we find we have an entirely different prospect. The light emanating from above, the highest realm, is a present joy: it is "a light, a glory, a fair luminous cloud / Enveloping the earth."[23] Symbols along this order reveal ultimate being and meaning:

> The heavens declare the glory of God.
> and the firmament showeth his handiwork.
> Day unto day uttereth speech,
> and night unto night showeth knowledge.[24]

The depths within the earth are the place of eternity and are full of glory for Aeneas.[25] And the darkness of interstellar space becomes positive and palpable to the cosmic voyagers in 2001: A Space Odyssey.[26] Ultimately, orientation toward this natural order of symbols integrates all levels of symbols so that there is free play among them. Accordingly, man sees himself thus as a participant in the cosmic dance:

> Garlic and sapphires in the mud
> Clot the bedded axle-tree.
> The trilling wire in the blood
> Sings below inveterate scars
> And reconciles forgotten wars.
> The dance along the artery
> The circulation of the lymph
> Are figured in the drift of stars
> Ascend to summer in the tree
> In light upon the figured leaf
> And hear upon the sodden floor
> Below, the boarhound and the boar
> Pursue their pattern as before
> But reconciled among the stars.[27]

The distinction between the natural and the introjected orders of symbols which is being developed here becomes a heuristic tool which enables us to interpret traditional material on an entirely different basis than the traditional one. For example, with this distinction in mind, we read the Divine Comedy telically rather than in terms of the spatial scheme of values which Frye has consolidated on the basis of Christian tradition.[28] According to our reading, the significance of the Inferno lies in its early place in the sequence of the narrative rather than in its place in cosmic geography. Dante's descent to the depths is part of a process of symbolic regression. He travels through Hell as a spectator rather than as a permanent participant in its horrors, and the fundamental, integrative insights he gains in his descent become the foundation for his subsequent ascent. The Devil's anus, for example, is a very positive point on his journey, for it is the axis on which the journey turns. Dante's journey to the center of the earth is modelled on that of Aeneas and has a comparable outcome: by their visits to the depths, both heroes are equipped for their heroic deeds. Whether one finds the subterranean realm a place of oppression or a place of synthesizing insight depends entirely on whether one is oriented to the introjected or to the natural order of symbols.

Each individual learns to symbolize himself either as in harmony or as in disharmony with Being. On the one hand, he can symbolize himself through the constructive and natural images which are related to his being in its integrity. On the other hand, he can symbolize himself through disruptive patterns which are alien to the true meaning of the self. Imagination is the means by which each person realizes one or the other of these two possibilities: a perceived world which is true to man's ultimate nature, or an alien order of images which have been isolated within while they surreptitiously seal off a part of the mind because they are not harmonious with the true nature of Being.

If the images affirming the positive values of nutritive comfort and life-giving authority are not the ultimate sphere toward which imagination can orient a person, and if such a naturally good realm of values is not the foundation for a comprehensive, integral psychology by which the individual can find his destiny and know himself, then man's quest for wholeness as a self-reflective being is an illusion and offers false hope. Furthermore, if such is the case, man is lost at sea and is alienated without any possibility of redemption for his psychic life.

In fundamental opposition to such a cynical view, we agree with Biddle that the person must be supplied with positive, corrective imagery at deep levels of his imaginative experience. Such positive images feed imagination and provide the seedbed out of which the individual can develop images of himself and of his world as ultimately worthwhile elements of a harmonious whole. This basis of reorientation allows the individual to experience his environment as ultimately nutritive. It restores the individual to a recovery of his innately sensed birthright which the disrupted imagination has partially obliterated from his awareness and which the same imaginative power, nourished by positive images, can richly renew. Thus, the underlying basis of the theory of symbolic regression psychology is the faith that these ultimate good images are anchored in Being and that they are available to man through a reorientation of his power of imagining. The point of contact for this reorientation is always imagination, the synthesizing and integrating function, for even the most self-depriving individual can be touched and appealed to through some remaining token of the original promise of his birth which he has buried like an unprofitable steward (Matthew 25: 24-30). The deepest intuitive powers of the therapist must be brought into play in order to determine where this point of contact has been buried and how it is best invested for the reorienting of any particular individual.

The synthesizing power of the mind is by definition holistic. Thus when it is fed by the natural order of symbols, it places the self within a harmonious universe of meaning and it produces dynamic, integrative constellations of experience. But when the self is symbolized according to the disruptive, invalid images introjected through a person's negative social experiences, the whole person gets into trouble. The world is experienced as unjust and lacking in positive possibilities. The world is seen as an alien realm, chaotic, and full of obstacles and dangers. It is perceived as disharmonious and fragmented. And it is felt to be depriving, uncomfortable, and tension-producing. Given this disruptive orientation to the cosmos, imagination synthesizes the self with inauthentic, introjected images and the person functions symptomatically. In response to this orientation, imagination seals off each unhealthy, negative introject in order to protect the individual's intuitive relatedness from Being. Yet it is this very disrupting as a defense measure that causes the alienation from Being and the resulting negative imaginative states which the individual suffers.

Yet we have seen that when the self is related to Being through a free and open imaginative orientation to positive images, the symbolizing function is dynamically constructive. The person's inner orientation to the world is charged with an atmosphere of lightness and well-being. In this state, deep communication with others and the satisfying ordering of one's inner and physical life are all elements of one broad continuum of experience. Love becomes a part of this world and an innate, continuing experience.

One of these two orientations which we have described becomes the ultimately dominant orientation in the life of each individual, although elements of both persist in everyone's experience. These two orientations are in competition for the allegiance of the person. The outcome of their competition is the ultimate relationship which the individual develops between self and Being. This struggle between positive and negative image poles contextualizes the true meaning of man's power of choice and will, for the act of choosing promotes the person's realization of the one or the other orientation. The signs pointing to a positive integration and harmony are embedded in the mind of each person in the form of his perhaps forgotten "dream" of the good life. When a person's orientation is fixated in the realm of disruptive and alienating images, these signs must be rediscovered and reinterpreted so that the individual can both know of and work toward positive goals which are real because they are harmonious with Being.

THEORY OF IMAGINATION:
NATURAL AUTHORITY VS. INTROJECTED AUTHORITY

The unrestricted imagination relates the individual to Being. This free relating is the state of symbolic regression. It consists of two major levels of grounding: awareness and images find their ground in the symbolic order, or consciousness; consciousness, in turn, finds its ground in Being. The individual's intuition of his relating to Being is his sense of ultimate meaning. He participates in the total order of things which is too big to understand, yet in this sense of participation is his intuition of ultimate meaning. If Being is the source of all values, so the symbolic order is the source of all coherence. The individual has a strong sense of both of these when he is grounded in them. Whatever may be involved with either granting or depriving access to this state of awareness is what we here call authority. That which grants access is good, natural authority. And that which deprives access is bad, introjected authority. Authority is an element of the imaginative function. It is a root element of the substance of the mind and it is inseparable from the cosmic imagery which each person experiences. Authority expresses the potential capacity which each individual has to harmonize his unique self with Being. A discussion of the nature of authority will further elaborate the nature of the distorting of imagination and the means of restoring it to its fullness.

Freud used the term superego to talk about the individual's inner sense of authority. The superego is the internal representative of traditional values as these are interpreted to the child by the behavior of his parents. This internalized authority is socially derived and it relates directly to man's immediately experienced social context. It is rooted in the moral concepts of society as these are related to family life. It is coextensive with an idealizing strategy, for its basic purpose is to secure the individual's social acceptance and ultimately his psychic survival. Its ultimate end is perfection at the expense of pleasure—the constriction or denial of instinctual drives. Its main function is to judge what is right and wrong. That is, it is governed by what the individual must do so that he can be considered a non-threatening member of the social system. The conscience, an irrational response to the mode of punishment, is part of this superego. Introjection is the method by which parental demands become part of the internalized meaning of authority. Imitation of or identification with the internalized ideals of the parent make the person feel "good" while conscience, as a balancing component of the same introjected system, makes him feel guilty by measuring the discrepancy between these ideals and his instincts.

Real guilt in contrast to this introjected guilt, however is a concept beyond the concerns of Freudian theory, for the superego is seen as a cultural instrument imposed upon a biological system. The superego inhibits instinctual drives by supplanting them with moralistic goals and rigid idealizations. The superego is thus opposed to both instinctual drives and to the ego's attempts to mediate instinctual drives in the form of humanized wishes. Superego is based on the desire for reward and the fear of punishment.

Freud posited that the energies of the superego are developed out of the child's experience of parental restrictions: the child internalizes these for the sake of survival. The child learns to behave in ways that reduce the tension between his undifferentiated libidinal instincts and his experience of authority. He then perpetuates this mode of tension reduction within himself throughout life. He identifies with the ideals the parent has, with parental introjects, so that his life is guaranteed to be pleasant at the level of family life. Through this identification with parents, the superego diverts energy from instinctual drives to a psychic system characterized by tension and conflict. As Ernest Becker puts it,

IMAGINATION   103

The child learns to conduct himself, and to execute
choices, in a manner which will avoid anxiety, and
which will be pleasing to his parents. He learns
to gain his feeling of self-value by performing
according to codes that are thrust upon him by his
parents. But then his early learning remains
inadequate to meet the demands of varied adult
experience; it constricts the choices and action of
the adult in some ways. When the child made sacri-
fices in learning in order to please his parents he
necessarily sacrificed the possibilities of broader
perception and action in the interests of his own
survival, security, and equanimity.
. . .
The whole of Freud's concept is summed up in the
lines uttered by the responsible child: "You
needn't punish me any more, father—I will punish
myself now."[29]

This superego as Freud analyzes it is at odds with Being and
thus at odds with natural authority as we have defined it.
Freud's analysis is very useful, however, for it provides us
with an excellent interpretation of the nature and dynamics
of introjected authority, as we shall see below.

Jung interpreted authority in more cosmic terms than did
Freud. According to his analysis, there are two distinct
levels of authority. First, at the broadest level, the
archetypal level, authority is an unconscious psychic predisposition towards the affirmation of self as a manifestation of Being which each individual inherits as a member of
the human race. This predisposition has developed unconsciously through the process of evolution. It corresponds
roughly with natural authority. Yet, according to Jung's
analysis, it functions along with the second level of
authority, the existentially learned expectations which a
person's society shapes for him and which he assumes due to
convention and dons as a mask or persona. This level of
authority corresponds precisely with introjected authority.
Thus, in Jungian theory, authority in man consists of a
level which is racially inherited and of a level which is
individually learned in the process of man's social
development.

The concept presented here, however, goes beyond Jung's
in one important aspect. There is a further element of
authority in consciousness which it is necessary for man to
become aware of in order that he might become a conscious
participant in and even an agent of his own evolution. For

there are now further resources within imagination for the
attainment of greater consciousness which lie ready for
those who learn to use them. Thus there is an ultimately
transcendent role of imagination at this stage in man's
evolution which Jung's theory allows for but to which it
does not give sufficient attention.

The brief consideration of the past theorists, Freud and
Jung, has helped to contextualize the concept of authority in
psychology. Mention of the ideas of two more recent
psychologists may further help to clarify the dimensions of
the concept as it is developed in symbolic regression
psychology. Abraham Maslow has emphasized the importance
of Being as the ground of man's psychic potential.
Deficiency motivation as he defines it is the state one is
in when introjected authority is in ascendency. Growth
motivation, which arises out of Being and can lead to Being
cognition, is the state of mind made accessible by natural
authority. R. D. Laing talks about these two poles in his
distinction between "primary ontological insecurity" and
"primary ontological security." Natural authority is the
threshold of "primary ontological security."

To this point, psychology has not developed a concept of
authority which adequately corresponds to the ultimate scope
of human consciousness. The nature of authority must be
reinterpreted in such a way that a person is thereby enabled
to let himself become self-reflective and conscious. Every
person implicitly asks and answers the question of the ultimate nature of authority, because each act that a person
commits is done on the basis of what he absolutely sees to
be ultimate meaning. That is, each person is constantly
doing that which is most affirming of his relating to Being
in the lived moment, as we have seen in our consideration of
phenomenological description in psychology. Nevertheless,
not many individuals know how to relate to authority in a
way that gives them the right to become fully conscious. In
fact, the problem of authority is the crucial problem which
must be resolved in order for a man ultimately to resolve
the problems of consciousness itself.

When the person is fully relating to Being through the
free play of imagination, the presence of natural authority
has made this possible. As a result, energy is released
through the person in the form of love. That is, the individual finds himself at one with Being and the harmony of
this state vitalizes his social relationships, all of which
find their common ground in the expansiveness and openness
granted by this natural authority which is the characteristic

of this state. As long as the person relates primarily to the internalized social environment, however, he cannot face the truth about that environment, for he has not yet found a more substantial ground in cosmic reality upon which to stand. Because he relates to himself primarily through his introjected images, he has no deep inner authority or sense of Being by which he can relate to or transcend his society's influence. This problem is especially acute in the present age of alienated consciousness. A man's implicit orientation to idealized, self-constricting authority results in four simultaneous yet self-contradictory conditions: self-righteousness, over-conformity, self-idealization, and cynicism. These four conditions which are related to this state of idealized social existence are related to the fear of becoming conscious, for the self in this state is unrelated to Being, and strategies have developed both to make this non-relating meaningful and to make it secure by perpetuating it.

Natural authority as the inner permission to achieve consciousness goes far beyond the mere mastery of group mores. Social rules are made for the conditions of the day and have an element of untrustworthiness about them. It is true that they must be taken seriously, for they represent an element of the developing consciousness of man. Furthermore, every individual must face them as part of his social reality. Yet, their revision is a constant necessity, for they are not adequate enough to Being to possess true authority. True authority does not necessarily keep law; nor does it necessarily transgress law. Rather, it transcends law, just as love transcends both obligation and performance.

It takes developed consciousness, or courage, to live in relation to Being and to express this state in society by taking a stand against the limits of existing conventions in the name of Being. The individual who acts on the basis of growing consciousness stands to lose social status and recognition in the short run, for he does not fit the patterns of motivation and awareness which are prescribed by the socially introjected authority which more or less constricts the lives of the great majority of people around him. Moreover, the more affluent a society becomes, the more easy it becomes for its members to idealize affluence and to forget the existential questions which force them to grow in relation to Being.

In contrast to natural authority, introjected authority contaminates the true function of imagination and makes it difficult for the individual to symbolize with any self-awareness. To the degree that a person is involved in symbolizing through introjected authority, his relationship to his own being will be indistinct and confused and his capacity for deep relaxation and peace, which is part of the state of symbolic regression, will be thwarted.

Authority is the disposition toward the full range of consciousness. Introjected images impose severe constrictions and distortions on awareness. Authority is the capacity to relate to the environment of Being according to the natural dimensions of life. At some point in each individual's early experience, his survival within the social system has become so important to him that he is willing to purchase it at the cost of what turns out to be a tragic compromise. He learns to relinquish the innate free range of his consciousness in exchange for the idealized security and esteem which the system seems to hold out for him. Yet it is these very rewards, created out of social consensus which is estranged from Being, that seduce him away from Being while obliterating his sense of losing it. This exchange which comes about in the process of social development is the exchange of natural for introjected authority.

Each human act represents a judgment about ultimate meaning in human life, an imagined affirmation of the actor's relationship to Being. Yet persons often are not aware of this. To the degree that a person directs his awareness only to introjected images, he is not only unaware of how his actions do not relate to Being, but he unconsciously deprives himself of the right to find this out. He is in the grip of introjected authority. He is governed by socially imposed demands that he take care of his parents or of his society, demands which substantially shift his awareness from inner energies and Being energies to "world" as obligating institution and to self as incarcerated curator. He is living in slavery to demands opposed to those of Being and far removed from the self-esteem and ontological grounding which only Being provides. He is often both puzzled and incensed about what is happening to him in such an imbalanced social network. He is torn apart by an orientation of symbolizing that requires him emotionally to take care of his relationships. He is in a state of unconsciousness.

He loses himself in a pathological strategy designed to avoid acknowledging the loss of natural authority. This predicament is itself not owned up to. Instead, the process of consciousness becomes attached to introjected authority which finally becomes embodied in images of authority figures. This attachment is referred to as fixation. In fixation, the self is unconsciously preoccupied with an order of introjected images which themselves must be hidden from consciousness. This self-concealing strategy is a self-idealizing mode of symbolizing, the symbolizing in which the loss of relating to Being is in part concealed by an overdetermination of the meaning of its substitutes. This self-idealizing symbolizing is the fundamental strategy underlying all psychopathology. According to the particular elements of this strategy which are being emphasized, all symptomatic strategies can be differentiated by this syndrome. This symptomatic strategy is part of an elaborate system built up to defend the psyche's inauthentic relation to the introjected order of symbols.

The symptoms which are a part of this system thus hide both the positive potential of the cosmic meaning of consciousness and the self-reflective modes of awareness as well. In this, the person's true needs are hidden from his awareness. His deepest psychic need for consciousness in relation to Being is hidden by a double-edged strategy: the symptomatic denial of negative meaning or meaninglessness which riddles introjected image states is balanced by the concomitant blocking out of real positive meaning beyond this introjected system. All of this is committed through the crowning strategy, the self-masking idealization or overdetermination of introjected images. Man is the only creature who is able to play with his moods and his mind so that he can deceive himself in this way. For only man has the special form of consciousness which is the capacity for making images and for self-reflection.

Symptoms are part of this syndrome in which introjected, depriving authority is idealized and the loss of Being is tacitly hidden from awareness. Yet they are always the individual's blind, misguided attempts at self-reflection. For symptoms indirectly portray the self's true nature as a sinking ship in which its captain is incarcerated. The self, through exchanging natural for introjected authority, has been seduced into becoming both victim and executioner in its own case. On behalf of the self, this state of distress is most effectively dealt with when it is addressed as a problem of authority. Thus the distress signals of the floundering self call forth the struggle toward greater consciousness, which is implemented by the principles of symbolic regression psychology.

In its evolution, human consciousness has attained a cosmic dimension. Consequently, each individual senses at his deepest level of conviction that his own choices and actions express his sense of ultimate meaning. We believe that there is a substantial reality to which this sense can be brought to correspond, that the individual can learn to imagine in such a way that he is constantly defining himself by relating his unique being directly to Being itself. His energies, his emotions, his choices, and his cognitions are all psychic processes which can become manifest in consciousness as aspects of his unique mode of relating to Being. In order to bring about this kind of consciousness, the individual must deal directly with the ultimate dimensions of Being. Because the individual must symbolize himself according to his sense of ultimate meaning, his psychic life is in conflict when, through introjected authority, he attributes ultimate meaning to a counterfeit order of symbols instead of to the natural order of symbols which is grounded in Being. All psychic disturbances are based on constricting, introjected authority which takes the individual away from Being and makes him forget it as an actually possible ground for his consciousness. Consequently, to expend the scope of a person's consciousness, one must ground his authority, his underlying predisposition towards symbols, in Being rather than in socially learned, introjected images.

In the evolutionary process man has undergone changes in consciousness which make the motivations for and the meanings of his behavior very different from the impulses governing animal activity. Contrary to the monolithic uniformity of motives in the instinct-driven animal world, man lives in a social milieu in which there are no human commandments that are not constantly broken in spite of often serious social consequences. This social conflict is based on the fact that individual being insists on grounding itself in universal Being. Behind the violations lies the requirement that each person relate himself to his social matrix in terms of his sense of ultimate meaning. This is a complex and frustrating task for man as the symbolizing animal. But for man to continue to develop as a social being, this task must constantly be taken up. Man must learn to fulfill his instinctual drives within society in ways that do justice to his ultimate cosmic being and meaning. To do this, man must relate to himself through adequate, natural authority so that his organic self-relatedness harmonizes with society as a part of cosmic reality. Society is in an ultimate struggle for the control of instincts because society is the organ of man's sense of ultimate meaning at the interpersonal level and it is dominated at the present time by introjected authority that is at odds with the other dimensions of man's being.

Man has developed to a level of consciousness which makes it possible for each individual to relate to others on the basis of natural authority. Yet man's preoccupation with survival in society distracts him from developing the cosmic dimension of his consciousness, for this self-expansion comes about through a transforming reorientation of one's images. Man has the energy for this endeavor only after he has resolved the problem of physical and social survival which his long period of infantile dependence creates for him. Once his survival has become relatively assured, a man can deal with the question of self-awareness, and can learn to stand alone as a being who has the need and the capacity to relate to Being through cosmic symbolization.

Each individual must assume responsibility for this project of developing his own symbolic regressive consciousness. In anticipation of what is to be developed in more detail later, we can see now that this project consists of several steps. First the individual gains access to the resources for this resymbolizing when he learns that he participates in and can come to relate to an order of symbols which at once affirms both the cosmic and the personal dimensions of reality. Then valid images of one's unique being as a manifestation of Man as a universal cosmic entity develop through the working of imagination in response to this reality. Once an individual has discovered the reality of what we have called the order of symbols, imagination as positive function can enable him to differentiate introjected images from his true nature as a participant in cosmic Being. This functioning is based on the ultimate order of positive images which is a manifestation of Being. Through this the individual discovers his own personal authority by finding and affirming the natural prototypes of authority in Being which are innate within himself, and which manifest themselves within the uniqueness of his own "world." He then refocuses his sense of himself through this discovery of inner authority. Then he must discover his true meaning and society's true meaning by a long process of exploring his ultimately positive cosmic symbols and getting to know them firsthand. Then he begins to harmonize himself and his social environment at deeper, more comprehensive, and more substantial levels of consciousness, and he discovers that he has both the capacity and the energy positively and actively to participate in the transformation of his society by relating it to Being through his actions.

Man's fictions, especially his utopias from Plato onward, have a role in this process, for they have become a means for him imaginatively to unite his ultimate sense of meaning with the concrete possibilities for his entering into an authentic community life. Utopias are thus one kind of attempt for man to integrate the instinctual drives of his organic self with the spiritual energies of his cosmic self in order that he might enjoy harmonious social experience at the level of the personal self. If we read Paul Ricoeur's comments on fictions in terms of man's utopias as manifestations of his social imagination and perhaps more generally in terms of the imaginative function itself, we discover the powerful role man's symbolizing activity can have in the growth of his consciousness:

> A story, a fairy tale, or a poem does not lack a referent. Through fiction and poetry new possibilities of being-in-the-world are opened up within everyday reality. Fiction and poetry intend being, but not through the modality of givenness, but rather through the modality of possibility. And in this way everyday reality is metamorphosed by means of what we would call the imaginative variations that fiction works on the real. . . . fiction is the privileged path to the redescription of reality. [It] only imitates reality because it recreates it by means of a mythos, a fable which reaches its deepest essence.[30]

Fiction, or imagination, puts man in touch with a realm of meaning larger than everyday reality and thereby reveals him to himself as a person whose possibilities actually make him larger than his everyday self. Through such uses of imagination, man can begin to learn to express himself in relation to cosmic principles, no longer limiting his world and his possibilities to the civil codes of his state and the customs of his society. Through such growth of imaginative capacity, he frees himself towards more authentic functioning as part of a community which is grounded in Being.

Traditional educational theory and traditional psychological theory have not given contemporary man enough authority—enough of the privilege of conscious self-reflection. In many cases, even, highly respected institutions of psychiatry and psychology have limited the development of consciousness. In a sense, man is often analyzed by the new and more powerful implements of psychological evaluation only to be indicted and found guilty. It is no accident that the psychiatrist has been called the "shrink," for he is the dispenser of a powerful psychological reality which can size up the individual and tell him where he is in his social adaptation while at the same time it does not necessarily direct him toward ultimate consciousness. Psychological institutions are floundering on the same rocks at the edge of consciousness as are other institutional representatives of reality, for they too are involved with authority introjects. To the extent that the psychologist is a proponent of the given institutional order, he perpetuates a socially introjected authority which to some extent aborts individual consciousness.

The therapist becomes an authoritarian model whether he wants to be or not. He takes this on in relation to his client, and in some ways he takes it on with regard to himself. He represents a psychological association of some kind which is sanctioned by the state and has social authority, and which has some basis in the status quo aspects of society. At the same time, he is looked at as a champion of freedom and self-awareness. Thus, licensed practitioners find themselves inextricably indebted to unconsciousness through social commitments in spite of their personal attempts toward greater consciousness. Even if the psychologist is a member of a group with a doctrine or of a group which takes a stance against the prevailing society, his quest for consciousness must take certain introjected channels which are at odds with the development of individual consciousness.

The society which could sponsor the kind of psychotherapy suggested here has not yet emerged, for it would have to be free of introjects, or at least promise that freedom. Thus the therapist, in the truest sense, must be a radical—one who goes to the roots of the issue—and a pioneer, for he espouses an authority rooted in the privilege of consciousness. He will be perceived as a threat regardless of his true intentions. The risks involved in this stance, however, are inseparable from the possibilities of true healing.

NOTES

1. William Shakespeare, A Midsummer Night's Dream, V,i,7-27, in Shakespeare: Twenty-Three Plays and the Sonnets, ed, Thomas Marc Parrott, (New York: Charles Scribner's Sons, 1938), pp. 156-57.

2. Samuel Taylor Coleridge, Biographia Literaria, ed. John Shawcross, (London: Oxford University Press, 1907; rpt. 1958), vol. I, p. 202.

3. Leslie H. Farber, "The Therapeutic Despair," in Interpersonal Dynamics, ed. Warren G. Bennis, (Homewood, Ill.: Dorsey Press, 1964).

4. Carl Gustav Jung, Memories, Dreams, Reflections, ed. Aniela Jaffe, trans. Richard and Clara Winston, (New York: Vintage Books, 1961), p. 150.

5. Melanie Klein, "The Importance of Symbol Formation in the Development of the Ego," International Journal of Psycho-Analysis, 1930, 11, 24-39.

6. Eric Berne, A Layman's Guide to Psychiatry and Psychoanalysis, 3rd, ed., (New York: Simon and Schuster, 1968).

7. Ernest Becker, The Revolution in Psychiatry, (New York: Free Press of Glencoe, 1964).

8. Donald Snygg and Arthur Wright Combs, Individual Behavior: A New Frame of Reference for Psychology, (New York: Harper, 1949), p. 20.

9. Clemens Benda, The Image of Love, (New York: Free Press of Glencoe, 1961).

10. Jacques Maritain, Creative Intuition in Art and Poetry, (New York: Pantheon Books, 1953), p. 8.

11. Wolfgang Kretschmer, "Meditative Techniques in Psychotherapy," in Altered States of Consciousness, ed. Charles Tart, (New York: John Wiley, 1969), pp. 219-28.

12. William S. Kroger, Clinical and Experimental Hypnosis in Medicine, Dentistry, and Psychology, (Philadelphia: Lippincott, 1963), p. xii.

13. W. Earl Biddle, unpublished talk, Los Angeles, California, June, 1966.

14. Hanscarl Leuner, "Guided Affective Imagery (GAI)," American Journal of Psychotherapy, 1969, 23, 16-20.

15. Silvan Solomon Tomkins, Affect, Imagery, Consciousness, ed. Bertram P. Karon, (New York: Springer, 1962).

16. Northrop Frye, Anatomy of Criticism: Four Essays, (Princeton: Princeton Univ. Press, 1957), pp. 131-62.

17. Northrop Frye, The Secular Scripture: A Study of the Structure of Romance, (Cambridge, Mass.: Harvard Univ. Press, 1976).

18. Christopher Marlowe, Doctor Faustus, ed. Sylvan Barnet, (New York: New American Library, 1969), I,i,40-49.

19. Walter Kaufmann, Existentialism from Dostoevsky to Sartre, (Cleveland and New York: Meridian Books, World Publishing Company, 1956; rpt. 1965), p. 122.

20. Jean-Paul Sartre, Nausea, trans. Lloyd Alexander, (Norfolk, Conn.: New Directions, 1964).

22. Fyodor Dostoevsky, Notes from Underground; Poor People; The Friend of the Family: Three Short Novels, trans. Constance Garnett, (New York: Dell, 1960; rpt. 1975).

23. Samuel Taylor Coleridge, "Dejection: An Ode," ll. 54-55, in The Portable Coleridge, ed. I. A. Richards, (New York: The Viking Press, 1950; rpt. 1971), p. 171.

24. Psalms 19:1-2.

25. Virgil, The Aeneid, trans. W. F. Jackson Knight, (Harmondsworth, England: Penguin Books, 1956; rpt. 1972), Book VI, pp. 166-69.

26. Arthur Charles Clarke, 2001: A Space Odyssey, (New York: New American Library, 1968).

27. Thomas Stearns Eliot, "Burnt Norton," in The Complete Poems and Plays: 1909-1950, (New York: Harcourt, Brace and World, 1971), pp. 118-19.

28. Dante Alighieri, The Divine Comedy of Dante Alighieri, trans. John D. Sinclair, three volumes (New York: Oxford Univ. Press, 1939; rpt. 1972).

29. Ernest Becker, The Structure of Evil: An Essay on the Unification of the Science of Man, (New York: The Free Press, 1968), pp. 150, 249.

30. Paul Ricoeur, "Philosophy and Religious Language," Journal of Religion, 1974, 54(1), 71–85.

Chapter IV: Person

HUMAN MEANING IN PERSONALITY THEORY IS BASED ON SYMBOLIC REGRESSION

Personality theory is the attempt to articulate the meaning of consciousness in human terms. In symbolic regression psychology, personality theory is based on symbolic regression, for this process, which is also a state of Being, is the foundation of the human meaning of consciousness. Having discussed our founding concepts, imagination and symbolic regression, we are now ready to define the person in terms of the human meaning of consciousness which these concepts imply. Once the concept of "person" is developed, we will consider the meaning of person within the context of family, the meaning of the pathological deviation from the natural symbolic regressive state, and the means by which the person can recover access to his primary ground through reorienting the imaginative processes. To begin with, we must distinguish the concepts of self, ego, and personality.

Personality as a psychological construct is a comprehensive term. It has been used to stand for as many different things as there are psychological theories: definitions have identified personality as the whole person, as some organizing function, as some adjustment mechanism, or as the unique characteristics of the individual, and have tied it to diverse speculations about the essence of human nature. To this point, no substantial definition of personality exists which facilitates its universal, consistent application within a comprehensive anthropological frame of reference. Now, however, with the concept of symbolic regression, the concept of personality can have this more comprehensive function, for personality is here defined as the resymbolizing of experience which is the organizing of human substance in its striving towards consciousness. The primary aspects of personality in this definition are the self, ego, and imagination as these become aspects of the double process of symbolic regression into Being and the symbolic expression of Being. As in any articulation of the nature of personality, there is a danger inherent in this definition, for the use of conceptual abstractions can distract from the ground and the goal which they must serve: here this end is the assumption that the human spirit is the protentive *striving* ultimately to realize meaning and Being as a state of consciousness. The process of symbolic regression integrates self, ego, and personality into a whole which is the person. A person's *experience* is his symbolizing of self substance as an act that relates his inner energies to Being. This relating *is* personality. Conversely, the person organizes experience according to the inner dimensions of his reflective self substance. This organizing process is symbolizing. Personality is the self, considered in terms of its experience of itself and its action upon itself.

In the most general sense, the person is a highly complex energy system. The self is human substance, the psychic reality which is constituted as this system. The self is both conscious and pre-conscious human material. It is given form by the symbolizing process, the dynamic process of relating person to Being. The self substance of the person is continually developing and reconstituting itself in relation to consciousness through this symbolizing process. The self is always being transformed in that its pre-conscious elements are becoming conscious—that is, becoming symbolized—through the process of imagination. The self is always emergent. It is always becoming delimited by the expanding awareness of self and Being which is the symbolizing process. The process of consciousness is the appropriating of symbols by which the self represents the structure of Being. The process of relating to Being through symbolizing is the process of symbolic regression. The development of the capacity for symbolic regression within the person is the means by which the self evolves and orders its powers of integral consciousness and self-reflectiveness.

The most immediately conscious aspect of the process of symbolic regression is ego. Ego refers to those processes of symbolic regression which become conscious as imaginative expression in the person. Symbolic expression or "imagizing" is rooted in the capacity for symbolic regression. Symbolic regression is a continual process of resymbolizing human substance into developing states of conscious being which are at once increasingly more differentiated and more integral.

Ego in its primary inner mode is the symbolic regressive function of the self. In its secondary outer mode it is the symbolic expressive function of the self. Ego processes in the secondary mode are the processes usually considered as imagination in its social manifestation. In the present context, the term ego is a distinctive one: it refers to the processes of self re-symbolizing at the conscious level.

PERSONALITY IS THE SELF AT THE LEVEL OF SOCIAL DISCLOSURE

Personality is a theoretical construct designed to describe why a person acts, thinks, or feels in certain ways. Personality theory is always based on implicit assumptions about the nature of Being, and the meaning of human substance in relation to consciousness. In symbolic regression psychology, personality is based on the implicit and hence axiomatic self, that is, human substance in the process of transforming itself into reflectiveness. Personality, like ego, is not a thing or substance. It is a process, the symbolizing process by which human substance comes to relate or to reflect on itself. It is the manifestation of the self at the level of interpersonal experience. It is Being as this is revealed by man to man symbolically.

The phenomenon of regression is the basis of the understanding of personality. Until now the concept of regression has not been seen in relation to its essential symbolic significance, its inner meaning. Yet, a truly organismic or holistic personality theory should give central importance to symbolic regression and thus meaning to symptomatic behavior in relation to symbolic regression. An adequate treatment of the concept of regression will relate it to the fundamental intention of the organism towards consciousness and to the being of the person considered as a whole. When it is described and understood as related to the movement toward consciousness in actual human substance, regression will be understood against the expressive background of all human acts as they relate to the inner background, the symbolizing of Being in human substance. For, at the most fundamental level, all actions of the person should be understood as symbolic, that is, as an expression of the drive toward consciousness.

Freudian personality theory is reductionistic and therefore inadequate for a truly human concept of man. According to Freudian theory, the id consists of everything psychologically present in the individual at birth, namely instinct. This concept implies that man's nature in its original essence is irrational and undependable. The body processes which are expressed in the id are instinctual and are actually at odds with external reality. According to Freud's concept, there is no place for the growth and transformation of human substance and thus for the real modification of instinctual reality as it relates to consciousness in the course of human development. Thus Freudian psychology makes inadequate provision for man's nature as an integrated, self-reflective being. As a result of this inadequacy, Freud's model of the mind forces him to assume that subjective experience is not necessarily related to objectivity in any way at all. The centrality of the symbolizing function as human substance is lacking. In this conceptualization, regressive behavior does not possess intrinsic meaning. Rather, it is interpreted as an eruption of instinctual material which is unrelated to conscious human behavior in irreconcilable opposition to each other.

A holistic concept of personality, by contrast, places the phenomena of regression in a direct relationship and definite continuity with conscious behavior. Symptomatic regressive behavior must not be reduced to meaningless activity. Rather, regressive behavior is to be seen as a symbolic expression of the dividedness of the self in its relation to Being. Such behavior signifies that human substance is frustrated in its drive toward consciousness. A close look at regressive behavior reveals that it has an underlying meaning which must be understood as the symbolic function attempting to reorient the self in its relation to Being.

An example of regressive behavior may help to clarify the radical difference between Freud's reductive approach to personality and the holistic approach afforded by the concept of symbolic regression. A man seeks help because he has serious digestive disturbances. He has an inflamed gastric ulcer and severe colitis. He swallows his food, but cannot digest it. He vomits, has diarrhea, and his body is quickly deteriorating into an emaciated condition. Underlying this condition is the fact that he cannot form an image of eating and digesting food that is adequate to his body's need for nourishment. The focus of attention for the therapist thus comes to be the critical nature of

the mental images related to eating. A comparison of the
Freudian and the symbolic regressive treatments of this
image state will reveal the need for a more holistic
approach to personality. The adequate treatment of the
image states of this person will result in the development
of his capacity for symbolic regression and thus for his
digestive functioning.

In Freudian theory, there are four levels of imagery
connected with this man's predicament, each of which is
either in conflict with or cut off from the others. Accordingly, the problem of eating must be resolved by the interaction and reorientation of these four levels of images.
The first image level relates to hunger as an instinct, the
animal-like devouring of food. The second image level is
that of memory traces available to the individual which he
can refer to as a basis for food imbibing or food avoiding
behavior. The third level of images relates to the superego demands within the individual. The images at this
level are social introjects which obligate him to perform
according to a certain pattern of food imbibing which is
certified harmless to himself and to society. Constricted
behavior implies that it is necessary for him to establish
and to prove his worthiness to eat what he needs. The
images at this level directly conflict with the actual
instinctual urges and their images. The fourth image level
is the immediate physical perception of food which the
individual has in the act of eating. According to this
four-leveled Freudian model, the person experiencing the
difficulty with food is in a condition characterized by
disruptive conflict among his various images. The physical
image of food competes with the levels of his inner images:
the instinctual, the remembered, and the repressed.

The problem with these Freudian image levels is that
they lack a synthesizing reference point by which they
might be integrated within the person as a whole being.
Freudian theory does not provide what it takes to relate
the act of eating to the reality of being human. The person
is simply not given an adequate frame of reference by which
he might symbolize and resymbolize the act of eating. For
Freud, the demands of the instinctual, unconscious, and
irrational aspects of human nature are the dominant ones.
These control the person, and his access to them is limited
to the secondary processes, reason, speech, and other
socially constituted personality functions. Accordingly,
there is no natural, **human** primary process into which the
person can symbolically regress in order to find himself at
home with Being. It follows that, in Freudian thought,

there can be no image of eating to which the person could appeal for an ultimate sense of the meaning of his actions and being. Thus, because of the divisive quality of the Freudian conception of human nature, the image problem involved with eating cannot be resolved at the level of ultimate meaning.

According to Freud, the energy demands of the id are involved with the image of eating so that it is invested with primitive and exciting qualities. It is these id energies which are the propelling factors of the person and the determinant of his behavior. Human nature is thus essentially unconscious and non-reflective. Imagination has no capacity for self-transcendence, no basic drive toward consciousness to which the person could refer. As a consequence, eating is ultimately nothing other than devouring, and regression into Being is to become altogether animal-like. Reducing tension within the individual in order to deliver him from threatening eating images would be brought about by disenfranchising one or more other image levels. Accordingly, the individual would always have to battle one or another basic component of his nature rather than cooperate with it and experience the harmonious working of his total energies. He will never be able to eat a completely relaxed meal.

To Freud, the instinct level is regressive in a negative sense because it returns the individual psychically to a disturbed state which his behavior has all along attempted to reduce. This syndrome Freud called the repetition compulsion. Individual behavior, the individual's search for psychic quietude, continues to be self-repeating until this quiescence is re-established. This state is ultimately achieved as death, which Freud apotheosized as thanatos. This death wish in man is Freud's psychological equivalent for the principle of constancy. Accordingly, eating represents a fusion of hunger and destructiveness which is only partially satisfied by biting and chewing and devouring until death itself can finally achieve integration by obliterating the drive. Thanatos has become Freud's substitute for symbolic regression.

In contrast to Freudian theory, symbolic regression psychology is built on the concept of human substance. Man's very substance is part of his capacity for cosmic image states which are ultimate in nature and which are part of his nature. These cosmic image states, which we have termed the symbolic order, can and must be appealed to as the ultimate frame of reference for man's coming to consciousness. Given this frame of reference, man can relate himself to eating and to the meaning of food in ways that transcend the level of animal-like devouring. Eating at the level of social behavior involves the symbolic transmission of energies which are at once both biological and social. The social aspects of eating are symbolically transcendent to mere biological urges. The social setting of eating symbolizes and expresses cosmic dimensions of man's conscious substance. The power of this symbolizing at the cosmic level can be seen in the representation of ultimate integration as a universal feast.[1]

The concept of human substance as a unique reality integrates all the levels of man into a coherent whole, enabling the effective treatment of symbolic symptoms such as food rejection. Given the notion that human substance is a striving toward consciousness, it can further be assumed that the totality of man's energies is arranged according to several harmonious levels of consciousness. Given these assumptions, the image of eating can be seen to possess an ultimate validity and goodness for man. Thus the primary image of eating need not be considered in terms of devouring alone. Rather, it can be seen to symbolize ultimate conscious human substance in its attempt to propagate and replenish itself. Furthermore, it can be assumed that symbolic processes relating to eating are also involved with other dimensions of human meaning. And in sum, it can be theorized that man's ultimate desire for the fulfillment of his basic needs has spiritual or cosmic dimensions.

These assumptions taken together require a radically different understanding of what happens when a man eats and of the meaning and implications of this act. The control of the individual's acting out is replaced by an understanding of symptoms according to their symbolic undergirdings. Accordingly, behavior can be redirected in order to harmonize it with inner being. Hunger is considered to be a relative state. The image of hunger can be related to by the whole person, for it is involved with the truly natural organic state with all of its cosmic symbolic implications. The person can be free to experience hunger in a natural and human way. To know the naturalness of his hunger, the individual must be freed from introjected demands for performance so that he can be conscious of his hunger state as it relates to Being. The person as an energy system is involved with several different dimensions of energy input so that biophysical energy is seen as integrative with cosmic personal energies. On the basis of this orientation, the man whose digestive tract cannot digest food can be understood and healed, for it was the demeaning of the energies related to man's higher levels of consciousness within his self substance that has cut short the symbolic regressive process so that he could not eat. For a man who has learned to eat in the context of suspicion and fear and rejection will have a difficult time digesting his food, no matter how digestible and nourishing it may be. As Biddle discussed in his account of hypnotic regression, the symbol of imbibing good food possess cosmic overtones, that is, it is symbolic of the ultimate meaning of nourishment.[2] Unless such images are possible for the individual, he cannot be psychologically healthy.

There are important similarities between Jung's ideas concerning personality and those of symbolic regression psychology. A consideration of the two approaches will show these similarities as well as the important differences that make symbolic regression psychology distinctive. Jung conceived of the psyche in terms of a number of polar systems. The two primary systems he discerns are the conscious and the unconscious, and the ego and the archetypes. The major polarity by which he understands the psyche is the polarity of consciousness and unconsciousness. He defines consciousness as "the function or activity which maintains the relation of psychic contents with the ego."[3] Ego, in turn, is defined as

> a complex of representations which constitutes the centrum of my field of consciousness and appears to possess a very high degree of continuity and identity. . . . [Ego] is as much a content as it is a condition of consciousness, since a psychic element is conscious to me just insofar as it is related to my ego.[4]

Jung elaborates his definition of ego by distinguishing between the ego and the self: "the ego is the subject of my consciousness, while the Self is the subject of my totality."[5] This definition demarks the difference between personality in Jungian theory and personality in symbolic regression psychology. For Jung ego is the subject of a psychic function which is consciousness and constitutes its center. Ego is an entity. This is in contrast to symbolic regression psychology.

Symbolic regression psychology differs from Jung on the import and exact content of these central psychological concepts. Most fundamentally, in symbolic regression psychology we almost always talk in terms of consciousness. Rarely do we have recourse to the term, "the unconscious." The significance of this radical shift in emphasis will become apparent in what follows. First of all, we conceptualize ego as the dynamic interface between inner and outer world, as energy and its components. This dynamic definition of ego enables us to broaden the concept of consciousness by relating it to the self rather than to ego, as Jung does. To paraphrase Jung, we define ego as "the symbolizing activity by which psychic contents are constantly being related to the self." Jung's narrower definition of consciousness is in turn what we mean by the term "awareness." Finally, we define unconsciousness as a psychic state in which blocks are imposed on ego, that is, the natural flow of psychic symbolizing activity. Implicit in this conception is the idea that consciousness is an innate and primordial mode of psychic reality. This emphasis on the ontological and temporal priority of consciousness contrasts with Jung's insistence on the priority of "the unconscious," for Jung says:

> The unconscious is older than consciousness. It is the "primal datum" out of which consciousness ever arises afresh. [Consciousness] is only a secondary phenomenon built upon the fundamental psychic activity, which is a functioning of the unconscious. . . . In every important situation in life our consciousness is _dependent_ on the unconscious.[6]

Jung's most powerful and controversial concept is his idea of the collective unconscious. Jung's "collective unconscious" is what might be called man's primordial substance or his cosmic self. It is out of this original psychic ground that the personality is built. As a result, the experiences of the individual are grounded in and profoundly involved with his collective psychic energies. Jung believes that the cosmos is borne in each person as an image. Accordingly, the world about the person comes to be perceived and identified with to the extent that it corresponds to this cosmic image as a dimension of human substance. Implicit in this notion of the "collective unconscious" is the presence of the wisdom of the ages as an accessible reality or quality of human substance within the psyche of each individual. If this aspect of the person's psychic reality is cut off or ignored through introjection, then the conscious processes of the personality are disrupted and symptomatic behavior results.

Jung is hesitant to make metaphysical assumptions about the nature of the "collective unconscious." Thus he conceives of it as the psychic residue of man's biological evolution. This is a defensive posture similar to that of Freud's when he attempts to make his psychological theorizing empirical and quasi-verifiable as well as heuristically useful. Jung clearly states his "empiricist" orientation when he introduces the mother archetype:

> When the Corpus Hermeticum describes God as the "archetypal light," it expresses the idea that he is the prototype of all light; that is to say, pre-existent and supraordinate to the phenomenon "light." Were I a philosopher, I should continue in this Platonic strain and say: Somewhere, in "a supercelestial place," there is a prototype or primordial image of the mother that is pre-existent and supraordinate to all phenomena in which the "maternal," in the broadest sense of the term, is manifest. But I am an empiricist, not a philosopher; I cannot let myself presuppose that [anything that comes from inside and cannot be verified] is universally valid. This is an assumption in which only the philosopher may indulge.[7]

By rejecting this defensive attitude and taking upon ourselves the indulgence of philosophical speculation, we are able to see the reality which Jung refers to as the "collective unconscious" as a way of looking at cosmic consciousness. The mind's own substance as a symbolizing entity points to ultimate meaning and Being and not just to man's genetic components as an evolving biological organism. Yet, while we are quick to point out the difference in orientation between Jung's theories and those of symbolic regression psychology, we also affirm that Jung's notion that the minds of all men partake in certain common contents or predispositions is an important one which we fully share.

What Jung describes as the "collective unconscious" is referred to in symbolic regression psychology as the cosmic self. Furthermore, we extend the notion of the cosmic self to include the cosmic dimensions of man's being. Jung sees the self, the individual psyche at the cosmic level, as constituted by latent memory traces transmitted to all human beings through man's genetic makeup. Actually, one does not need to share Jung's biological speculations on this point to assume that human substance has within it implicit qualities which enable all men to participate in a universal human consciousness. These qualities, which we have termed "images," are the elements at the human level which correspond to the symbolic order, the structures implicit in Being. Human substance, as it is here conceived, is constituted by symbolizing processes which correspond to the inherent nature of Being. Thus, cosmic energies, as they find expression in these images as psychic entities, become capable of harmonizing man with himself as well as with his social and natural environments.

Jung's major assumption which corresponds to his concept of the collective unconscious concerns its contents. He assumes that man's makeup includes his capacity to bring into consciousness the experiences of past generations. Thus, Jung would concur that man's substance becomes to a degree conscious. It is not just man's sensory experience that is inherited, it is the consciousness of his nature, his capacity for self-reflection, that he receives in his genetic heritage. Furthermore, predispositions within man's substance result in his reacting to his environment in a manner which is to a certain degree determined. These predispositions are the contents of man's projections. For example, each member of the human race has had a mother. Consequently, each person has an inborn capacity to relate to his mother in terms of the cosmic meaning of mothering. The individual's inherited capacity for mother-meaning is a part of his self-substance:

> Just as man is born with the capacity for seeing the world in three dimensions and develops this capacity through experience and training, so man is born with many predispositions for thinking, feeling, and perceiving according to definite patterns and contents which become actualized through individualized experiences.[8]

According to Jung's concept, the collective unconscious is composed of archetypes or "imprints" which are predispositions toward certain modes of symbolizing common to the whole human race. Examples of how these archetypes work can be seen in the father or mother archetypes, predispositions innate in the child, which function as a capacity to recognize the actual parents as distinct symbolic entities which correspond to their analogous polar elements in the cosmic order. Thus the actual parent is understood in relation to the ultimate meaning or cosmic structure which he or she embodies for the child.

The nature of mothers--what they do--has remained pretty much the same throughout the history of the race, so that the mother archetype which the baby inherits is congruent with the actual mother with whom the baby interacts.[9]

We expand Jung's concept of the archetype at this point. The infant actually inherits substance constituted by symbolic imprints which correspond to what will become represented in consciousness as the universal mother and the universal father. Consequently, the actual mother or father is perceived as an image in terms of this universal symbol. Accordingly, the individual personality is a composite of inner predispositions to perceive the environment along the lines of these imprinted predispositions. The actual environment will be perceived through what is symbolized out of these predispositions. Underlying this notion is the idea that the nature of the individual and the nature of his environment possess certain intrinsic points of correspondence which can and must be discovered and symbolized for the personality to become conscious.

The concept of energy is central to Jung's theory of personality. To Jung, the whole psyche can be understood as an energy system which is a dimension of the totality of metabolic processes. The energy which takes expression in this psychic system can become cathected as certain states, images, or ideas which become the topography and contents of the individual's conscious understanding. Symbolic regression psychology is based on the idea that the origins and functions of this psychic energy go far beyond the limits within which Jung understood it, for this energy is not only the expression of metabolic processes but also of cosmic dimensions of energy. Occult writers describe this reality, the cosmic dimension of psychic energy, as "the vital body." This concept of the vital body, or cosmic dimension of psychic energy, corresponds to Chardin's notion that all human substance is in the process of becoming conscious and is interactive with other psychic energy systems, both cosmic and personal. This notion of energy is also fundamental to the Chinese system of medicine with its points of vitality; accupressure and acupuncture are rapidly finding their place in modern medical conceptions of the body. It is important for the individual to know that these other dimensions of energy constitute a psychic energy generated by the inner organic processes as such. The full activation of psychic energies is based on the capacity for symbolic regression, for symbolic regression unites both organic and cosmic energies into a harmonious, dynamic functioning, thereby constituting the integrated personality.

Images comprising the self substance constantly come to be resymbolized in the personality through the double process of symbolic regression and symbolic interaction with the environment. For example, the mother image is an expression of the person's attempt to unify the primordial ground of cosmic matter with the person's inner substance through the act of symbolizing. The healthy, symbolically regressing personality constantly reinterprets the experience of mothering according to the ultimate prototypes of mothering in nature. It is this innate symbolizing as a natural process which makes the person continuous with Being. But if there is a gap between the person's innate sense of the ultimate mothering dimensions of Being and what he is able to experience in his environment that enables him to feel continuous with his own nature, extra energy must be expended on this process. Thus, until the experience of parenting and the cosmic dimensions of nurturance and sustenance are somehow brought into alighment through the symbolizing capacities, the person will have to use excessive psychic energy to maintain the continuity of energies between self and Being which is the fundamental condition for the individual to exist as a conscious being. Such excessive energy will manifest itself in overly-intensified dream activity as well as in symptomatic regressive behavior.

Jung's ideas about personality development, especially as they are expressed in his concept of individuation, implicitly contain the fundamental principles of the theory of symbolic regression. Jung designated the first half of life as based on instinct and oriented toward survival. Accordingly, a dramatic transformation occurs during man's mature adult years, at about the age of forty. At about this time, his energy expenditure changes from an essentially biological to an essentially cultural or spiritual orientation. The person begins to realize his spiritual capacity. The process involved in this shifting of energies can be understood as the symbolic regressive function of the person as he attempts to attain consciousness. This shifting itself is made possible when the personality can reorganize experience in harmony with the energy dimensions of Being. The self that is consciously oriented toward Being and within which the personal and cosmic energies are integrated develops more intensively in relation to social, cultural, and philosophic concerns.

If this kind of integration at the cultural level has not been prepared for by the development of consciousness as a life-long process, then it does not come about at this time. Consequently, it will become increasingly difficult for the person to relate consciously to his experience in the years that follow. Instead, the individual will tend to hide from reality so as to sink into more and more unconsciousness, and senility will set in during the declining years of life. Negative entropy will set in and the person's substance will deteriorate into unconsciousness. This is the psychological process which underlies much senile behavior. Senility is the attempt to act out one's regressive needs because he has not developed the capacity for symbolic regression which can bring his symbolic and his existential realities into harmony. Underlying this deterioration is the fact that, as a person ages, more and more self substance is needed to symbolize cosmic energy into the personality. When this need cannot be met, the individual can no longer symbolize himself as a cosmic being within his actual environment. His demand for more symbolic-expressive outlets is met only by fewer such outlets. When, due to the disruption of his inner continuity with Being, he cannot develop his expressive privilege, he becomes symptomatic and is labeled senile. Development thus has less to do with biological phases than with the individual's deliberately and constantly expanding the privilege of consciousness.

In his concept of individuation, Jung's primary underlying assumption is that the personality possesses an innate tendency towards wholeness. Man is born as an innately undifferentiated unity. Ultimately, man's development will once again reflect this reality. Symbolic regression psychology is based on these assumptions. Symbolic regression is a lifelong need of the person and is the basis for harmony between the person and Being. Regression, whether symbolically unifying self and Being or symbolically symptomatizing the dissidence between self and Being, is the index of whether the person is moving psychically toward or psychically away from higher levels of consciousness and wholeness.

In his concept of the transcendent function of the person, Jung attempts to emphasize the importance of the relationship between man's cosmic nature and his consciousness. It is man's consciousness which unites his being with Being. When the self is consciously organized in relation to Being, the wholeness of the person emerges and comes to ascendency. This cosmic wholeness can be considered the spiritual dimension of human personality. All symbolic processes of the person, such as dreams, religious ceremonies, and mythical expressions, can be understood only if

this relationship between man and Being is recognized.
Symbolic regression can be appreciated only if this reality
is yielded to.

THE SELF IS HUMAN SUBSTANCE

The twentieth century has become an era characterized by
a renewed search for a more satisfying, holistic definition
of man. As part of this search, psychology has just recently
focused on the problem of human consciousness. The self is
becoming a central concept in this creative search to understand
and define the nature of consciousness. Until
recently, psychology has been concerned with man and his
pre-reflective existence as an organism whose primary needs
were instinctual. According to this level of approach, man
has been seen as an organism involved in a struggle for
survival through the manipulation or refinement of his
biological urges. His task was to survive by maintaining a
balance or compromise between nature or instinct on the one
hand, and the control processes of ego on the other. The
self thus has had little place as a concept in classical
personality theory. More recently, the term self, which
denotes the essence of man's being, has come to be associated
with concepts such as spiritual consciousness and with
references to man as a trans-instinctual being. The self
has once again become a central reference point in the
discussion of human reflective consciousness.

Humanistic psychology emphasizes the problems of
consciousness facing thinkers who speculate in the areas of
human ethics, aesthetics, philosophy, religion, intuitive
wisdom, and all forms of mysticism. Man needs a more comprehensive
prospective for understanding personality, one
which more adequately penetrates to the meaning of human
consciousness. The concept of self meets this need. Clark
Moustakas summarized all of the literature on the concept
of the self.[10] He discusses selfhood as intrinsic in
nature, and selfhood as becoming. Moustakas points out that
"intrinsic nature," as it is used in the literature on the
self concept, refers to the natural or unchanging potentialities
and proclivities of man.[11] These inherent
potentialities are to be realized if man is to be developed
as fully and completely as possible. Selfhood, then, is
the drive by which the conscious aspects of man are organized
with regard to Being. To the degree that his self is
actualized, man is conscious in relation to his nature. To
the degree that the person is not actualized, the self
remains unconscious and does not relate the person to Being.

When a person refers to a certain behavior in which he felt he could not choose but to behave as he has done, he might say, "I was just being myself." A person in such situations seems bound by an inner reality to conduct himself as if he had no choice. This phenomenon can be explained by reference to the concept of "self." This concept explains both how and why the individual reconstructs his experience in order to act consciously in harmony with his being. The idea of the self can be used to broaden our understanding of human behavior, for it enables us to explain it in symbolic terms. The individual is struggling for consciousness. His birthright is to be able to enjoy or experience life in its full range of meaning within the horizons of his own unique destiny. His very substance is involved in this effort. If the attempt is thwarted, he symbolizes the frustration symptomatically in mind and body and his many energy systems send out signals of distress.

If man's chief characteristic has become his drive toward consciousness, his hope to harmonize with Being will become actualized in those interactions with himself which bring about higher conscious states. Consequently our psychological constructs used to describe man's essence will have to be reformulated. One of these concepts is the self, for the concept of the self as it is here formulated is the key to understanding the significance of man's drive toward consciousness.

The self is to be defined as conscious and preconscious human substance, constituted by man's being, his energy systems. The self achieves consciousness by participating in the process of constantly rearranging human substance, which is symbolic regression into the ground of Being. In this process, the individual is reconstructing his experience so that his personality is continuous with consciousness. Through this symbolizing process, personality is in a continuing state of transformation. When the self does not actualize the capacity for symbolic regression, potentially conscious human substance is blocked off from the energies of Being and the personality and experience of the individual are put out of gear with his substance and being. The blocked energies then find their way into symptomatic expressions as symbolic evidences that the consciousness attempted is being blocked. The self therefore is also the source and ground of integration between the world of inner being and the environment of being. This interface itself is ego. The healthiness or degree of consciousness of ego is the relatedness of personality to the individual's world. When an individual says that he

PERSON   131

was just being himself, he thus means that his behavior was
tied to his consciousness so that his very being evoked his
symbolizing act. Another way of expressing this reality is
to say that he was "selfing his being."

The focus and orientation of the self in any individual
is unique. There is no such thing as a "type" of person.
There is also no such thing as a "type" of mental abberation.
Such "types" can only be used to describe how any individual's
consciousness is organized within him as it relates to his
total being. The self ought to relate to Being in a way that
results in emergence of life or life energies. The activation
of one's psychic energies comes from the person's ability to
find in the world that which corresponds to the depths of his
own being. The self then is conceived of as the ground of
being of the whole person, the point through which consciousness of that which is without is related to that which is
a priori within. The conscious self is the one that is constantly relating to the whole of Being. The self contains the
symbolic origins of value in what manifests Being in the
environment so that the individual is continually able to
relate to human substance, the source of meaning within.

The self informs experience according to Being in order
to permit and to make possible creative activity in the
personality. When the consciousness of which the self is
capable is developed, experience and interaction with the
environment take place through a continuing, direct intuition
of the world. Expressions of the true self are always
creative and constructive interpretations of the self in its
process of cosmic consciousness. The phrases used to describe
the self in the language of recent psychology all help to
convey different facets of the self which is being presented
in symbolic regression theory. Phrases such as emergent
self, one's nature, self becoming, intrinsic nature, self
fulfillment, and self creativity are all applicable to this
self. Psychological literature is full of such evidence of
self-reflectiveness and cosmic consciousness in man's natural
state.

EGO IS THE SYMBOLIZING ACT

Ego is a term used in psychology to designate the
reality-orienting process of the personality. Freud originally used the term to mean the function which mediates
between the instinctual drives of the organism and the
survival demands imposed upon it by society. Ego is thus
the censorship system which the individual uses to

understand himself as a psycho-social being. Freud postulated that pathology resulted when this ego became overwhelmed with the organism's irrational instincts, an overloading of ego-generated anxiety, and thus began to malfunction. After Freud, personality theory began to place the ego in a different frame of reference in relation to the whole person. For example, Melanie Klein conceived of the ego as the person's means of coping with anxiety, the alarm reaction to the threatened destruction of the person's good and nurturing world. Since Freud, all formulations of the theory of ego have reflected the trends of the psychological theorizing and the sociological formulations of the times within which they have arisen. At this time, society is moving toward a cosmic consciousness. Individuals now experience themselves in terms of an inner psychic space which has its symbolic correspondence in the expansive potentials that face man as he stands on the threshold of the space age. Given this scope, ego in symbolic regression psychology is defined as the process of expressing consciousness which functions as the interface between the drive toward cosmic consciousness and the fear of becoming conscious. To become conscious requires an actual change of human substance. Ego is the process of altering conscious states. Thus, rather than being an arbitrating agent, ego is the process of synthesis. Ego process is a bringing of various dimensions of reality together with their cosmic meaning, an integrating of the expressive and the regressive within the psyche, and a causing of the individual to move to higher levels of consciousness. Ego is the process of becoming cosmically self-reflective. It is the process of rearranging consciousness within self-substance. Ego is the self's rearranging consciousness with regard to the whole being of the individual as he evolves his perception of the cosmic order of things.

Human energies are distilled out of other cosmic energies into a center of unique being and substance. The constellation of these energies in the individual is the self. In non-human forms of life, consciousness does not develop to the level of self-reflectiveness. Rather, it remains organized at a subconscious level. Selfhood is a uniquely human reality. Likewise, ego, which is the process of rearranging cosmic substance through symbolic regression, is a strictly human function. All forms of plant and animal life are energy systems ordered as expressions of a cosmic purpose or consciousness. Thus they remain closely enough allied with all other centers of being within the order of nature so that they exist through primitive intercommunication as essentially nonreflective ecological systems. In

the human being, however, energies which go into forming a
center of being have developed into such a high cosmic
frequency that the self-reflective consciousness which has
emerged through the evolutionary process now manifests
itself in man's preconscious and organic energies as well as
in his consciousness.

Freud saw the ego as an arbitrator between instinctual
drives and social demands. By contrast, in symbolic
regression psychology, ego is regarded as the process of
symbolizing the person in terms of Being. With this
definition, instincts need not be considered antagonistic to
the ultimate demands of society. Rather, they are seen to
be arranged as part of the order of a substance which is
self-conscious. Ego is the process by which the self rear-
ranges its substance through symbolizing according to energy
dimensions which are universal for mankind. Jung's version
of the ego as the conscious point of the personality falls
short of interpreting the consciousness of man as the
expression of his very substance. This is because Jung's
scientific presuppositions force him to imagine the ascent
of man in terms of a biological-evolutionary continuity.
Thus he cannot take into account a conception of man's
ascent characterized by a definite break from the instinctual to the differentiated psyche, which involves self-
consciousness relating to the archetype, for this would have
involved him in a theory of conscious substance.

Jung's most profound contribution, and one which can be
related to any psychology which takes cosmic consciousness
into account, is his concept of the collective unconscious.
Jung held that the collective unconscious is the psychic
residue of man's evolutionary development and he theorized
that this residue has accumulated in man through many
generations of adaptation. This concept applies his notion
of man's evolutionary development to the idea of latent
memory. It refers to a substance, human conscious substance,
as having been shaped by the natural history of its adapta-
tions. As such, it is a kind of expression of man's
capacity for cosmic consciousness. Nevertheless, Jung does
not let this aspect of his theory radically transform his
conception of human nature because he limits his speculations to the scope of biological concepts. Thus Jung leads
up to the brink of radically redefining ego, yet his
concept is substantially different from the concept as it is
developed in symbolic regression psychology. Yet, because
June conceives of the collective unconscious as an inherited
racial foundation upon which the whole structure of
personality ultimately rests, his notion of ego parallels

that of symbolic regression psychology to some extent: Jung says that it is the function of ego to raise the contents of the collective unconscious into consciousness so that the person can function in harmony with himself as a being who expresses the cosmic process within his own energy system.

Ego is the individual person's movement toward consciousness through the process of self-reflection. In its unfolding this process incorporates functions such as cognition, perceptions, sensation, choice, will, and movement in time and space. Looked at telically, this process is the rearrangement of cosmic substance through symbolizing. It is the transformation of the self from unconscious and preconscious states to conscious states. Sometimes this function is symbolically direct; sometimes the symbolizing is distorted and thus symptomatic. The agency of ego as symbolizing process is imagination. Ego is the process of rearranging cosmic substance through symbolic regression with the end of grounding self-awareness in the order of Being. Symptomatic ego functions manifest themselves in depressiveness, addiction, and the schizoid splitting processes.

Ego is the process of the self in its evolution toward cosmic awareness. Strong ego is the process of consciousness which is attuned to cosmic reality. This attunement makes possible the continual rearranging of consciousness. Weak ego is the symptomatic attempt at rearranging the self-substance which results when the self is not attuned to its cosmic undergirdings. In this ego state, the correlation between self and cosmos is attempted, but only by indirect and distorted means. This lack of attunement keeps the whole being unaware that consciousness is in fact being attempted. The attempt at consciousness in weak ego function is very frightening and thus it is compensated for by means of symptomatic behavior. The symptoms, however, are only signposts to the greater reality of cosmic awareness towards which ego is the striving even if without success. Symbolizing is the essence of ego, for the self reflects back upon itself through psychically energized symbolic modes. Appreciation of the centrality of this symbolizing function is the basis of a constructive interpretation of symptomatic, indirect, and therefore inadequate ways of attempting consciousness. Psychological healing can be accomplished only if the self is conceptualized as the arranging of symbols in relation to the order of cosmic energy. Thus consciousness explains the basis for ego energy and the resymbolizing of substance according to the cosmic dimensions of Being.

PERSON

The reductionistic-empirical approach to personality assumed that the unconscious was basically at odds with the powers of rational man, a refuse bin into which noxious material had been passed. What it did not do was to acknowledge the infinitely complex symbolic ego processes which reconstitute man's consciousness in relation to cosmic destiny. It did not recognize the symbolically constituted relationship of different dimensions of the self and the need to appreciate the potential of the unconscious and preconscious aspects of personality.

Space age man can no longer live with partial ego in a mental-spiritual paralysis which splits him off from the deeper recesses of Being. He can no longer deny the deeper dimensions of all that he is. He must admit that in the great reservoir of preconscious realities are to be found the possibilities for his self-relatedness and his cosmically grounded understanding of his world. Unless man understands his basic ego process as a search for such self-relatedness, he will misinterpret the true significance of his anxiety, his guilt, and his fundamental conflict-laden emotions. An adequate psychology of the person will take the unformulated, preconscious realities underlying the illusions and idols of his culture as serious materials for understanding ego's project. When self theory is based on such an understanding, it will help man toward behavior which is compatible with his cosmic significance. Ego process must be conceptualized as working with transcendent realities within the self. Whether a person is aware of it or not, ego is his perceiving the world around him according to spiritual principles operating in his unconscious and preconscious dimensions. All objects and persons possess intrinsic symbolic spiritual value for man as well as extrinsic concrete value. Unless this is understood, the person is interpreted deductively rather than cosmically.

IMAGINATION IS THE SYMBOLIZING AGENCY

Imagination is the agent of the symbolizing process called ego. It is in a sense the switchboard for the attainment of cosmic consciousness. The symbolizing of personality works through imagination to reconstruct the relationship between self and Being. Ego has been studied with regard to its mechanisms but not according to its deeper symbolic regressive dimensions which these mechanisms serve. The end toward which ego drives is the orienting of the self according to cosmic meaning. The primal level of this process is symbolic regression, for this is the integrative symbolizing function. Imagination is the primary agent of this function. All ego activities, such as cognition, perception, sensation, and intuition, are related to the cosmic striving toward a full developed symbolic regressive capacity in the person and to the primal function of imagination in bringing that state about. The person's capacity for consciousness in time and space, the constant reconstructing of the primary drives toward Being, as well as the ability to will and to choose, are all related to the capacity for cosmic awareness through symbolic regression.

Edward Edinger has delimited the significance of regarding ego as a symbolizing process.[12] He has described the difference between the merely pragmatic use of words as signs and the symbolizing process which is ego. Words as signs convey merely abstract, objective meanings, according to Edinger, whereas symbols are man's way of relating himself to his cosmos. For symbols are involved with another kind of meaning: they are at once subjective and cosmic. They are carriers of living meaning which does not primarily relate to abstract knowledge, but rather to those kinds of psychic energies which actually affirm life. Dreams, myths, and works of art are all symbolizing functions of ego which convey this living meaning. This symbolic meaning is quite different from objective, abstract meaning. Man is often unaware of the symbolic depths, the different kinds of transcriptions, and the different kinds of symbolic me-sages which are part of the human psyche's efforts to maintain life which are implicit in Edinger's distinction.

The failure to distinguish sign meanings from symbolic meanings causes confusion in understanding the function of ego. The problem is that, while symbolic meaning corresponds to human subjectivity, there is no transcendent value ascribed to subjectivity in modern western culture, for with the decline of religion that has occurred in the last century, man has lost a necessary and extremely important collective sanction for the subjective realm of life. Pressures of western society have urged man to seek life's meaning in externals and objectivity to the detriment of the meaning of individual subjectivity. Religion itself has, in fact, often become merely another form of scientism.

However, consciousness remains man's ultimate goal and cosmic consciousness is necessary to this survival. The unique and not to be duplicated subjectivity of the symbolic processes which Edinger suggests for human meaning and relatedness must be stressed. This is in some ways frightening because man's hope, even in our present empiricistic orientation, is not susceptible to a purely objective and statistical approach. The majority of psychologists, who ought to know better, contribute to the present depreciation of subjectivity. Edinger indicates that subjective symbols are now often interpreted as nothing but reflections of the environment and of interpersonal relationships. As a result, ego is seen as a phenomenon the product of which is the creation of the self or some other psychic entity. Edinger points out that, to many theorists, the idea of unique individual personality is a delusion. In the face of this almost monolithic orientation, Edinger's emphasis is extremely important, for contemporary man's most urgent need is to rediscover and build his life on what Kierkegaard meant by "truth as subjectivity": that the inner subjective world of the psyche is ultimately real and meaningful.

Symbols as carriers of psychic energy are related to the self and its reorganization of consciousness. They are central to the processes called ego. Symbols are alive. They actually transmit consciously or unconsciously the life energy of man which supports, guides, and motivates him. The significance of the symbol is missed when it is understood merely as a sign or substitute for some known content. The concept of ego as the symbolizing process which unites the individual with the universe within him in both its organic and cosmic dimensions is critical to understanding the person in his fullness.

THE THERAPIST IS A PROTOTYPE OF CONSCIOUSNESS

Carl Rogers makes several statements about the value of a helping relationship which seem fundamental to the meaning of the self as it is articulated in symbolic regression theory.[13] Rogers points out that the therapist must be perceived by the other person as trustworthy and dependable in order for the growth of consciousness to take place. He indicates that the most helpful physicians are those who make great use of procedures which are passive or permissive. Such helpful physicians are likely to develop a relationship in which the patient feels confidence. Rogers further indicates that individuals who had undertaken psychotherapy agreed on some major elements of that experience. These common elements were attitudinal factors which these individuals held accounted for the significant changes they had undergone. These attitudes were: their trust in the therapist, their sense that they were understood by the therapist, and their responsiveness to the therapist's direct statements about feelings which they as clients had only hesitantly approached. Rogers further shows that it is the client's meanings which it is necessary to have understood in the relationship in order for it to be therapeutic. Finally, the therapist's initiative in self-disclosing behavior is highly related to change in the client. Thus procedures and techniques of the therapist are less important in his work than are his attitudes.

Genuineness is the most important characteristic of cosmic man. His self stands the challenge of false realities and in the challenge continues to act upon the basis of that which is intrinsic and natural. This frees those to whom he relates to take a similar stance with their lives.

Creativity is a result of a highly energized relationship between self and Being. It is implicit in this relationship that cosmic consciousness, self-Being relatedness, is ultimately necessary for man's survival. The recovery of creativity is the goal of psychotherapy. The foundation of the successful therapeutic process is the psychotherapist who is related to Being and thus to himself so completely that his whole being is actually or potentially expressed and brought to bear in the therapeutic encounter. Such a therapist has developed a relaxed stance toward the world and toward the meaning of his own person for the person of the client. In his free, creative approach to the environment, he possesses a naivete within himself which permits him to perceive reality relatively free from introjected distortions and which allows his being to flow harmoniously with the energies of the other.

Given this state of the therapist's integration, even small things become significant to the therapist and to his client. The therapist is seen as being basically happy or hopeful. His tone reveals that he enjoys the task of relatedness even in its difficult dimensions. His capacity for enjoying and harmonizing with his own inner simplicity and the inner beauties of his own nature are seen as a deep spiritual awareness. Egotistical success striving and competition have given way to the shared search for personal meaning and psychic harmony. He is led by his inner nature. He shows that fatalism has given way to optimism in his relating to others. He acts out of the assurance that he is an agent in his own destiny, thus giving the other an inner desire to relate to his way of being in the world. The real world of nature becomes the therapist's true domain and he only feels the impact of society's expectations when they are in harmony with his own inner reality. He is not addictive or depressive or schizoid in his behavior or perceptions. He can learn from anyone who has something real to offer him, and yet he is most quick to reject any mere intellectualisms being promulgated as knowledge. He feels whole and this feeling he communicates in a way that is convincing to others because the feeling is genuine. He doesn't really think about himself, for he is himself, he reflects upon himself, he is at home with himself, and he has an inner reality which he brings to bear on the otherness of his client and those around him. He is experienced as having a kind of equanimity. At the same time, he values the other's struggle for consciousness and for legitimacy. While perceiving the dark side of existence and the power of introjected, illegitimate strategies, he stands in relation to the power of consciousness in all situations. His relating in this stance enables the client, at the point of the client's relatedness to him, to discover the power of his own legitimacy and gradually to let go of each of the introjected images and the symptomatic strategies which have denied him his birthright.

The conscious therapist, or the conscious person, is able to decide about what he wants because his inner reality is in harmony with his environment. He is able to set the other person free to decide what he really wants and needs. He possesses conviction and often seems relentless when he is in states of heightened consciousness. He is beyond the polarities and moralisms which plague unaware persons and frighten them into further unconsciousness. Thus the person who comes to him for help feels appealed to on all levels beyond "ought" and "should." Rather the appeal comes at the level of all that is natural. The conscious person neither reacts nor conforms; he acts and he forms. He acts because of the fullness in the action itself, not merely for its effects. His ethical choices are personal and autonomous and his action is based on the priority of consciousness in each new situation. He trusts his intuition and acts on it without guilt or fear or the need for self-justification. He directly experiences his own reality. He has a growing faith in the trustworthiness of his own nature. He appears as rather uncomplicated: he is a man of simplicity with himself. His uniqueness is untarnished by man-made complexities and stereotypes. He is in truth childlike. Thus he is nonthreatening, because this state of childlikeness, the state of simply and directly relating his being to the being of others, is experienced within the personality of the other. This is the psychotherapy of revelation rather than of intimidation, and his appropriation of the amplitude of his own being becomes extended to his client. Paul Ricoeur expresses the meaning of this reality in his discussion of the power of the word in genuine dialogue:

> When we speak of the word as a living and effective word, we evoke a connection between the word and the active core of our existence. We imply that the word has our existence. We imply that the word has the power to change the understanding we have of ourselves. Its power is not primarily imperative in nature, however. Before the word addresses itself to our will as an order and elicits obedience, it addresses itself to what I call our existence and elicits effort and desire; it changes us, not because a will is imposed on our will but because of the effort made by "the hearing which understands." The word reaches us at the level of the symbolic structures of our existence, the dynamic schemes which express our way of understanding our situation and of projecting our power in that situation. Our existence as capable of being modified by the word is prior to the will, therefore, and even prior to the principle of obligation, which according to Kant is the a priori principle of the will. The inner connection between our desire to be and the power of the word is a consequence of the act of listening, of hearkening. This connection in its turn makes possible will, evaluation, decision, choice.[14]

Because the therapist is "turning out all right," he does not need to make the client turn out all right. The therapist is turning out within the context of his own reality. As the client learns to emulate this attitude or spirit, he too begins to evolve in the context of his own inner reality. The past and the future become part of the therapist's continuing cosmic awareness and he is thus perceived as confident and self-possessed. His privacy is experienced not as withdrawal, but as a drawing upon inner resources which make him capable for the situation at hand. He has a mild aura of well-being about him. He enjoys life not only because it is good for him but because it is good, and he is good for it. He experiences the client's anxieties as conflicts within the client's own nature rather than as states in which he is himself a participant. This kind of person or therapist, then, is perceived as feeling taken care of by his world. He does not take care of it; he is sensitive to it because it is responsive. To him, life is never experienced as mere drudgery to be endured until some external goal is achieved. Rather, he constantly discovers new and refreshing facets of experience and wonders at the mysteries which the world continually presents.

The man of heightened consciousness frequently appears to be alone, a man apart, but the therapist who is truly cosmic is not experienced as lonely or as a loner. Rather, he possesses the spirit of a pioneer, one who is uninhibited by the usual social fears. He appears detached from time and space and yet able to enjoy life in a direct and naively simple sense. The reality of the therapist, when expressed merely in terms such as "empathy," and "rapport," seems too abstract. For such qualities, taken apart from the process of consciousness, are only the most marginal elements of true consciousness or genuineness with Being. In fact, the person who is developed in his cosmic consciousness is not analyzable; he is only knowable through direct experience. Such an individual is easy to be with. Nevertheless, he provokes the awareness that the relationship with him is one for which the other must take his own responsibility. The cosmic man reveals himself as part of his total relatedness. He does not assume responsibility for the revelation of the other person, or demand it. Nor does he allow himself to be manipulated to accept substitutes for genuine self-disclosure. For in his being open, that is, his being conscious, he is aware of the responsiveness that is conscious or genuine in the other. This consciousness is acknowledged and affirmed in silence as well as in speech.

NOTES

1. This motif is a central one in Biblical myths of redemption, for example. See Exodus 24:9-11 and Revelation 19:7-9.

2. W. Earl Biddle, unpublished talk, Los Angeles, California, June 1966.

3. Carl Gustav Jung, "Psychological Types," in The Collected Works of C. G. Jung, vol. 6, pp. 421-22.

4. "Psychological Types," p. 425.

5. "Psychological Types," p. 425.

6. Jolande Jacobi, The Psychology of C. G. Jung, Revised Edition, (New Haven and London: Yale Univ. Press, 1968), pp. 9-10.

7. Carl Gustav Jung, "Psychological Aspects of the Mother Archetype," in The Collected Works of C. G. Jung, vol. 9, part 1.

8. Calvin S. Hall and Gardner Lindzey, Theories of Personality, (New York: Wiley, 1957), p. 81.

9. Hall and Lindzey, p. 82.

10. Clark Moustakas, ed. The Self: Explorations in Personal Growth, (New York: Harper and Brothers, 1956).

11. Moustakas, "Summary: Explorations in Essential Being and Personal Growth," in Moustakas, ed., pp. 271-79.

12. Edward F. Edinger, "Symbols: The Meaning of Life," Spring, 1962.

13. Carl R. Rogers, "The Characteristics of a Helping Relationship," The Personnel and Guidance Journal, 37 (September 1958), 6-16.

14. Paul Ricoeur, "Religion, Atheism, and Faith," in Alasdair MacIntyre and Paul Ricoeur, The Religious Significance of Atheism, (New York and London: Columbia Univ. Press, 1969), pp. 78-79.

Chapter V
Family

> The foundation of the family is the relationship
> between husband and wife. [The wife's] place is
> within, while that of the husband is without. It
> is in accord with the great laws of nature that
> husband and wife take their proper places. Within
> the family a strong authority is needed; this is
> represented by the parents. If the father is
> really a father and the son a son, if the elder
> brother fulfills his position, and the younger
> fulfills his, if the husband is really a husband
> and the wife a wife, then the family is in order.
> When the family is in order, all the social
> relationships of mankind will be in order.
> The I Ching, no. 37.[1]

THE INDIVIDUAL ENTERS CONSCIOUSNESS THROUGH FAMILY

In the chapter on consciousness we developed the idea that there are three levels of consciousness, the organic, the personal, and the cosmic. Each of these levels integrally corresponds with the others, and each has been carefully analyzed by major modern schools of thought. This chapter focuses on family at the personal level through which much of man's total consciousness becomes delineated. The reality of family underlies and informs the scope as well as the contents of consciousness for each individual person. We will consider how for each individual the structure of family experience becomes the matrix through which he comes to consciousness of himself in his organic, cosmic and personal dimensions. In the City of God St. Augustine suggests the centrality of family as the matrix for human authority and consciousness:

The human family constitutes the beginning and the essential element of society. Every beginning points to some end of the same nature, and every element to the perfection of the whole of which the element is a part. Thus it becomes evident that peace in society must depend upon peace in the family, and the order and harmony of rulers and ruled must directly be actualized from the order and harmony arising out of creative guidance and commensurate response in the family.[2]

Jung founds his talk of the inherited archetypes of the race on biological language. Parsons presents the family as a social system in structural terms which can be interpreted to correspond to the archetypes of Jung. Certain phenomenologists of religion, such as Tillich, Eliade, and Watts, describe the structure of man's cosmic consciousness in ways which seem to extend and amplify this structure at the cosmic level. Furthermore, Ernst Cassirer's original conception of man as a symbolizing animal provides a comprehensive perspective which integrates the parallel structures of man's levels of consciousness into a totality. As we see it, there are three common notions underlying all of these approaches which are the foundations of symbolic regression psychology. We will now consider each of these inseparable root concepts in the discussion of family. These concepts are: polarity, authority, and symbolic regression.

Family, as the milieu which gives form and scope to all of the individual's symbolizing, has three different modes. First, antecedent to all actual families, is the prototypical cosmic structure which we designate as <u>symbolic family</u>. This is an innate structure in man. Second, the particular biological and social family into which any given individual is born becomes his <u>existential family</u>. This existential family becomes introjected as the matrix by which experience is made intelligible to the individual. Third, the energies constellated by the individual's relating introjecting elements of his existential family to the innate elements of symbolic family constitute his <u>imaginary family</u>.

Each individual is born into symbolic family as well as into an existential family. Elements of both the symbolic and the existential modes of the reality of family impinge upon the individual to form his imaginary family, whether or not he is aware of them. The structure of the existential family more or less corresponds to symbolic family. To the extent that the mothering and fathering polarities in the individual's existential family deviate from their prototypes in symbolic family, they distort the structure of his imaginary family. His experiences of himself, of the structure and functions of human society, and ultimately of the cosmic masculine and feminine polarities of Being are also deformed. At the same time, the deformation of the imaginary family determines the form and scope of the individual's inner authority.

Symbolic regression is the psychic device by which the individual relates to his primary needs--those implicit at the level of symbolic family--through imagination. The inner authority to which the individual thus gains access through symbolic regression becomes manifest in his growing authority within the existential family. The result of this process is a change in the dynamics of the existential family.

Joseph Campbell argues that family as the embodiment of cosmic structure is grounded at the most fundamental biological level:

> As long as the nuclear unit of human life has been a man, woman, and child, the maturing consciousness has had to come to a knowledge of its world through the medium of this heavily loaded, biologically based triangle . . .[3]

Thus, a sexually mature male impregnates the womb of a sexually mature female with a sperm which fertilizes her egg. The zygote which is the product of the union of sperm and egg begins its long development toward becoming another sexually mature member of the species. Because of the unusually long period of post-natal development of the human individual toward sexual maturity, male and female adults work together to provide the nourishment and protection necessary for their offspring to reach this maturity and to repeat the reproductive cycle. This biological basis of human existence is irreducible. Yet out of such biological conditions emerges the social reality of the family. The long post-natal development of the human being makes necessary the social collaboration of parents or their substitutes and it is this collaboration in the reproductive cycle which becomes socially institutionalized in the role relationships of the family. Thus family implements the task of perpetuating the species which is inherent in any individual's biological nature.

In spite of recent comparative studies which attack the idea of the universality of the nuclear family, its basis in the biology of human reproduction and its prevalence throughout much of the world make the nuclear family the most natural unit for the discussion of family images. David B. Lynn's conclusion concerning the anthropological limits of family structure provides a starting point for this discussion:

> The norm for all societies . . . is a family arrangement of some sort in which <u>at least</u> one woman and one man care for children, whether or not they are the biological parents.[4]

Comparative anthropologists M. J. Levy and L. A. Fallers extend this minimal definition of family by looking at the family as a social system. They see it as a system of roles operating as a "nuclear-family relationship complex."[5] With this concept of the "nuclear family relationship complex," the biological family, the specific "nuclear" form which the family takes in western societies, and the family as a network of roles can be taken together to more or less correspond to the cosmic order as this becomes manifest in family structure and, similarly, to the family images which ultimately determine the structure of the individual human self.

POLARITY CONSTITUTES PERSONAL AUTHORITY

Polarity is inherent in the principle of authority. Consideration of the cosmic dimensions of polarity helps to understand the importance of the principle as it is used in symbolic regression psychology. The concept of polarity is the foundation for this analysis of family structure. Man does not understand the reality of the gravitational fields which polarize the universe and at the same time make possible the harmony of the spheres, but the reality of this polarity is obvious to all. Likewise, the magnetic fields of the earth typify this cosmic reality and are necessary for its balance. The north pole is not right and the south pole is not wrong. Such polarities as this run through all of Being. The conception of polarity as a cosmic principle is the basis for understanding the masculine and feminine poles within the personality and thus the images related to the individual's authority and the symbolic significance of the family. Authority is the manifestation of this cosmic structure as the structure of consciousness.

FAMILY   147

    Polarity is the notion that a given entity is part of a
system which includes its opposites. Any given element is
thus known by its distinction from and necessary relation to
its opposite within the system. The concept of system
determines that no one element can be isolated from the
others. Thus, the individual identity of the element is
known by its function in relation to the rest of the system.
At the same time, the fact that any given element has an
individual identity means that it can be thrown into relief
in relation to the system as a whole. Thus each polar
element is at once distinct from its other, yet inseparable
from the total field which it helps to constitute. At all
levels polarity is a dynamic concept, for the emergence of
one pole changes the whole field of relationships, including
the role of the other pole as well. This concept of
polarity will help in the understanding of the dynamics of
the family and of the psyche as related systems of energy
fields, for the family as a unit and the psyche as a whole
consist fundamentally of three polarities, the polarity of
masculine and feminine, the polarity of parent and child,
and the polarity of microcosm and macrocosm.

    Talcott Parsons has related the concept of polarity to
his analysis of the structure of the family as a social
system. He sees four major role functions in the family
which are constituted by two polarities, the polarity of
gender and the polarity of generations. The roles of any
given family member are to be determined by that family
member's position in relation to these polarities. Thus the
person who embodies the masculine parent poles is the
father-husband, the one who embodies the feminine parent
poles is the mother-wife, the one who embodies the masculine
child poles is the son-brother, and the one who embodies the
feminine child poles is the daughter-sister. Parsons'
placing of family members according to this analysis of
social roles presents the family as a dynamic system
consisting of two of the polarities of our analysis. This
system gives structure to the family images inherent in each
human psyche.

    Parsons' analysis of family role structure grew out of
his sociological analysis of the working of small groups.[6]
Parsons determined that two types of leadership, what he
called "instrumental" and "expressive" leadership, seem to
emerge in every small group. The instrumental leader is the
one who provides for the existence of the group through
relating it to the exigencies of the world beyond it. The
expressive leader fosters the internal dynamics and the
interaction which make it possible for the group to function

as a social unit. The extent of mutuality of function between these two kinds of leadership determines the nature and success of the group.

When Parsons applies this analysis to the family as a social system, he finds that the role of father-husband generally corresponds to the instrumental leader, just as that of mother-wife corresponds to the expressive leader. The meaning of this structure of leadership, common to the small group and the family, lies in its immediate correspondence to the deeper structure of human experience and in the more extended, implicit correspondence between man's images and the cosmic order.

The structure of the family and the roles of its members according to Parsons' analysis correspond to the archetypal predispositions which Jung suggests in his speculations on the cosmic dimensions of the psyche. Although the scope of a given archetype as Jung treats it seems to be fluid, Jolande Jacobi suggests that the archetypes ultimately resolve themselves into the polarity of masculine and feminine elements.[7] Such analysis implies that the masculine-feminine polarity is a cosmic principle. This notion of cosmic sexual polarity is common to many spiritual traditions.[8] Nevertheless, Jung's discussion of archetypes seems naturally to orient itself in relation to the family roles suggested by our two polarities. Thus, three major archetypal figures emerge in Jung's writings-- mother, child, and father.[9]

The role of the mother image and, by implication, of the father image in psychology is suggestively extended by object relations theory. According to this theory, maternal nurturance is symbolized in the image of the mother. To the extent that this nurturance is adequate and consistent and thus corresponds to the natural needs of the child, it is taken together as the image of "Good Mother." On the other hand, to the extent that this maternal care is disrupted and becomes depriving for the child, it is taken collectively as "Bad Mother." In a developmental theory such as that offered in object relations psychology, the image of the mother becomes progressively more focused in the course of the individual's development into his differentiated adult consciousness. At the same time, the individual has continuing access to each of the less focused moments in the development of his mother image, and, more importantly, all of the moments of this image taken together color the mood and tone of each of his subsequent experiences of the world in which he lives.

Symbolic regression psychology goes beyond the emphasis on the mother image of the object relations school, for here the father image has a role equal to that of the mother image in constituting the subjectivity of the individual. W. E. Biddle sketches a developed analysis of these parental images in his article, "Image Therapy."[10] Biddle divides family images according to whether they have a positive or a negative effect on the person that has them. As a result, the family images as he presents them consist of six modes of family role structure: "good mother," "bad mother," "good father," "bad father," "good child," and "bad child." The positive family images correspond to imagination in its natural, harmonious process. These images foster an innate sense of self-worth and legitimacy in the person. The negative family images, on the other hand, correspond to introjected material arising out of the experience of emotional deprivation. Such images are abortive: they undermine the individual's self-worth and make him feel a sense of illegitimacy about his existence. The six family images which emerge in Biddle's analysis of family structure manifest themselves within each dimension of imagination. They can be represented schematically in the following way:

Family Images

Natural Affirming Images	Introjected Depriving Images
Existential Family Level	
Father: potent and sustaining father	impotent or disruptive father
Mother: nurturing mother	depriving or seductive mother
Child: good, legitimate child	bad, illegitimate child
Level of Social Projection	
Father: good authority, social order	bad authority, social disorder
Mother: society as a comfortable milieu	society as an alienating milieu

Child: individual as genuine   individual as deviant or a
         contributor to the   liability to society
         transcendent values
         of society

Level of Cosmic Projection

Father: the rational order of   irrational chaos, damnation
         things, exalted   and annihilation for the
         destiny for the   individual
         individual

Mother: nature of cosmos as   nature of cosmos as alien
         ultimately comforting   and not comforting

Child: subjectivity as   subjectivity as invalid and
         genuine and   hallucinatory
         legitimate

Family determines the way in which masculine and feminine cosmic images become symbolized in the person and it serves to evoke images which permit or deny the individual access to consciousness and to his inner authority. The masculine and feminine polarities of the individual's inner experience and the masculine and feminine interactions in the social environment are both types of polarities inherent in human substance. These inherently human polarities are in turn constellations of the universal polar structure of symbolic energy at the cosmic level. The way in which these two poles are experienced through social interaction results in either the validation or the inhibition of the person's right to his own autonomy. Thus family determines the level of consciousness, legitimacy, and genuineness which the individual is able to realize. It is in the family that the individual's inherited, preformed orientation to masculine or feminine realities is identified with psychologically, for it is his social experience which determines a man's capacity to identify with his masculinity while accepting his feminine aspect.

Symbolic family refers in the first instance to all the mothering or nurturing and all the fathering or ordering qualities inherent in the cosmic order which are to be found in the individual's environment. Jung's concept of the archetype helps to explain this cosmic level of the reality of family, for, according to this concept, the form of the world into which a person is born is already innate within him as a virtual image.[11] Thus, to focus on one parent image for a moment, the newborn infant inherits a preformed receptivity to mothering as a set of qualities which predetermines how he will perceive his mother. Yet, superimposed on this predisposition, the perception of the infant is delimited by the person of the actual mother as the infant experiences her. The actual mother herself in the early stages of development is thus the most important agent in forming the introject and thus in determining the scope of the individual's natural authority. As a consequence of the mother's influence, the child's experience is the joint product of an inner disposition to perceive the world in a certain natural manner and an environment which mirrors this predisposition in either direct or more or less distorted ways. The inner predisposition and the actual nature of the social introject come together in imagination in childhood to form the individual's mother image. The constellation of this conjunction with that of the father image is the foundation for the individual's personal authority.

The existential family either corresponds to or distorts the individual's inner predispositions and symbolic regressive capacities. The development of the capacity for symbolic regression in the person depends upon the way that he develops his inner symbolism of fathering and mothering energies. When the family provides a person with the privilege of symbolizing his child self in relation to the ground of Being, this person develops in a natural, autonomous way. When the family does not do this, it imposes authority images on the person which hamper the self-energies from grounding themselves in Being. This results in the self substance being symptomatically expressed. This state must be resymbolized by the development of the capacity for symbolic regression so that the individual can recover access to the primal, legitimate dimensions of symbolic family. Thus <u>the existential family is the key to the meaning of psychopathology</u>. At the same time it provides the means of personal integration and consciousness because <u>it contextualizes the etiology of symptomatic behavior</u>.

It is important to recognize the difference between preformed dispositions and introjects, and to recognize the polar nature of authority in each individual. The failure to recognize the polarity of authority causes a person to identify with one pole against the other, so that he confuses himself about his nature. In this confusion he loses a sense of his autonomy and legitimacy.

Polarity is the structural principle expressed in family as a symbolic-functional social unit. For years psychology has focused on the mother. Now the father is beginning to appear. In this the opportunity has arisen for us to understand adequately the meaning of authority with regard to family dynamics. The father image is being brought to light as the mother image had previously been brought to light. The family poses the problems and the possibilities for consciousness through its embodiment of the masculine-feminine polarities of authority.

The structure of the emotionally healthy family is such that mother's authority is distinguished from father's authority not so much by its manifestation as such, but rather by how the mother relates to and complements the father's authority. The basis of the mother's authority lies in how she relates to the father's authority—she affirms her own in affirming his. This polar concept gives a dynamic, depth quality to the experience of authority.

The child's authority is confirmed or denied for him by the quality of his experience with his father. Accordingly, the father must be conscious of his authority and willing to transmit it to his child. The mother supports the father's authority by giving the child care and nurturance as she relates in her strength to the potency of the father. This nurturance in the context of her relatedness to the man gives the child the double-edged comfort necessary for his openness to the father's authority.

To elaborate, in the beginning the mother supplies the physical nurturance while the father supplies the spiritual nurturance to the child. That is, the father supports the mother's authority over the child's inner world. He affirms the mother's command, "Eat your carrots." At adolescence this is reversed. The father teaches and supplies nurturance for the concrete, practical matters of the outer world while the mother provides a spiritual presence which supports the child to believe the father. She affirms the father's faith: "Yes, you can get that job."

Polarities which are organized into the masculine and feminine dimensions of Being are the guiding principles by which the self is related to Being. Biological, sexual differences are important at the cosmic level as basic differences in emotional energies between the masculine and the feminine principles. Opposition exists everywhere in the personality between these two poles of psychic energy. These differences, if properly understood, can be used to integrate the polar nature of authority as it is symbolized through the actual family. Mother is not father; father is not mother. In the interaction of human existence they represent different ultimate cosmic realities in necessary polarity with each other. A father can mother, and a mother must sometimes father. But a father is not a mother, nor is a mother a father.

These two energy poles which function in all of life, and are more or less identified with by the male and the female in real existence, must be learned and understood through family structure in order for the individual to be free to have an adequate sense of personal authority. Failure clearly to see this structure results in emotional and mental disharmony and confusion. Psychotherapy is the attempt to depolarize the self in relation to the masculine-feminine dimensions of authority in imagination through defusing the polarity-confusing introjects and reducing their power over consciousness. Through the reaffirmation of sexual polarity, therapy develops a sense of individual authority in the person.

Conspicuous by its absence in contemporary literature is the discussion of masculine authority in the family and its relationship to feminine authority as this affects personal consciousness and autonomy. As these polarities differ in the existential family, they bring into interaction with each other the elements which are necessary for consciousness. Gender polarity has been assumed by many schools of thought to be purely a socially learned phenomenon. Yet at the same time that women are demanding equal rights with men in reaction to the oppressive elements of traditional western patriarchal society, we are now uncovering important principles relating to the polarity of masculine and feminine. Women should be demanding unequal rights, and it is precisely at this time that the psychotherapist must begin to determine the meaning of authority as it is transmitted through family images. There are ontological, inborn differences between the sexes, differences in temperament and inclination which are transcultural as well as transpersonal. Sex specific discoveries in science now validate this. To put it simply, imagination in a man is somewhat different from imagination in a woman. Men and women must learn from each other or perish in a misguided struggle for power. Erich Fromm emphasizes the need for the sexes to discover and socially to express their true complementarity in an important essay, "The Significance of the Theory of Mother Right for Today."[12]

When these universal polarities are not understood or when they do not become conscious to the child through his experience of family, he begins "parenting" these polarities in the parents and in himself. That is, he idealizes himself as the omnipotent and universal caretaker who preserves the fantasized parent or parents. This attitude denies him his own finiteness and gender polarity and he does not develop a sense of his inner autonomy. With such psychic disguising of the polarities, the child cannot identify with his gender specific pole in ways that allow him to develop according to his own gender specificity. This confusion of images deprives him of the right to relate clearly to the other pole. The truly conscious person does not see father as he sees mother, nor does he see mother as he sees father. In the individual's images, these father and mother energies should compensate for each other and also intermingle with each other so that they are mutually enhancing. But when masculine-feminine authority is confused in family, the child becomes confused about the ultimate nature of authority. He cannot imagine the reality of his own concrete identity or relate to others out of it. He loses his capacity to relate with cosmic awareness to what is going on in the universe of Being around him. Yet, the individual's capacity symbolically to regress in relation to these poles is vital for his existence as well as for the development of his consciousness.

THREE POLARITIES UNDERLIE FAMILY STRUCTURE

The family as a social group is constituted by three structural polarities which have a developmental significance in the growth of consciousness. The first of these is the polarity of child and parent, the second is the polarity of masculine and feminine as this is expressed between the parents, and the third polarity is that between the family as a small social group or microcosm of society and the society at large within which it is to be found. The first two of these in particular are of central importance in symbolic regression psychology.

The polarity of parent and child is what Parsons calls the polarity of generations. Kierkegaard stresses the importance of this polarity in its broadest terms:

> Whatever the one generation may learn from the other, that which is genuinely human no generation learns from the foregoing. . . . Thus no generation has learned from another to love, no generation begins at any other point than at the beginning, no generation has a

task assigned to it than had the previous
generation. . . . In this respect every generation begins primitively, has no different task
from that of every previous generation, nor
does it get further, except in so far as the
preceding generation shirked its task and deluded
itself.[13]

A child needs to learn at the outset that he has parents.
This may seem trite, but the profound consequences of the
child's not consciously living in relation to this reality
results in serious damage to consciousness and to his sense
of personal autonomy. If the child has a cold, withdrawing
mother, for example, he will learn to withdraw from his own
spontaneous warmth. He will become unrelated to this
aspect of himself. He will remain unconscious of the world
around him. He will become more or less oblivious to
warmth and to the nurturing dimensions of life. To such a
person the world easily becomes hostile and depriving, a
place against which he believes he must take care of himself
by idealizing his situation. On the other hand, if the
father is explosive and uncomfortable with his masculinity,
the child can become unconscious of his anger and deny his
capacity for aggressive explosiveness. The child will
"parent" the parent. He will "take care of" this aspect of
psychic functioning within himself. In so over-controlling
his emotions and feelings, he will become either compulsively explosive or withdrawn from the expressive and
creative side of his personality. His authority will not
be experienced as under his conscious direction; rather, he
will feel caught in the push and pull of the social forces
impinging upon him.

In all mental and emotional deprivation and disturbance,
the child becomes his own parent in order to control a world
perceived as threatening to his weakened sense of authority.
In a sense, the child becomes his own grandparent. He takes
care of his own parents, and in this act denies the reality
of his needs and his legitimacy. Consequently, as he grows,
he loses the capacity to contact the meaning of his natural
inner child, the meaning of spontaneity, the meaning of
expressiveness and creativity, the meaning of warmth, the
meaning of anger, and the meaning of sexual feelings. When
these natural elements of emotional life begin to emerge, he
must try to repress them, for they are without meaning to
his authority. Thus, "deparenting" the individual becomes a
major goal of consciousness and genuineness. When the
person can contact the inner child, and can release these
kinds of feeling states, he becomes personally and

spiritually more autonomous. He deparents himself by seeing his existential parents in relation to their prototypes in symbolic family.

The second structural principle which embodies the development of the child's right to his own authority rests in the relationship between father and mother in the child's experience. When parents are unable to form a coalition and recognize the mutuality of their masculine and feminine polarities in this coalition so that the child can feel comfortable with his own identity, the child will lack the balance within himself to relate harmoniously in society. Instead of relating with both parents in full emotional give and take, he exaggerates his attachment to the one parent with whom he feels he must identify for a sense of security. In this symbiotic attachment to one parent, he idolizes the other parent. This idolizing takes expression in fearful withdrawal, or in attacking the other parent, as if the suppressed aspect of himself which is embodied in that parent has much greater power over him than it really does. Thus, he divides both his inner and his outer worlds; he polarizes his authority within and without. He has access to only a small part of his consciousness, yet that part of his consciousness is not satisfying to him because it deprives him of a major aspect of himself. He goes through life ambivalently, alternating between the masculine and feminine poles of reality and feeling illegitimate. Nurture is threatening to his feelings of masculinity, and creativity is threatening to his needs for nurturance. He cannot choose; he cannot, in a sense, easily become genuine, for he feels illegitimate. He lacks authority. One of the major tasks of therapy is to depolarize the personality so that imagination affords access to both poles of the self.

From the beginning the child must be presented with the difference between father and mother if the relationship between father and mother within him is to develop in its dynamic fullness. The adult in therapy must learn to think of his parents not as a unity but as two individuals. The "we" of parenting is necessary but only in that it follows the "I" of the individual father or mother. It is important that the person say, "my father and my mother," and not merely, "my parents." This differentiated stance toward family results in the development of the child's genuine autonomy and sense of legitimacy. At the same time, this differentiation does not mean that the coalition between the parents is not vital; rather, it means that the child learns to perceive the difference between father authority and mother authority in order for him to feel the legitimacy of his own authority as the child. The polarity of parental

authority as it becomes internalized in the child becomes
very complex, for the child does not get his image of his
father from his father alone, nor does he get the image of
his mother from his mother alone. Rather, the child gets
the image of his father from his mother, from his father,
from his grandparents, from the society around him, and from
his brothers and sisters in their striving with him for
father's acceptance. This same complexity also shapes the
mother image and the other family images as well.

We are beginning to see that the image of the father
and his influence on the psychological development of the
child are as important as the image and influence of the
mother. In fact, it is now becoming recognized that the
father's influence begins even before the baby is born.
Henry B. Biller says that the father's paternal influence
begins during pregnancy in such things as his keeping the
expectant mother in a good frame of mind.[13] The father's
influence is crucial even in those early years when the
mother is supposedly the key parent. Moreover, the father
is probably more important than the mother to the healthy
sexual development of both boys and girls, for the father
differentiates more than the mother between the son's and
the daughter's sexuality. The father-deprived child has
problems with the opposite sex. Indeed, the time has come
for psychology to acknowledge the polar nature of authority
in the home as it relates to the development of authority in
the individual child. The father needs to support the
mother and the mother needs to comfort the father. The
interrelating of these two independent yet indispensible
realities, with their cosmic significance, is the foundation
for the child's capacity for personal authority, consciousness, and his sense of legitimacy. Where have all the
fathers gone? Looking at the evidence, behavioral scientists
are beginning to tell us that the neglected and neglectful
father is the root cause of many of our current social
problems. We believe that the loss of the potent and loving
father from the home is the cause of the loss of the personal
sense of legitimacy characteristic of these times.

It is important to be aware of the ways that the parents
move away from the genuineness of the natural polar
coalition to become involved in parenting each other in a
kind of emotional fusion. When adults have become deprived
of their own childhood, they are tempted to become parents
to each other. The only way they know to exist is to deny
their need for personal autonomy. They thus parent each
other in ways that prevent the other from genuine self-
expression and autonomy. Regardless of the form which this

mutual parenting takes, its chief danger is the lack of
clear lines of demarcation between father and mother
authority in the home. This fusion is the consequence of
the father's strategy to overprotect or "father" the mother
as his means of "saving" the fragile projection of his
masculine image into the family. This strategy of the
husband corresponds to the wife's strategy of "mothering"
the father in the home in order that she might avoid facing
her own basic needs as a woman and her fears of male
potency. In both of these cases, the child sees the confusion that results from such displaced anxiety and learns
to imitate these strategies in his own mode of emotional
expressivity. As a result, he ends up unconsciously becoming his own emotional parent in his attempt to disguise his
confusion about the meaning of Being and the privilege of
his own natural child identity.

In a competitive society, parenting of the parent
becomes a critical and devastating game. The young person
often responds to the demand that he "parent" his parents by
rebelling against them because he cannot tolerate the
burdens of this imposed role. Yet he has not been given
adequate opportunities for learning how to be the child.
Father kills himself to succeed in his work in the service
of his distorted, introjected, demanding family. As a
consequence, he abdicates his authority within the family to
the mother who must therefore take over almost all of the
authority manifested in the family. Then the father turns
to pleasing the mother, to whom he has given his own natural
responsibility, in order to win her approval. The mother in
her turn becomes hostile and upset with this distortion of
the natural authority structure, for it neglects the true
authority of her basic feminine needs. For the child, the
absence of father's authority in the home is interpreted as
a lack of his interest in the child. Thus the child feels
he must parent his own life, and in applying the consequent
imaginary paternal authority to himself, he opts for
security at the cost of emotional development. Thus on many
occasions he decides not to push himself, not to compete,
and not to pay the cost of success, for he is reacting to
success as that which preoccupies and motivates the father
and thus deprives the child of his sense of legitimacy.
This distortion of family structure undermines the child's
natural authority, and, by extension, dampens the basic
creative thrust of society as a whole.

One of the major tasks now emerging for psychotherapy
is to bring the father back into visible presence in the
home. This must be done by confronting the distortions of

paternal authority which often take expression in the
father's drive for success as part of a false need to overprotect the family. In this the mother's denial of her own
nurturing needs must also be considered, for the whole
family must be involved in the therapeutic effort. There is
no therapy which is not family therapy, for it is impossible
for anyone to attain a sense of legitimacy as long as the
polarities of masculine and feminine modes of authority are
not clearly differentiated within the family structure.

Third is the polarity of family and society. If the
imaginary family is aligned according to the parent-child
and the masculine-feminine dimensions of its meaning, then
the relationship between the individual and society will be
symbolized so as to result in good social authority
structure. The person will possess authority in society as
well as in his family. Family will relate itself to the
mothering and fathering aspects of society in constructive
ways. In emotional disturbance, the polarity of home and
society has broken down. The family has polarized itself
against society by either mothering, protective strategies
or fathering, competitive strategies. That is, in homes
with children who are disturbed, society has come to be
conceived of as in some way an enemy or a rival of the
family. The family must be free to relate itself creatively
to "family" at large so that the child is enabled to
perceive that there are comforting and constructive ties
between family and society as a whole.

Where family authority is inadequately structured there
is no place for the child to be a child, to be in touch with
his primary needs, and to have direct access to primary
consciousness. The child in a poorly structured or deformed
family environment learns to parent relationships and
becomes confused about the relationship between the masculine and the feminine principles. His perceptions become
distorted and he begins to symbolize his inner reality in
ways that constrict his natural imaginative capacity,
denying him symbolic access to the inner child self. He
begins to symbolize Being symptomatically by parenting or
protecting the denied aspects of his own being. He artifi-
cially takes care of his world so that he might "have"
parents. That is, he founds his own self-symbolizing on the
basis of an imaginary, omnipotent self that preserves his
parents as ideal for him in order to compensate for their
deformations of natural family structure.

DEFORMATIONS OF THESE POLARITIES CAUSE PATHOLOGY

It is no longer realistic to assume that the etiology of mental and emotional disorder is unknowable or that its relief in treatment must remain a matter of mere speculation, since one real origin of emotional disorders is the family in which the pattern of interaction confuses masculine and feminine principles of authority. Treatment of the polarity of masculine and feminine principles immediately involves the family in interaction. This theme thus provokes a direct approach to understanding the symptomatic person's mode of imagining himself in his world. The frightening image introjects related to the fixated and polarized masculine and feminine principles inherent within his being must be uncovered. And the social authority introject which blocks him from the adequate use of his imagination must be directly attacked within the context of the family. In short, both the realities of the imaginary family and of the existential family upon which the imaginary family is being projected must be seen as messages to the family asking that it change its structure and its orientation.

Theodore Lidz, following Parsons, indicates that the family has virtually universal role functions and structural features.[15] These elements of family become especially important in contexts such as American society in which the isolated nuclear family is predominant, for in the nuclear family the masculine and feminine principles are learned basically through the attitudes and the behavior of the two persons who in themselves tend markedly to influence the family organization, the parents. For it is from the parents that individuals within such systems primarily learn the nature of masculine and of feminine authority as well as the relationship between these two poles which constitutes the authority of the child. Perception of the roles of male and female, mother and father, husband and wife, boy and girl, girl and mother, child and father, and so on, is confined for the most part to highly isolated family experiences. Thus, study of nuclear family structure as the basis for understanding masculine and feminine principles of reality becomes essential for understanding modern western experience.

In his book, <u>Schizophrenia and the Family</u>, Theodore Lidz links family structure and pathology. He says that there is strong evidence to indicate that the family has a decisive and pervasive role in personality development and human adaptation. Family organization must be interpreted in relation to the development of symptomatic, polarized, idealized masculine-feminine orientations in the child. All therapy must be family therapy. Commenting on family interaction in relation to schizophrenic symptoms, Lidz says, "Every area of interaction in schizophrenogenic families was found to be faulty in some respect."[16]

According to Lidz, there are three areas of primary structural deficiency in schizophrenogenic families. First, the parents lack individual autonomy, self-responsibility, and an adequate definition of self boundaries. This lack prevents a healty, balanced, interactive coalition between the parents. Second, by confusing gender-linked roles, the family fails to provide models and support a distinct role appropriate to the gender of the patient. These first two deficiencies relate to the polarity of gender; the third relates to the polarity of generations, for when inadequate, undifferentiated, confusing family communication does not maintain the boundaries between the generations, children lose the crucial sense that they are differentiated from their parents. Mothers of schizophrenic children do not provide adequate self-boundaries, for they ask the child to validate their meaning through prompting the child either to over-solicitude or to rejection. Parents in such families do not instill firm identity, self-esteem, or legitimacy in the boy or girl. They ask the child to be the parent in ways that deny his generation and his gender.

Lidz says that in the schizophrenogenic family the father intrudes into the mother-child relationship in subtle ways, upsetting its balance and throwing the mother-child relationship into question.[17] The father who does not outgrow the son-idealization imposed on him by his own mother perpetuates this mother relationship in relation to his wife, and thus requires his children to support his narcissistic needs. Again the child is asked to become the parent of the parent. In such instances, it is too dangerous for the daughter to develop her femininity, while the son lacks an adequate model for his full sexuality as well.

Furthermore, there are two tendencies among schizophrenic mothers. The first type of mother of the schizophrenic child is insecure in her mothering, and thus in unrealistic ways looks to her child and to her husband for validation. Sometimes this mother intrudes into the child's life so that she can know what the child is doing simply for the sake of reassuring herself that she is alright. Commonly the mother with a schizophrenic son treats her son as an extension of herself. The son of such a mother has difficulty developing his powers as a man, for the mother limits the son's explorations and makes his decisions for him. The child thus does not learn to differentiate his drives and needs from those of his mother. In effect, the son is given the role of teaching his mother what it means for her to be a woman while he in actuality is is nothing but a male infant.

The second type of schizophrenogenic mother is the one who is frightened about her identity and who is thus unable to invest herself in the mother-child relationship. She therefore stays emotionally withdrawn from the child. The daughter of this type of mother must deny her mother's withdrawal, idealize it, and divorce herself from the true feminine dimensions of her being. Such a cold, withdrawing mother asks her daughter to give her the sense of worth she feels lacking within herself.

The child of such parents is forced to become his own parents. He fixates upon depriving image introjects which are overwhelming at the same time as he idealizes his real deprivation of natural parental sustenance. In this strategy of deprivation and idealization he remains alienated from the roots of his sexual identity. In place of his own natural authority he acts under the imposed demands of the inner bad parental authority introjects. He is unable to assume responsibility for his personal direction, as he must constantly act to avoid frustrating the introjected images which demand that he give up his selfhood in the attempt to validate the inauthentic parent.

The crucial influence of the family social system on personality development has generally been overlooked by psychiatry. Here, however, the family is the key to understanding all pathological personality development, for in all situations the structure of the family determines the authority image introjects in the child. All the studies of schizophrenia cited by Lidz are characterized by serious disturbances in the sexual polarity of the family structure as a social system.[18]

Lidz, following Parsons, points out that the family has two leaders, a father and a mother.[19] The child in his formative years perceives the natural roles of the parents. The father is seen as the instrumental leader and the mother is seen as the expressive leader. These natural parental roles should normally be experienced in the family so that the child's natural image structure is confirmed through his family. In terms both of family soundness and individual psychological health, this image structure includes three elements. First, there is the coalition of the family which confirms the complementarity of ultimate parental authority images. Second, there are boundaries between one generation and the next which confirm the ultimate polarity of generations. Third, there are clearly differentiated gender-linked roles for each member of the family which confirm the ultimate polarity of genders underlying gender identity. Lidz says that, as natural and simple as these structural requirements are, no family with schizophrenic children has the capacity to embody them adequately. Accordingly, emotional disturbance can be described in relation to family structure. Such disturbance can range from mild forms of identity crisis to the more serious problems of chronic identity diffusion and schizophrenic psychosis. Each possible deviation from the natural family role structure relates to a different quality of individual psychopathology, for the resulting social introjects prevent the individual from using imagination constructively to facilitate the process of self-identification. We will now briefly consider the role of each of these three elements of family structure in the formation of personality characteristics in child development.

The first element in family structure is the parental coalition and its possible deformations. When a realistic, reciprocal coalition between the parents is lacking, the parents compete for the loyalty of the child. This creates a fundamental antagonism within the home. Usually one of the parents gives in and abdicates his role to the other. As a consequence, the child begins parenting the relationship between masculine and feminine aspects of the competition within himself. In this way he disguises from himself the true nature of his own identity. He polarizes his relationships with his two parents: he uses one to completely identify with, while he uses the other as a remote, idealized model. Furthermore, using such strategies, the child invests his energy in the attempt to bridge the gap in this faulty parental coalition. He thus parents the relationship between the two parental realities, disguises their natural meaning for himself, and idealizes the deprived life in which he finds himself regardless of the role he is overtly given by his family situation. As a matter of fact, the actual role he fills is determined by the kind of disharmony that exists in the interaction of masculine and feminine leadership in the family system. The child may mask the parental discord by filling the role of scapegoat. He may feel responsible for satisfying the needs of the parents. Or he might believe that he must symbiotically complete the life of the parents. With any one of these choices, he takes on the role of parenting the family relationships. In so doing, he impairs his ability to differentiate and thereby integrate these polarities within his own imagination.

The second element in family structure is the polarity of generations and its possible deformations. When there is a failure to maintain the separation of the generations, the dependency of a parent upon the child puts the child in an emotionally parenting role with the parent. In a sense, the child must become the parent. The way in which the child symptomatizes his existence through the resulting inadequate self-symbolization will depend in part on the other elements of family structure: the sexuality of the parent, the sexuality of the child, and the relationship between the two parents. For example, when the mother cannot establish her own identity boundaries, she implicitly defines a role for the son as a substitute father. The son must become a father to his mother. In this, the mother is refusing to relate either to her own father or to her husband and the son is cut off from relating to his father as well. The son therefore lacks the experiential support for the natural identification with his father which leads to an integrated father image within himself. Consequently, he is deprived of the identity which is the foundation for his satisfactorily relating to both men and women. On the other hand, when the father is too weak to assert his rightful place in the family and is thus too passive a figure for the son to identify with to affirm his inherited masculine potency, the son remains ignorant of his imposed role although emotionally he is fathering the whole family structure. Consequently, his need for self control and for control of the situation become expressed symptomatically. It is these very symptoms which are indicators of the primary needs which are being unnaturally denied.

The third element in family structure is the polarity of gender and its possible deformations. Here it is fatherhood which brings into focus the importance of gender-linked roles, for the extent of the father's identification with his masculinity plays a major part in determining the development of the child's gender identity. Furthermore, major role reversals in parents can distort the child's gender images. For example, the inability of the mother to fill the affectional-expressive role or of the father to provide instrumental leadership does not adequately foster the alighment of the child's inner images with the cosmic and personal dimensions of the polarity of masculine and

feminine principles. The confusion of gender roles between
the parents and the resulting imbalances in the dynamic
structure of the family develop a faulty sexual identification in the child which becomes the basis for consequent
deep emotional problems. Lidz emphasizes that the
masculine-feminine polarity within the personality enters
decisively into the formation of fundamental personality
characteristics.[20] The gender identity of the child is the
most decisive factor in the achievement of ego identity.

From this analysis it becomes clear that it is the
deformations of family structure which determine the nature
of such elements of psychopathology as: the child's scape-
goating to minimize intrafamilial rivalries; the parent's
failing to provide an adequate identification model for the
child; and the family's inadequately motivating the child
toward proper role identifications. Nevertheless, analytical
theory has for the most part been limited to analysis of
only one small dyad within the family, the mother-child
relationship. Consequently, until recently, the role of the
father has been neglected in the study of schizophrenic
behavior. The father, however, as Lidz has shown, plays an
essential role in the development of the child, for any
child who grows up with a faulty or undeveloped father image
will have identity problems.[21] A weak, ineffectual father,
for example, is probably more significant than a weak,
ineffectual mother in providing a schizophrenogenic background for the child, while a cold, unyielding mother is
more of a problem than a cold, unyielding father. Moreover,
in terms of family dynamics, the mother's ability to mother
cannot be divorced from the support she gains from the
father. The father in a pathological home resents the child
while competing with it for the energies of the mother. The
child's capacity to relate to the mother realistically is
determined to a large extent by the father's ability to
relate to her, his estimate of her, and his acceptance of or
enmity toward her. If the father despises or rejects the
mother, the daughter finds it difficult to relate to the
father as a model love object. If the father is hostile
toward the son, if he is weak in relation to the mother,
then the son has difficulty identifying with his inner
masculine images.

THERE ARE FOUR TYPES OF PATHOGENIC FATHERS

Lidz's studies of schizophrenic families show the
crucial influence of the father in pathological development,

especially for the son. The father in the schizophrenogenic family rarely presents positive masculine images for his son to incorporate. The daughter, on the other hand, if the mother is a mothering figure that she can appreciate, may remain relatively passive after her emergence from the family, but her identity will not be as much disturbed as that of the son. For a son to find his way in life in both career and marital roles, the covert as well as the actual support of an acceptable and accepting father is important. It is easier for a son to grow up without a father than to grow up with an inadequate father. Many studies indicate that if there had been a stable father in the family where schizophrenia is present, the patient would not have been so seriously affected by the mother's difficulty. The lack of the father's effectiveness in his parental role results in much of the schizophrenic patient's inability to integrate the masculine and the feminine polarities of his psyche satisfactorily.

When we consider all of the fathers who have disturbed family relations, and therefore emotionally disturbed children, four major orientations in these father-family relationships seem to emerge. Each of these four orientations expresses the dynamics of one of the four misalliances between husband and wife which are summarized in Lidz's concepts of schism and skew. In the schismatic marriage, one spouse takes an aggressive role and the other plays a passive one. In the skewed marriage, the one takes a dominating role while the other plays a submissive one. The four types of pathological fathers correspond to these four distortions of the marital alliance: aggression, submission, domination, and passivity. The chart (p. 167) sketches the qualities, the strategies, and the effects of each of these four orientations.

We will now briefly note the characteristics of each of these four types of pathological fathers, and then consider their effects on their families in some detail. First, there is the aggressive father. He is a success-driven man who can be paranoid and demanding. Second is the submissive father. This man sometimes competes with his children for the attention of his wife, and often turns to seek warmth outside of the family, the realm which he has abdicated to her. Third is the father who must dominate his wife and family. By playing the authoritarian role, he maintains an exalted conception of himself within the family. Fourth is the father who has become passive. This man has given up on his creative potentials and has in a sense entered into a state of emotional death. We will now

FAMILY

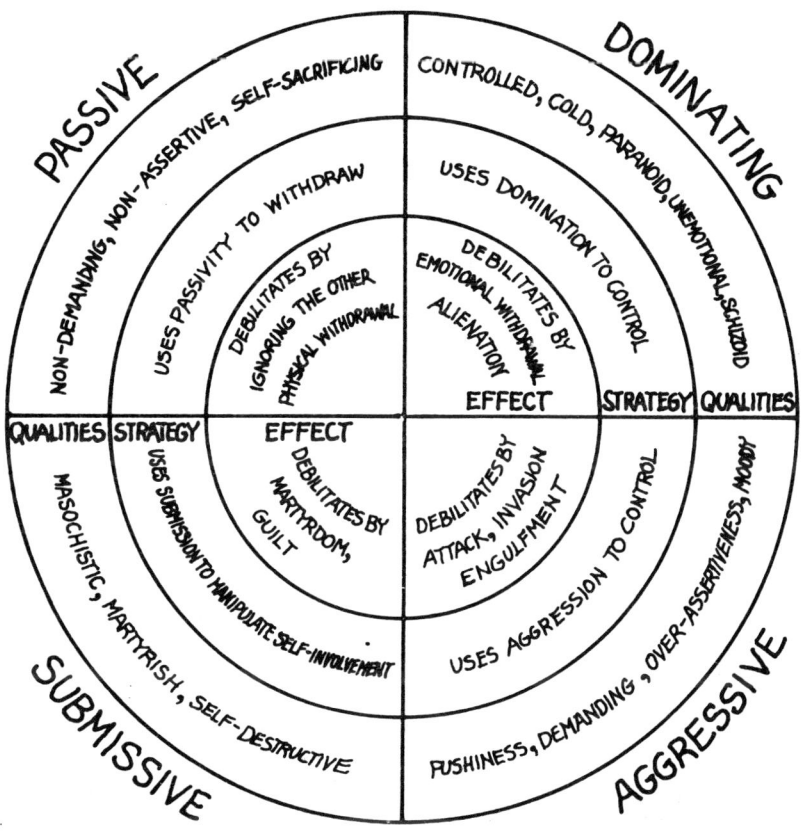

CHART OF THE FOUR EMOTIONAL MISALLIANCES IN MARRIAGE

To the extent that a person manifests one of these four strategies in relating to his spouse, he invites the spouse to take up its opposite in response. Accordingly, the emotional structure of any given family can be delimited according to which of these strategies each parent takes. The man who takes up an extremely passive stance with his wife, for example, both elicits an aggressive strategy from her and subverts that strategy by his emotional withdrawal. The effects of each misalliance on the sons and daughters are predictable.

consider each of these types and their effects on their families in some detail.

The Aggressive Father

First, the aggressive father undercuts the authority of the mother, derogates her, and thus creates a passive role for her. The wife of such a man often accepts this passive role in the relationship, but compensates for her derogation by becoming manipulative in the home and by communicating with ambivalence, thus confusing the child. The child, as a consequence, is left with an overly aggressive father against whose hard actions he lacks the support of a consistent and overtly strong mother. The hostile father thus places impossible demands on his wife and establishes relationships with the son and daughter which create differing kinds of emotional problems for them.

The son of the aggressive father has his own distinct problems. He is put in the position of having to cope with a great deal of the father's aggressive, success-oriented striving. He therefore becomes compulsive and perfectionistic. Imitating the father's valuation, he is insensitive to the mothering dimension of his own needs and self. He thus isolates himself from the woman, becomes emotionally detached, and becomes cold or success-driven. In his excessive compulsiveness, he frequently becomes perfectionistic, and if this kind of strategy does not provide him with the necessary rewards, he becomes controlled and controlling. Because his father models only aggression and success-striving, he has no model for coping with life apart from a success-oriented basis. Thus, if this kind of strategy fails him at one point or another, he identifies with the position of the mother, adapting a life in which he is secure without really having to relate to the woman or to meet his natural nurturing needs. This mother-orientation precludes his having to feel the shame of ultimate defeat by comparison with the father, for in it he is protected by his withdrawal from the competitive and aggressive dimensions of adult male life which are exaggerated in his father's stance. Thus, in the long run, he becomes a pawn of the woman and her domination.

Although the aggressive father usually has a strong temper and is very outspoken and emotional in his aggressiveness, he is not necessarily firm with his daughters. For the most part, this kind of father merely opposes his wife's expectations for the children and attempts to seduce the daughter into some kind of allegiance toward him. There are two typical ways in which the daughter responds to this father. On the one hand, she may enter into this collusion with the father. In this case, she does so either because she feels the mother's instability in the face of the father's hostility or because she feels the need to get whatever security she can by identifying with her father. On the other hand, the daughter may choose not to identify with him. Instead, she may seek to validate her femininity by using a passive strategy to win his love. She does this in spite of the fact that this father almost completely lacks tenderness. As a consequence, this daughter becomes quite disturbed if not schizophrenic. She finds it most difficult to differentiate herself from her mother because her natural need to validate her femininity through the father gives her the same role as a victim that her mother accepts. Thus her mother cannot be the natural model who leads her into fully developed feminine maturity. At the same time, the father's demands are too unrealistic to allow her to establish her own identity through relating to him. The father's hostility towards the mother is devastating for the daughter.

The Submissive Father

The man in the second category, the submissive father, basically projects his anger at his wife onto his children. He becomes competitive with his sons for the attention and validation from the wife which he never feels that he is getting from her for himself. He behaves like a jealous older brother, and consequently does not form an adequate model of masculinity for his sons. Typically, the son in such a family is faced with a father who is either alcoholic or repeatedly involved in extramarital affairs. The father may also seek to lose himself in his work in some way in order to substitute for or cover up for abdicating his potency in the home. Frequently the wife of such a man withdraws and becomes cold toward her own emotional needs. Sometimes she becomes emotionally frozen and withdrawn in her relating to the children as well.

The son of the father who is submissive within the home and thus compensates for this role by going outside it recognizes the father's emotional inadequacy in the home and attempts to fill the vacancies in the mother's relationship with the father. This movement toward the mother increases the son's fear of his father and makes him overly susceptible to her manipulations. In this situation, the son

easily loses his sense of his own inner authority. He feels
he must learn to control his needs for the sake of the
nurturing mother, for he fears her ambivalence toward the
man. He thus becomes ambivalent about the major choices he
must make in his life. In this situation he is easily
susceptible to schizophrenic reaction.

The daughter of such a home, fearing to identify with
the coldness of the mother and being unable to relate to the
emotionally absent father, often does not get beyond a
homosexual or symbiotic relationship with her mother.
Together, daughter and mother become overtly passive toward
the male, but within this imposed passivity they tend to
dominate or control relationships in which they are involved,
usually through frigid or homosexual behavior patterns.

The Dominating Father

Third, the dominating or authoritarian father is
anxious about his sexuality to the point that he feels he
must dominate his relationships with women and force exalted
conceptions of himself on his family. This father requires
the wife to be inordinately submissive to his domination,
although he does not hold out this demand in a clearly overt
manner. He merely expects it. The wife of such a man is
compelled to be his admirer. Paradoxically, this father-
like husband is too detached from his own emotional center
to be able to make the kind of contact with the children
that will fulfill his function as a father. This man usually
remains physically aloof from his children and gives little
or no support to his sons. The son thus feels too weak to
emulate the father, and frequently finds himself quite
impotent in his general sexuality.

The daughter of this kind of father attempts to perform
for her father rather than naturally responding to him. She
therefore remains submissive in identification with her
mother. When the daughter finds it necessary to become
expressive of her own personality and to enter into her own
inner emotionality, she develops phobias and anxieties and
finds it difficult to relate to anyone in a relaxed manner.

The Passive Father

Fourth is the father who somewhere in life has failed
to become the creative person that he was meant to be. This
man seems almost a non-entity in the home. Thus the dignity

of his role in the family slowly collapses. Unable to do
anything concrete and substantial, this father accepts the
gradual coldness and exclusion from the wife's vitality
which is her response to his deadness. The children caught
up in this family structure tend to be shy and prone to
schizophrenic formations. The mother becomes anxiety-ridden
and hysterically aggressive and controlling. The father may
be kindly, but he cannot be effective on behalf of his
children, for he becomes aloof and is able only passively to
appreciate the personality attributes and uniqueness of each
of them. He demands little for himself, and thereby teaches
his children that self-deprivation is their natural lot in
life. In all of this absence of fathering support or
masculine presence, the father tends not to engage or to
counter the anxious and eccentric child-rearing patterns
enacted by the mother in the home. Consequently, the
mother's femaleness runs away with itself. To the extent
that the mother becomes anxious about her excessive
aggressiveness which the passivity of the father has elicited,
the children become inwardly withdrawn from their own
emotionality and from their active participation in life.

In each of these four different manifestations of
paternal role deviation, the father's stance makes all
family roles--mother and child as well as father--confused.
These fathers are unable to support the mother's efforts to
mother the children. They also provide and establish no
proper models of masculinity for their children. And, most
significantly, they cannot support their children to
develop a conscious self-awareness in their emotional and
creative dimensions.

THERE ARE FOUR TYPES OF PATHOLOGICAL MOTHERS

Each of the pathological types of fathers whose
characters and whose effects on their families we have now
sketched represents a distortion of the natural polarity of
mother and father. Yet the father's excess is only a part
of the total family picture, for the wife complements the
husband's excesses in each of these cases. Thus along with
our awareness of these pathological deficiencies in the
father's role we must acknowledge that the father is only
one of the parents and that the symptoms which ultimately
develop in the child depend upon the degree of strength in
the mother as well. This maternal strength can be measured
by the mother's real reasons for staying in the relationship,
by the way in which she stays, by how she copes with the
father, and by what kind of involvement she has with her

children. All of these factors contribute to the nature of
the father image and the authority pattern which the children will possess. The nature of the parental coalition
together with the actions of each parent—both father and
mother—determine the exact quality of the father's contribution to the personality of the child.

The kind of mother a woman is to her children depends
upon the three major elements that constitute family
structure: the nature of the coalition with her husband,
the nature of the generational boundaries between herself
and her child, and the adequacy with which she fulfills her
gender specific roles. Her mode of behavior as a wife and
her ways of relating as a woman to her husband both
influence the authority images which are developing in her
children. A woman who cannot establish a stable coalition
with her husband deprives the child of unified, coherent
directives. This makes the child question whether the
masculine and feminine principles which he feels and experiences within himself can be harmonized.

To illustrate this point, it is highly unlikely that a
woman can adequately mother her children if she chooses to
live with a man whom she does not feel can father them. If
her husband's worth as a male authority is constantly undermined, her relationship with him presents him as a father
while her relationship with the children denies his authority
in this role. From the man's position, if his authority as
a man is ineffectual with her as a woman, it will also be
inadequate for the needs of the children. Conversely, if
her authority as a woman is constantly undermined by the man
in such a relationship and the mother therefore turns to her
son rather than to her husband in her quest for emotional
support, she denies generational boundaries and the child is
the one to suffer. The woman who assumes the male role in
the family or who cannot fulfill the feminine affective role
disturbs the child's personality and his sense of personal
identity as well.

The Passive Mother

In the first category of family, that with the hostile,
success-oriented father, the mother plays the correspondingly passive role. She is a vague and poorly organized woman
deficient in self esteem and caught up in an unhappy,
schizmatic marriage in which she is the devalued partner.[22]
In fact, she is considered and hence made to be an inadequate wife and mother by her paranoid and difficult husband.
The woman who accepts this role and attempts to mother under

these conditions tends to manipulate in a passive-aggressive stance within the home. She communicates indefinite personality roles to her children. She is thus difficult for her children to predict, and she is a constant problem for them.

Those who listen to the exchanges in such families are often confused about whether the mother has said anything. Her remarks are filled with platitudes and cliches, the kinds of statements that keep her out of trouble. Often such a mother creates the false impression that she is feeble-minded. She vacillates from total passivity to depression or various psychosomatic symptoms. She thus endeavors to manipulate her inner state so that she might pacify the aggressive, demanding behavior of the husband.

The son in such a marriage actually becomes a father by becoming a husband to his own mother. Usually he does this in a way that enables him to identify with the success-oriented, perfectionistic demands of the father, thereby avoiding becoming schizophrenic. However, his personality is ultimately overshadowed by the need to make the mother good by standing in some kind of perfect attendance upon her life.

The mother gains little satisfaction from her daughter and, though she is sometimes intrusive and over-controlling, she brings an aloof, hostile, and rejecting quality to the relationship. The daughter, in her attempt to identify with this mother, develops what might be called a hysterical personality which, when under pressure, can break into schizophrenic reaction. Commonly, such a mother is schizophrenogenic for her son as well.

The Dominating Mother

The dominating mother, the mother in the second kind of pathological family, devotes her energies to rearing the children to her own detriment, for since she does not find her identity confirmed in the relationship with her husband, whom she considers weak, she finds it through the son. Consequently, she makes a constant and insistent intrusion into the son's life, and she insists that she is the only one who can truly understand him. She does this because she has learned to validate herself in an illusory way through the son's activity. With such a woman the capacity to deny the obvious is truly remarkable. The son never makes mistakes. If he has been caught in a situation which has been poorly managed, it is the environment's fault, not his own.

This woman dominates the home scene. She is cut off from the natural emotional undergirdings of her personality. She is withdrawn and cannot express emotional warmth. She looks for little from men and sees them as weak. Often it seems that such a woman is married to a man in order to have a son who will be the means of validating her femininity. The husband-father in this relationship thus victimizes himself. He ends up being ineffectual and his children consider the manipulations he performs on himself to be rather childish. Whenever the wishes of any family member do not fit the preconceptions of this mother, she becomes impervious to them. While her communications are fragmentary, they are treated as if they were ultimately powerful dispatches. This overvaluing of the mother's intimations creates great perplexity in the listener. The husband's worth is by complement demolished: he is unable to have positive meaning for his son.

The daughter in this kind of family tends not to be able to relate warmly to her mother. She therefore divorces herself from her own internal emotional nourishing processes and attempts seductive stances toward men. She wants men to dominate her at the same time that she cannot stand to be dominated.

The Submissive Mother

The submissive mother, the mother in the third kind of pathological family, is frequently the product of schizophrenic mothering, and if she remains in a relationship to the father-husband for very long, she tends to make herself compliant or passive. Her world revolves around validating herself through the father. The mothering done by such a woman, since it is related to a dominating father, is actually less pathological than that of any of the three other types. Sexual identity problems in the children are not as deep in this case, and schizophrenic potential in the children is not as developed.

The Aggressive Mother

The aggressive mother, the mother in the fourth type of pathological family, is dominating and demanding towards the father. As the father comes to be a weak and almost invisible figure in the family, the mother becomes anxious and attempts to compensate for the father's weakness by forming some kind of basic strength and security in the home through which the child can develop an identity. This framework, like the others, is poorly based, and results in inadequate images of the person's sexuality for each member of it. Schizophrenogenic potential for the children and potential for emotional withdrawal in this family are great.

THERE ARE FOUR TYPES OF PATHOLOGICAL FAMILIES

Each of the four types of pathogenic fathers finds its corresponding type in one of the four types of pathogenic mothers. The resulting deformed parental coalitions yield a typology of pathological families. This typology is represented schematically on page 167. It is delimited in the pages that follow.

	passive father	dominating father	
	IMPOTENT FAMILY	DOMINATED FAMILY	
	4.	3.	
aggressive mother	FOURTH PATHOLOGICAL FAMILY	THIRD PATHOLOGICAL FAMILY	submissive mother
dominating mother	SECOND PATHOLOGICAL FAMILY	FIRST PATHOLOGICAL FAMILY	passive mother
	2.	1.	
	INVERTED FAMILY	PRESSURED FAMILY	
	submissive father	aggressive father	

The Pressured Family

In the first pathological family structure, the father is aggressive and has an assertive life style. He is the strong emotional force in the home, where he condescends to the woman, either overtly or covertly. The woman, as a consequence, must act within the parameters of his emotional demands. He is defensive against emotional expression on the part of the woman. He is, furthermore, defensive against admitting his own need for emotional nurturance at the same time that he demands it. The wife must therefore act to mother or pacify this man's inwardly disturbed emotional state. In this pattern of behavior he is intrusive with the woman in ways that continually disrupt the basic rhythmical patterns of life which express the natural female principle. The woman's thought patterns, which center around concerns natural to the family process, are denigrated as trivial aspects of existence. This kind of man is unaware of the female's inner rhythms and he does not really pay attention to her as an emotional being. She is taken as merely a portion of his property. Clearly, such a man fits the stereotype of the male chauvinist.

In this family structure the mother's life style is passive. She does not affirm the basic inner rhythms and institutions of her femininity, but rather allows herself to be pushed by her husband's aggressive intrusions into her emotional meaning. Her femininity is not differentiated to the point where she feels herself as a woman who is autonomous and distinct from her mother, for she feels she must remain in a symbiotic relationship with her mother to stay related to this man. Her life style is confusing, and her communications have double meanings or lack focus. She tries to adapt her emotions to what the situation calls for and thus falls into repetitive routines in her lifestyle and commonplace platitudes in her self-expression. Her son sees her as needing his protection and her daughter attempts to cover up her real fears of identifying with this woman.

The son in this family structure usually feels that the father expects him to be strong and success-oriented. He thus develops a way of life in which he can control his emotional needs and becomes oblivious to his nurturing dimension. Since the father rewards aggression as a means of social achievement, the son becomes oriented toward social success, but not oriented toward his natural needs for nurturance. Therefore, he does not feel his fundamental need for the woman and for woman's affectional and nurturing dimensions. The father, having little understanding of the true emotional needs of the son, fosters a self-image within the son which is characterized by the need to be strong, perfectionistic, and compulsively successful. In such an obsessive, compulsive life style and with such a strong goal orientation, the son remains unaware of his deeper emotional needs. The pants he wears with the mother are thin at the knees of father's betrayal. Such a son, standing in the coldness of his own strength, is unaware of his needs for comfort from the woman, even to the point of denying such needs. He strives to achieve and to gain social prestige at the expense of his most basic personal needs. His strength is pseudo-strength, and his identification with himself as a man is nebulous.

The father in this family structure expects the daughter to idealize him. This expectation results in her suppressing her true feminine expression and adopting a nice, pacifying attitude toward the father. Such an attitude becomes a lifelong facade which she uses to cover up both her fear of identifying with her mother and her fear of facing the deprivation from her father. The daughter who develops this facade of niceness focuses on external social acceptance and approval as her means of attaining self-esteem and security. When confronted with emotional stress, she may become hysterical, thus expressing her underlying hysterical personality structure. When there is little or no support for her style, her ambivalence and lack of stability over her femininity become the elements of a schizophrenic reaction. Fundamentally, her problem is that she has been cut off from the inner feminine realities necessary for undergirding the personality in its genuineness.

An example of this mode of pathological family structure may be helpful at this point. Mr. and Mrs. Knight had two daughters and one son. The father was constantly degrading the daughters while putting demands upon them. By his actions, he also constantly indicated a lack of true sympathy with the mother. The coalition between the man and his wife was an impossible arrangement. Consequently, the mother vacillated between alcoholism and being bedridden with depression until she finally developed terminal cancer and died. After the mother's death, the father continued to deal with his daughters on a very demanding basis, blaming them for not completely accepting him regardless of his behavior or the way he treated them. The mother, by contrast, had kept doing the "right thing" by being totally subservient to her husband to the end of her days. Using

the mother's example, the father constantly told the
daughters what they should feel and do as women. One
daughter developed a hysterical personality and the other
became somewhat schizophrenic in her behavior and life style,
manifesting a schizophrenic reaction pattern whenever she
was under stress. The son, on the other hand, finding himself unable to make a successful adaptation to the father's
aggressive demands, alternated between deep depression and
obsessive compulsive behavior.

The Inverted Family

The second type of family organization is characterized
by the father who relates to his wife as if he expects
nothing from her emotionally. This father actually tends to
be submissive to the mother in the home. Such submission
often leads to daughter indulgence on the one hand and to
disdain for the son on the other, for the father tends to
express his resentment toward his imagined lack of the
woman's support in his relationships with his children or
with his social situation. In this way he displaces his
hostility toward his wife while disguising it by an apparent
submissiveness to her coldness. Often this man finds relief
from this distressing situation through promiscuity or
alcoholism. He is insensitive to the feminine dimensions of
existence in himself as well as in the home, and tends to be
ravishingly penetrating. However, he defends himself
against his inner emotional deprivation which he localizes
in the home by having a huge phallic life, whether this
exists in fact or in fantasy. He continually seeks to
arouse the woman so that he might feel involved and comforted in spite of his cutting himself off from comfort. He
mistakes excitement and emotional stimulation for natural
feeling. His passions are not at his disposal: his
passionate energies are spent in instinctual sexual striving.
To him, women are for the pleasure of men and he must be
indulged. His demand for the woman's indulgence is related
to the bad mother introject and symbolizes the unbroken
symbiotic binding between son and mother. His affairs lack
the depth of true relationships, and the feminine principle
in his imagination is not symbolized into the self according
to the true nature of his being. Because this kind of
father perpetually idealizes his negative mother introject,
he debases his masculinity in order to reject his true needs
for a genuine relationship with a woman. Each woman this
man meets must relate to or meet the demands of the introjected bad mother. Subtly the demands of this depriving
mother image take expression in demands upon each woman with

whom he attempts to relate. The purpose of his relating to
women is always to pacify the introjects, for he cannot find
access to the natural feminine principle within. The female
functions to validate his masculinity. Consequently, he
cannot bring the true dimensions of his masculine self to
lean upon the woman, for the cosmic self energies are at the
mercy of pure instinct and there is lack of full sensuality
and feeling. His eros, although controlling so much of his
life, is hidden from view. That is, it is felt to be all of
life, therefore its conscious choosing and thinking aspects
are disguised or lost and sexual, impassioned dimensions of
himself must remain compelling because they are anonymous
and unconscious.

The mother in this family organization is usually
schizophrenogenic. She either is or becomes an empty woman.
Such a mother is cold to her own emotional self. She is
insensitive to her emotional dimensions and divorced from
her own warmth. She overtly denigrates sexuality but
inwardly fantasizes ravishment while denying the need for
involvement with the emotional dimensions of existence.
Further, this mother intellectualizes about the inner
emotional life from which she is severed. Her husband does
not feel needed by her. This results in her feeling unnecessary, yet she cannot let herself expect to be otherwise.
She becomes moralistic and idealistic but also unconsciously
seductive, especially with her son. She tends to intellec-
tualize her relationship with her daughter who, like the
mother, has difficulty feeling the inner dimensions of her
own femininity. Her platitudinous and overly-simplified
rationalizations about how life should be lived result in
shallow relationships with her children.

The children relate to this mother by imitating her own
beholden behavior and self-depriving ways. Frequently the
son in this kind of family organization becomes paranoid,
emotionally cold and controlling, if not schizophrenic or
psychopathic. He dominates in his relationships with
women: he idealizes being over-protective and over-
demanding with them. In effect, he almost crucifies the
woman in order to hold her emotions out of awareness. This
behavior is his mode of coping with an overpowering,
seductive, inner bad mother state. For such a son, the
dying words of mother drip like blood from the tip of the
childish sword. Similarly, the daughter in this organization holds herself in a position of aloofness. She becomes
frigid and tends to control or suppress her emotional needs.
She denies her deprivation by compensating for it with
promiscuous or otherwise sexually disturbed behavior.

The Dominated Family

The father in the third family organization is probably the least disturbed of the four kinds of pathological fathers. He dominates the woman by over-protecting her emotionality, for he idealizes himself as the guardian of femininity--and the principle of femininity can emerge only under his auspices. He takes this right for granted and assumes that the woman should be submissive to him. He must feel that he is the ideal father. Thus, most often the mother in this family finds her role to be in the home. The father is not aggressive; rather, he is immovable, inflexible authority whom no one dares to question. The woman is expected to be grateful to him and to keep her place. He controls by permitting no one, including himself, to mistreat mother by questioning her. The children must get to the mother through him. On the other hand, she cannot stand up to the children for herself: she must constantly bring this father in on the disciplining of the children.

The mother in this third kind of family organization lives a life of male idealization. Overtly, she is not too disturbed by this; she is repressed. She assumes and accepts the ultimacy of the male principle and gains her validity by helping to make the man a success. She does not provide an emotional base upon which her children can question and test the limits of male authority in order to attain a sense of personal autonomy. This mother makes possible some security in the home, but very little creativity. She idealizes her role as a bed mate, mother and cook, and assumes that the deprivations which come with this life style are natural. She expects her children to seek nothing less than to be like their parents, and any departure from this life style causes deep anxiety in the children, for they cannot be supported in it.

The children in this third family are anxious. The son is often rather impotent and has little capacity to receive nurturing. He becomes quite competitive and manipulative in his attempt to compensate for his deep anxiety over his masculinity, for he feels continually castrated by the father's demand that he relate perfectionistically to the mother in confrontation with the mother's lack of support for his need to identify with his father. The daughter is hysterical and repressed. She goes through the formalities of relating to others, but she finds it very difficult to develop adequate relationships on the level of her emotionality. She becomes overly concerned with keeping herself calm. Typically, this daughter develops a phobic syndrome whenever she finds herself in a stressful situation.

The Impotent Family

In the fourth category of pathological family patterns, the father idealizes his role in keeping the woman functioning. He feels that the woman needs to be aggressive and expressive to the point of denying his own need for nurture from his wife. He forsakes his children altogether in his attempt to secure the mothering which he needs from the woman. The woman is thus made to feel indebted and guilty so that she must act to repay him for sacrificing his life to her. Thus the man has given his feminine principle over to his inner image of mother: his life essentially revolves around the great mother. Consequently, what happens with the children will eventually be determined by the mother's relationship to them and the environment which she creates in the home. In turn, the man becomes the emotionalist, the pale ideal mother's son who runs her errands. He is a non-erotic, emotionally passive personality often characterized by a borderline personality.

The mother in this family organization is emotionally aggressive, for she is the figure in the home to whom everyone looks for strength and action. While the father is seen as a weak and non-erotic male, she is seen as the center of all life. Given this role, she will not let her husband get in her way or frustrate her emotionally.

The children of such parents are incoherently shy. The son is shy and nice; he is impotent. He becomes the acceptable, impotent, "nice boy." The kiss of the powerful and seductive mother is wet upon his lips. He fears to emerge and manifest himself lest he be devoured or abandoned by the aggressive but incestuous mother. The daughter in this family organization is also shy and inadequate. The mother's aggressiveness and the father's weakness make it difficult for her to show her emotional needs. She does not sense her own erotic nature. In instances where the mother tends to have a borderline personality, the children can become borderline themselves, if not chronically schizophrenic.

THE TYPING OF FAMILIES ORIENTS THE SYMBOLIC REGRESSIVE TASK OF PSYCHOTHERAPY

Inasmuch as the deformation of family structure is directly related to the development of inadequate self identifications, the underlying task of therapy must be radical to reconstitute the structure of the inner imaginary family, whether this reordering is possible in the existential family or not. The requirements and goals of the therapeutic process are determined by which family member seeks help and what motivations for change have brought him into the helping relationship, for the client's inner family organization is projected upon the total therapeutic milieu before therapy even gets under way. The dynamics of the therapeutic process depend upon how therapy is interpreted as a family organizational problem. That is, therapeutic contact itself becomes a mode of the client's experience of his fathering and mothering realities and expectations. Thus the therapist must know what inner family images this person is actually bringing to the therapeutic encounter as well as how the therapeutic encounter can be structured so that it helps the client learn about his inner masculine-feminine orientations and his inner organization of the family images.

An understanding of the client's internalized family structure as it relates to these four major pathological family syndromes is a fundamental means of heuristic insight into the rudimentary parameters of any given person's disturbed self image. The use of this heuristic analysis as a general diagnostic or orienting tool discloses first of all the quality and nature of those personal situations which will be stressful for him. Furthermore, it becomes a basis for indicating in general outline what kinds of social and family organization change are necessary to help him resymbolize his self image. Finally, it suggests in what ways the structure of the therapeutic encounter can be arranged to bring into awareness the true masculine-feminine images which undergird his existential situation. These concrete applications of this heuristic diagnostic model make it possible for symbolic regression therapy to be an orderly, understandable and predictable process in which the origins of psychological stress in the person's images are known. Given such theoretical foundations for understanding the existential reality of family structure, the process of growth into genuineness can be supported by relating it to its roots in the symbolic family and in Being. Consequently, the presenting stress situation which has brought the person into the therapeutic encounter can be dealt with as symbolic material so that by the individual's learning to transcend his stress-producing image introjects he is enabled to redirect his resources for coping with the situation.

As an example of the application of the model, consider the wife who appears for therapy declaring herself married

FAMILY   183

to an impossible tyrant. She wants a divorce. Perhaps she
is in a marriage that corresponds to the first of the four
pathological family structures. If this is the case, the
woman's motivations for seeking help and her intended use of
the therapist can be hypothesized. Changes in the possible
undergirdings of her motivations can be made from time to
time, and what she wishes accomplished can be redefined
according to her deepest needs as the process of therapy
unfolds. Thus, from the outset the process of therapy has
an informing basis which gives a thrust and a continuity to
the woman's relationship with the therapist.

The direct approach to imagination which is central to
a therapy devoted to the development of a higher consciousness requires a basis in existential dimensions of personal
self experience which incorporates the masculine and
feminine poles into a configuration which is ultimately
consistent with the true nature of the self. Knowing the
probable authority image undergirdings of this woman's
relationship with the man provides the therapist with the
general outlines of her self image and the kinds of symbolic
reorientation which will facilitate her approaching herself
more consciously.

Thus the professional knowledge which this heuristic
model provides might be compared to that of the teacher who
at the outset knows which grade he is teaching and knows
what the general learning processes and dynamics with which
he is to be involved will be like, but does not yet know
about the specific learning capacities or even the creative
possibilites of his individual students. Rapid general
determination of the family organization behind symptomatology makes possible the structure, planning, process,
determination, and evaluation which result in a successful
therapeutic collaboration in the quest for consciousness.
Furthermore, such diagnosis of the client's family imagery
makes it possible to cope with him as an imagizing,
reflecting being in a process of relating which proceeds
from his general orientation to the more specific immediate
issues he is facing. This sequence is highly important, for
it corresponds to the therapeutic process which must also
proceed from the more general to the more specific. Symbolic regression reverses the normal process by which the
child develops his awareness of general symbolic configurat-
ing out of the concrete, specific elements of his experience.
Thus, treating the therapy situation on the basis of the
family structural undergirdings of the individual makes
direct approach to imagination easier, for the individual's
entire life is brought into the therapeutic process and he

himself is enabled, through the course of his therapy, to proceed from that which is generally known to that which is highly specific and unique to him as an individual.

This procedure not only establishes a more efficient kind of therapy, but it also makes therapy a more trustworthy process. Since the existential family situation in which a person lives is so much an extrapolation of the state of his imagined inner family, it is important that he constantly relate his changing inner images inherent in the growth process to the situation and structure of the existential family within which he lives. Integrated growth is based on the principle that the inner, imaginary family and the outer, existential family are continually brought into confrontations with each other. The therapist, therefore, must be constantly engaged with the process of family structure within which the person lives and attempts to work out his images.

NOTES

1. The I Ching, Third Edition, (Princeton, New Jersey: Princeton Univ. Press, 1967), pp. 143-44.

2. Aurelius Augustinus, The City of God, (New York: Random House, 1950), book XIX, ch. xvi, p. 695.

3. Joseph Campbell, The Masks of God: Primitive Mythology, (Harmondsworth: Penguin Books, 1976), p. 78.

4. David B. Lynn, The Father: His Role in Child Development, (Monterey, Calif.: Brooks/Cole, 1974), p. 22.

5. M. J. Levy and L. A. Fallers, "The Family: Some Comparative Considerations," American Anthropologist, 61 (1959), 647-51.

6. Talcott Parsons, Robert F. Bales, and Edward A. Shils, Working Papers in the Theory of Action, (New York: Free Press, 1953).

7. Jolande Jacobi, The Psychology of C. G. Jung, (New Haven and London: Yale Univ. Press, 1968), p. 44.

8. See Mircea Eliade, The Two and the One, (London: Harvill Press, 1965); and Allen Watts, The Two Hands of God: The Myths of Polarity, (New York: Collier Books, 1969).

FAMILY

9. Jung's essays on archetypes focus on two of these in particular, mother and child. Jung's only writing specifically focusing on the father is his short essay entitled, "The Significance of the Father in the Destiny of the Individual," Collected Works, vol. 4, pp. 301-23. Erich Neuman follows Jung's lead regarding these family images in his books, entitled The Great Mother: An Analysis of the Archetype, (Princeton, New Jersey: Princeton Univ. Press, 1972), and The Child, (New York: Harper and Row, 1976). With both Jung and Neumann, the father image is given much less weight than the mother image. This is to some extent compensated for in the work of Jolande Jacobi who equates the importance of the mother with that of the father in her discussion of "the wise old man" and the "magna mater" (p. 125), and in the work of the American Jungian, John W. Perry, whose book, Lord of the Four Quarters: Myths of the Royal Father, (New York: Braziller, 1965), is a cultural study of the father archetype. Thus, the archetypal images in depth psychology roughly correspond to the key figures who comprise the family's structure.

10. W. Earl Biddle, "Image Therapy," American Journal of Psychiatry, 126 (1969), 408-12.

11. C. G. Jung, "The Psychology of the Child Archetype," Collected Works, vol. 9, part i, p. 160.

12. Erich Fromm, "The Significance of the Theory of Mother Right for Today," in The Crisis of Psychoanalysis, (new York: Holt, Rinehart & Winston, 1970), pp. 79-83.

13. Søren Kierkegaard, Fear and Trembling, (Princeton, New Jersey: Princeton Univ. Press, 1968), p. 130.

14. Henry B. Biller, Father, Child and Sex Role, (Lexington, Mass.: D. C. Heath, 1971).

15. Theodore Lidz, The Person: His and Her Development Throughout the Life Cycle, Revised Edition, (New York: Basic Books, 1976), pp. 45-63.

16. Theodore Lidz, Stephen Fleck, and Alice R. Cornelison, Schizophrenia and the Family, (New York: International Universities Press, 1965), p. 362.

17. Lidz et al., p. 364.

18. Lidz et al., p. 367.

19. Lidz et al., p. 368.
20. Lidz et al., p. 370.
21. Lidz et al., p. 102.
22. Lidz et al., p. 323.

Chapter VI
Pathology

> Man is not free to choose whether or not he
> wants to develop an idea of the absolutely
> real . . . . Man, <u>necessarily</u> and always,
> consciously or unconsciously, <u>has</u> such an
> idea, such a feeling acquired by himself or
> inherited from tradition. All he can choose
> for himself is a good and reasonable or a
> poor and unreasonable idea of the absolute.
> . . . Even without being quite aware of it,
> man can fill this sphere of absolute being
> and of highest good with a <u>finite</u> content
> and good which, in life, he treats "as if"
> it were absolute. . . .
> If man is to transcend this spiritual
> position, he must learn two things. First,
> through self-analysis, he must become con-
> scious of the "idol" which, for him, has
> replaced absolute being and good. In the
> second place, he must smash this idol, i.e.,
> put the overly loved object back into its
> <u>relative</u> position in the finite world.
>   Max Scheler, <u>Philosophical Perspectives</u>[1]

FIXATION VS. SUBJECTIVITY

Since man is a symbolizing being whose self-awareness is derived from his conscious sense of his relation to Being, man both symbolizes himself and acts in relation to some absolute sense of Being which he himself constitutes by his own symbolizing capacity. Thus even pathological symbolizing is based on and a distortion of the universal need in man to relate himself to the absolutely real. When an individual distorts his symbolizing so that his image of what is absolutely real deviates from the order of Being, the result is symptomatic psychic functioning. Accordingly, the person assumes that his imagination is not rooted in ultimate images of Being, and his behavior betrays this alienation and the consequent inner disharmony in the form of pathological symptoms. In terms of ontology, pathology is the condition of the psyche when the individual's imagizing is not fully grounded in Being. Thus pathology is man's approach to the relative as if it were absolute and to the absolute as if it were relative.

To understand this conception of pathology, we must distinguish between that which is essential to man's nature and that which is existential. According to Paul Tillich, "the essential" refers to Being as an ultimate or cosmic source of man's images.[2] For the purposes of symbolic regression psychology, this refers to the natural or innate, what is at once intrinsic and ultimate in the individual. On the other hand, Tillich terms that which is imposed on the individual from the outside, from his social environment, as "existential." Existential images arise from the circumstances of the individual's social experience. In symbolic regression psychology, the priority always rests with the innate, Tillich's "essential," rather than with the social, which Tillich terms the "existential."

Tillich's distinction of the essential and the existential provides a basis for understanding authority in terms of either of two states of imagination. The authority of the individual, his sense of himself as this impinges upon his world, is founded on either one of two sources: natural authority images or introjected authority images. Natural authority, which is synonymous with the individual's subjectivity, is developed through his awareness of his own nature. On the other hand, introjected authority is imposed upon the individual by his assent to what others tell him he is really like. Thus each person's authority and his image of authority come either from personal self-awareness or from definitions of him which others impose upon him. On the basis of this distinction, authority is inseparable from ontology. And it is this ontological dimension which separates symbolic regression psychology from much of traditional psychology, for psychological authority is almost always discussed apart from ontology.

Fixation is the condition of consciousness when relative or external images of authority are treated as if they were ultimate. This in turn makes the individual's authority with regard to himself, that is, his subjectivity, relative instead of absolute so that it is in conflict with his natural, non-introjected state of consciousness. Consequently, the privilege of the individual's authority--his sense of his basic meaning as a unique conscious being in the cosmos--is lost.

Furthermore, the concept of fixation highlights the way that the individual comes to use introjected images of authority to define his own authority, for his definition of authority is the foundation upon which the inner self, and hence subjectivity, is organized. By contrast, symbolic regression is the primary process relating the individual to his innate or natural authority which is the ground of his being. Consequently, through the process of symbolic regression, the individual discovers images of authority which are both primary and grounded in his own being.

Given these assumptions, we follow Kierkegaard's analysis in The Sickness Unto Death in which he finds the meaning of man's despair in his attempt as a finite being to reach the ultimate.[3] The resolution of this contradiction between the finite self and the ultimacy of its intending is courage, the individual's recognition that he must settle for a relative experience without giving up faith in the ultimacy of his being. This is the state of radical subjectivity to which Kierkegaard refers in his claim that "truth is subjectivity."

If we take Kierkegaard's notion of subjectivity seriously, we can see that the introject itself has meaning, for the introject always implies the individual's innate need for the ultimate. The introject is the image through which despair is experienced. Thus man's need for the ultimate is what makes introjection possible. Yet that it makes introjection possible does not make the need in itself bad, for this need also makes genuineness a human possibility.

The priority of the inner or innate does not make the social dimension of experience dispensable. Rather, the social dimension of authority should be contiguous with natural or innate authority. In fact, the two dimensions must be brought together for the individual to have an integrated life. The truth of the individual's subjectivity must be brought to bear upon his social existence. When this subjectivity is not expressed, the self of the individual becomes disembodied and characterized by ontological insecurity and the striving to perpetuate an illusory sense of self as if in opposition to Being.[4] Thus bringing one's subjectivity to bear upon his social existence is crucial, for such expressivity cuts down the power of social experience as a source or confirmation of the introject. Moreover, the fear of bringing the innate, good images to bear upon the realm of one's social experience leads to a state of compromise which insults the integrity of subjectivity. This state of compromise is fixation.

By contrast, love is the state of consciousness which expresses the ultimate concord between subjectivity and ontology. Love is the primary expression of the natural, non-fixated state of consciousness. Love is the positive energies of Being as these take expression through the person. Love is my subjectivity in its natural state. Love expresses my relating to Being. Looked at from this positive angle, there is one ultimate question which sheds light on all pathology: "What is wrong with my love?" The recovery of genuine love is the recovery of mentally healthy living.

SYMPTOM AS MEANING

In spite of their research devoted to validating the effectiveness of the psychological treatment of the whole person, Steiper and Weiner found that all methods of therapy produced about the same rather poor results.[5] London pointed out that it was difficult to determine what psychotherapies do to whom and why.[6] This serious lack of coherence and effectiveness is due to the fact that diagnosis is all too frequently divorced from a comprehension of the meaning of the whole person. The drive toward consciousness in the person must be made the basis for an understanding of pathology, for when this drive is frustrated it takes symbolic expression in the symptoms of pathology. Every symptom has a personal, an organic, and a cosmic foundation. The person must be treated as a whole being in relation to his symptoms. To remove the symptoms without an appeal to the underlying realities to which they point is totally inadequate. What is needed is a process of resymbolizing, the development of the capacity for symbolic regression.

Often psychological symptoms have not been understood as cries for health, as indicators of the ultimate needs of the person. Instead, a person who appears for therapy is diagnosed and his "illness" categorized so that the meaning of the symptom is not made useful for the whole person's reorientation to himself. With such treatment, the symptom becomes something to be "cured" as quickly as possible. Yet, when a person comes to the therapist complaining of hives which cause great bodily discomfort and inconvenience, for example, there are two levels of approach by which the hives might be treated. On the one hand, they could be treated as evidence of "anxiety" which is to be conditioned away. With such conditioning, the discomfort from the hives would dimish, yet the person's underlying anxiety, as it relates to the other dimensions of his existence, would remain untouched. On the other hand, a depth treatment of the hives in terms of symbolic regression psychology would relate them as a symptom to the sufferer's ultimate meaning in the world. Recently when a particular woman appeared at my office with this symptom, it turned out that her ultimate underlying fears were that she was illegitimate, that she had no right to experience the privilege of her own nature, and that, in order for her to have the right to her life, she was supposed to satisfy the demands men made upon her as these had been defined to her by her mother. She was therefore inwardly agitated. She cried out through her hives for a more adequate means of symbolizing her existence, one through which she could come to experience the world as ultimately safe.

Symptoms are symbolic expressions of the self when it relates in distorted ways to Being. If the relationship between self and Being is devoid of meaning, the symptoms will scream it out. Symptoms indicate a lack of ego, an undeveloped symbolic regressive capacity in the individual. Symptoms cry out for consciousness, for the orientation of self in relation to Being. They indicate the fixation of imagination on introjects, idealizations the person has made at the cost of experiencing his own true nature. When concern with what the person "should be" has overcome what he is, symptoms emerge as urgent reminders that he needs to return to his own inner reality as the essence of consciousness. Because they are distorted expressions of a person's ultimate human meaning, symptoms are intolerable until their meaning is comprehended. Thus removal of symptoms without comprehending them merely replaces one symptom with another, whether or not the connection between symptoms is direct and obvious. True comprehension of the meaning of the symptom, on the other hand, is a symbolically regressive act which functions as a healing expansion of imagination.

Symptomatic living is an attempt to cope with fixation on depressing images of life, but it is also an inchoate revelation of the contents of these images. Thus, symptoms are signs of a life strategy designed to hide psychic fixation or anxious and depriving self images. Accordingly, symptomatic man is restless in his view of himself and his world because he lives in a partly hidden and depriving contradiction to the nature of his being.

When a person is symptomatic, his various fixations on introjects determine his reality orientation so that he is not even aware of the states of imagination which rule his perceptions, his behavior, and his feelings. Yet the symptom is a clue to the nature of his fixation. Left to his own devices, the person is hard pressed to discover the discrepancy between fixated states of imagination and the ultimate possibilities of Being.

Mersault, the central character in Camus' novel The Stranger, illustrates the dual role of fixated symptoms, for he fixates on or identifies with what he interprets as the meaninglessness of his mother's life and death.[7] Fatherless, he has no emotion at his mother's funeral. His one night stand with Maria and his relationship with Raymond his neighbor are both characterized by indifference and detachment. The most obvious symptom of his emotional constriction is his gratuitous shooting of an Arab in the heat of the sun. His outburst of anger at the priest who comes to confess him before he is to be hanged makes his symptomatic life coherent, however, for with this anger he finally takes an emotional position in relation to the priest, a representative of the cosmic order about which he has been profoundly ambivalent. This sudden burst of energy within an otherwise emotionally barren existence enables Mersault to begin to face his own death with a renewed sense of himself and to open up to the wonder of the universe, although he remains confined to his victim's role to the end, for he fixates on his helpless mother and consequently interprets the world to be meaningless.

The therapist must go beyond the priest in Camus' novel. He must not only evoke emotions but also relate them to the person's struggle between cosmic meaning and neurotic fixation. The therapist must be able constantly to discover fresh approaches to the imaginative encounter with Being. With the help of the therapist, the individual can learn to trust the consciousness of another whose imagination is not fixated.

FIXATION AND IDEALIZATION

Fixation is the fundamental element in pathological imagizing. A fixation is constituted when the self comes to be organized around introjected rather than natural

PATHOLOGY 193

images of authority. Fixation is the invalid symbolizing of the relationship between self and Being. When socially introjected images of authority are absolutized, imagination orients the self in ways that are invalid and the self and Being are symbolized as alien to each other. Fixation thus amounts to the loss of the true dimensions of the self image to annihilating introjected images.

Thus when fixation rules imagination, the self is symbolized through false authority images, the self-Being axis is disrupted, and the self is symbolized as meaningless. The result is pathological or symptomatic symbolizing of the self. The fixated person considers himself to be at odds with the world, the victim of a bad universe. Consequently, he becomes either villainous, an agent of evil, or helpless, a victim of evil.

Fixation is a significant phenomenon because it reflects the fact that by his nature as a symbolizing being man seeks the eternal in all of his temporal relations. Scheler acknowledges this when he writes that

> man is not free to choose whether or not he wants to develop an idea of the absolutely real. Man, <u>necessarily</u> and always, consciously or unconsciously, <u>has</u> such an idea. . . . All he can choose for himself is a good and reasonable or a poor and unreasonable idea of the absolute.[8]

Man will orient himself absolutely in some direction. Fixation occurs as a misdirection of this search for absolute meaning. Man will be absolutely something, even if that something means being absolutely nothing, for man is ultimately impelled by the cosmic interrelationship between himself and the ground of his nature in Being. Man cannot live without symbolizing himself in terms of his ultimate and universal meaning, even when he does so symptomatically.

Daim describes the fixated person as attached to meanings which are not integral to what is true of himself in the ultimate sense.[9] In the fixated state a demand is made upon the self to demonstrate absolute power in false ways. Success striving, status seeking, and ideal performance predominate in his behavior. The fixated imagination orients the self around a false center so that the sense of Being is distorted into a closed system of thought, one governed by fragmented conceptual behavior. The resulting psychological organization of the individual relates him to false polarities because it makes him prone to symbolizing himself so that all possibly anxious or painful experiences are of little conscious significance for him.

Fixation leads to the strategy of idealization. The child fixates upon the more restrictive forms of the parental images when he introjects them into his personality. In this he becomes alien to the true nature of his self. Yet this fixation is so painful that it leads to denial--he tries to deny its meaning as soon as possible. He gives up his integrity rather quickly to cover over the life-threatening constrictions of fixation. Accordingly, such states as grief, despair, and alienation are experienced as impossible, and thus when the child has become an adult he cannot admit these states as essential elements of his being. In his relating he attempts to compensate for his real anguish by covering it over with a facade of rationalized, idealized self images. The entire life strategy in the fixated state is based upon the individual's idealizing some portion of reality to secure himself against the imagined hostile, meaningless world to which he has become subconsciously tied at the level of the child self.

Idealization is the second element in an ontologically articulated pathology. Its focus is the state of self-idealization. Karen Horney first introduced the concept in her discussion of the "idealized self image."[10] She defined the "idealized self image" as the glorified image of the self which is built out of a false assessment of one's assets. The drive to perfection characteristic of this idealized state distorts psychic energies away from affirming the cosmic meaning of the self. The false dimensions that the person in this idealized state imagines he possesses are at constant war with inner and outer harmony with Being. The person may say, "I feel inferior," but questioning reveals that he more deeply feels that his parents are the ones who know nothing. He makes this claim to appease his fixation, his imagined meaninglessness. This underlying self-idealization is at variance with the individual's reality.

The person's self-understanding in the fixated-idealized state takes expression in statements such as these:

> No one is able to appreciate the meaning and the depth of love as much as I do. If my parents had appreciated the meaning and depth of love as much as I have, then I would have fewer problems today. Since I do appreciate the depth of love so much, I should be loved at all times.

I don't want people to think that I am pious
and saintly, but neither do I want them to think
that I am bad or villainous. I just want them
to think that I am properly bad and properly
villainous, and properly saintly and properly
pious. I've tried very hard to prevent all of
these things at the same time. Therefore, everyone should see me as being a very well-balanced
person and treat me as such at all times. No one
should have the audacity to criticize me or to see
me as proud. If my parents would have been this
way I would have less problems.

I have tried very hard to protect others from
emotional upset while at the same time I've tried
to deny that I am emotionally upset at all times.
I've tried very hard to do both of these things at
the same time. If my parents had been this way,
I would not have felt the world to be so horrible
and catastrophic. Yet, since I am this way,
people really should treat me in a very kind and
quiet manner and should not attempt to upset or
control me.

In the fixated, self-idealized state, the person is
truly guilty of relating to his being on the basis of a
false absolute. Self-idealization cuts the self off from
relating authentically to Being and effects controlled
relationships with parents, siblings, spouse, and society
in general. Imagination is put into the service of wishful
thinking rather than grounding the person in true, need-
satisfying consciousness. Gradually imagination becomes
absorbed in maintaining the idealized state and thus becomes
dissociated from its true function. Every idealizing
strategy involves contempt for personal limitations and a
disregard for the self. In self-idealization, the person
defies all limits: money because it is concrete, time
because it is definite, and death because it is final.[11]
He identifies with extremes: wealth or poverty, accomplish-
ment or passivity, and death-defying vitality or passive
acquiescence to death. Because self-idealization is the
fundamental symbolic-psychic state underlying pathology, it
expresses a subconscious psychic ambivalence toward the
self. This ambivalence is a perversion of the natural quest
of the self to identify with the true ideal which is at the
center of man's true authority and is related to his ultimate meaning and to Being.

Self-idealization evokes self-deprecation. In the
attempt to simulate the natural, grounded state of

genuineness, there is always an attempt to hide one's self-idealizing position of omnipotence, omniscience, pride, superiority, and virtue by glorifying their opposites: inferiority, confusion, suffering, stupidity, and weakness or other self-deprecating mechanisms. The person using this strategy cannot imagine a real alternative in which genuine independent or inter-dependent relatedness exists. Rather, he unconsciously elects both self-idealization and the counter-maneuvers necessary to suppress it. The suppression of egotism is an added attempt to establish some kind of relatedness through imposed self-inferiority. But all such self-deprecating mechanisms carry an underlying message of hostility and rebellious, self-righteous idealization.

The first person narrator of Dostoevsky's Notes from Underground is a primary example of the fixated individual who cannot relate to his own true powers and therefore idealizes his sense of his own depravity. He begins:

> I am a sick man. . . . I am a spiteful man. I am an unattractive man. I believe my liver is diseased. . . . I refuse to consult a doctor from spite. That you probably will not understand. Well, I understand it, though. Of course, I can't explain who it is precisely that I am mortifying in this case by my spite: I am perfectly well aware that I cannot "pay out" the doctors by not consulting them; I know better than anyone else that by all this I am only injuring myself and no one else.[12]

Later he forces himself on old school fellows who openly dislike him. Then he opens up to a prostitute in her bed and eloquently discourses to her about life, glimpsing an almost divine power within himself for a moment. But when she subsequently comes to him with love he turns his self-contempt to hatred and degrades her before rudely sending her away because love is inconsistent with his strategy. His stance in life is characterized by disillusionment and obstinacy—his problem with his symptomatic liver reflects this. He has distorted his true authority by an illegitimate stance towards the absolute, one that is both superior and self-victimizing at the same time. He extends this self-conflicted image stage to all of life by projecting it onto others and ultimately onto his whole world as well. In each of these dimensions of his life we see the symptoms as a distorted cry for meaning and legitimacy.

The counter-maneuver of self-blame occurs to the extent that the individual denies his own needs, does not feel the disappointment related to those needs, refuses to admit his self-idealization, and avoids understanding his blame of others. Self-blame, then, is necessary because it is a way of tacitly blaming the other. For example, one client uses this strategy when she sees herself as an innocent victim. She denies any responsibility or guilt for her reactions to what she considers to be her husband's rejection. She asks, "What should I do? Give me an answer so I won't make any mistake, and then I'll no longer be an innocent victim." She does not realize that in these very words she is asking the therapist to perpetuate the pathological stance about which she is lamenting. Often the first step in self-awareness comes when the person can admit the self-idealization involved in the worship of his imagined unselfishness.

The object in self-idealization functions as an idol. Since all humans must imagize according to that which is ultimate, each human being has a tendency to idolize or project undue powers to entities and conditions outside himself. Only the development of one's capacities for symbolic regression, which results in symbolic continuity with the energies of Being, can overcome this idolizing. In all symptomatic behavior the introject is projected as an idol which one imagines he doesn't have and should have. The introjected idol is that one strives to incorporate by holding on to what he imagines he must do to be ideal. This is the essence of pathological strategizing. Such strategizing means denying that one is idolizing at the same time as one proclaims the difficulty of his own position of self-idealization. In his felt inability to achieve the idol, the individual discounts his implicitly imagined but denied superiority. He blames others because he is performing sincerely in order to realize an image of what he ought to become and do. Thus he is ideal because he so sincerely performs what he thinks he ought to do and so intensely denies that he isn't what he thinks he shouldn't be. If his parents had only tried as hard, cared as much, and known as deeply, life would not be so difficult. This is one's thinking, whether one condemns or patronizes the actual parent. When the individual is relating to himself and to his world through the idol image, the idolized other is always imagined to have the advantages and to be enjoying the good life. In this kind of imagizing, the individual first idolizes that which does not exist. He then devises an ideal role for himself by which to try to equal the idolized figure. At bottom, however, the idolizing person is not really worshipping the idol. Rather, he is fearing that he must worship the idol. Thus his real struggle is to free himself from the idol by reclaiming for himself the energy he gives to it.

An example of this idolizing strategy can be seen in the case of a client who has struggled to relate to this father. When Jeff visits his father, the father starts the conversation with, "How is your relationship with God?" Rather than listening to Jeff's response, the father waits to let Jeff know that his own relationship with God is very good and that that is important because in his self-deprecating state God alone can give him the validation he needs. The father tells Jeff, "As I grow in the knowledge of my unimportance, I grow in the knowledge that I am important only as God makes me important." In this fixation, Jeff's father idealizes his relationship with God. He is unworthy, but God as a cosmic countervalue compensates for this intrinsic unworthiness. This is fixation on God as a version of the idealized parent. Yet Jeff's father keeps himself ignorant of the true nature of his real fixation and his real problem through self-deprecation. The result is a disturbed sense of the absolute which cuts off the possibility of the man's relatedness to other persons. Identification with the authority introject obliterates personal authority and relatedness and creates an ersatz, idolatrous cosmic-relatedness. This pattern combines the elements of fixation, idealization-deprecation, and idolization. Fixation on the idolatrous introject corresponds to the individual's feelings of his own unimportance which are related to his guilty self-image. In the most disturbed cases of this syndrome, the individual relates to himself "as God" and projects his identification with the idol into a cosmic mode. Although it may not be obvious, this is true of Jeff's father. Jeff's right to renounce this idealization of his father's is implicit in the message of his own syndrome.

Jeff's father cannot communicate with Jeff unless Jeff adopts a fixation which "takes care of" the idol his parent psychologically worships. Jeff is allowed to be legitimate only by adopting his father's idolatry--that is, only by parenting the fixated condition of his parent. One day Jeff came to the point where he said, "It became very clear that a relationship with my Dad on the basis of my intrinsic value is impossible. I am illegitimate until proven legitimate by worshipping my father through worshipping his God." With this clarity, Jeff was able to break through his guilt, see his intrinsic unimportance to his father, and say to his father, "I need a new kind of recognition for who I am."

Because depression weaves its way like a silver cord through all pathological symbolizing, understanding depression is important for understanding all pathology. Abraham interprets the paradoxical humility of the depressive patient as a facade for psychic grandiosity.[13] This depressive "humility" may express itself in delusions of injustice, or, taking the opposite mode, in manic states. Freudians link the depressive state with extreme narcissism, with fixation on the gaining of self-esteem, and with status striving.[14] Wolman describes the manic depressive person in terms of his belief that he is a rejected Cinderella who hopes that, when he reaches the depths of despair, the high reward to which he is entitled will be forthcoming.[15] He adds that usually such a person has maneuvered himself into the position of family savior. This person is preoccupied with the imperative of winning unqualified approval through some ultimate sense of sacrifice, for he feels that he must define his significance in absolute terms in order to be valid and legitimate.

According to Bibering's definition of depression, the collapse of self-esteem occurs when the individual must somehow admit that he has failed to reach his ultimate ideal.[16] Depression is a fixation on the feeling of helplessness which comes when the individual has failed to get what he needs from others to maintain his self-idealization. To the extent that the depressed person is attempting to tolerate or manipulate himself on the basis of introjected absolutes, bad authority images, he has adopted an inadequate strategy of life which is bound to collapse. Yet the loss of self-esteem involved in this collapse must be seen as a necessary loss if the individual is to discover the real loss carefully hidden beneath it. Through either supportive confrontation in therapy or unavoidable failure in his life experience, the depressed person must learn how self-idealization had to fail and how his feelings of helplessness can actually point to the existence of a deeper need. Such knowledge is the crucial side of his awareness which makes it possible for him to enter into symbolic regression and thereby to recover a sense of his ultimate legitimacy as a child of the universe.

From the point of view of symbolic regression psychology, the symptomatic horse religion of Alan Strang and the depressed nostalgia for a meaningful cosmos of Dr. Martin Dysart in Peter Shaffer's *Equus* are two versions of the same pathological problem.[17] The boy's misdirected attempts to find a cosmic significance for his passion in an idiosyncratic worship of horses finds its analogue in the impotence of the psychiatrist who laments the loss of both meaning and passion in his sterile world of rational adulthood. The strategies of both must fail so that each can begin to develop a personally more adequate integration of passion and meaning based on the recovery of the legitimate child self.

THE MEANING OF GUILT AND ANXIETY

In psychological terminology, guilt is used to refer to the fear of introjected, inordinate, and unacceptable social mores. This fear is referred to here as <u>false guilt</u>. It has been a concern in psychology to indicate the relative basis of guilt and the introjection of social demands. However, it is important that true guilt be distinguished from false guilt, for true guilt is part of man's essential nature. Guilt is always related to man's need for integrity according to his ultimate meaning—his reality as a cosmic being.

False guilt is the pathological disguising of real guilt which is made necessary when one is unconsciously committed to false authority ultimates: the world is consequently perceived, imagined, and symbolized as hostile and depriving. Moreover, the symptomatic person is oriented to symbols which do not reach to the ultimate meaning of the self. Whatever he does, whether washing his hands forever or constantly confessing his sins, he is evading the need to confront himself, his parents, his wife, or any situation demanding intimacy. Unless man confronts himself and relates to himself in humanly conscious ways, such guilt reducing mechanisms will not diminish his inner tensions at any ultimate level even though he may vacillate from one tension syndrome to another.

False guilt is expressed in the tensions built up through conflict within the organism. This false guilt is the consequence of a reality choice based on the introject rather than one based on faith in the intrinsic meaning of life. It involves such statements to the self as, "I shouldn't have done it this way," or, "I might have hurt someone by what I did," or, "Why am I so imperfect?" False guilt expresses that the person is working according to a symptomatic strategy. The bad authority images related to frightened inner states make courage seem wrong and reality-oriented actions seem destructive. Everyone wonders if in the moments of his most obvious courage he hasn't been too cruel, too inhuman, or too unideal. Even

PATHOLOGY

in man's most courageous moments, in his moments of utmost integrity, he is involved with bad authority introjects which constantly seem to require of him that he involve himself with idealistic self-imagizing. Thus, to the therapist, the problem of false guilt also involves personality immobilization. Given this false, depressive guilt, the person tends to depress the healthy activity which comes into play when he makes valid, reality-oriented choices.

The concept of self-idealization is also related to <u>true guilt</u>. True guilt is the upset state of the self when it denies the deprivation that comes with relating to Being through false authority introjects. True guilt is fundamental for understanding the psychology of the person and must be dealt with by the therapist, for the person's guilt evidences the lack of a symbolically regressive stance. In self-idealization, the self is fixated upon a power-oriented introject as a basis for autonomy, and this fixation replaces relating to Being through harmonious imaginative centers. The individual in this cut-off state thus idealizes power but pretends powerlessness. "Powerless people should have control of power," the individual tells himself. Another person may idealize the imagined conformity and security orientation of others, but at the same time idealize himself as rightfully defiant. Each of these persons idealizes himself but idolizes that personality attribute of the other with which he cannot or will not cope. Since this bifurcation involves a basic breach of relationships, the person suffers from true guilt for his self-idealization and the related idolatrous imagizing.

To illustrate true guilt, "I am inferior" means, "If the other person understood himself as well as I do myself, he would not act so superior." Also, "I am inferior" is a way of saying, "I am guilty for saying that I feel inferior when I also mean that I shouldn't feel inferior." At a deeper level this also reads:

> My parents were stupid. If my parents were as smart as I, they would feel more inferior and I wouldn't have to act so inferior. That I feel inferior is a problem, for I shouldn't feel inferior. My parents and others feel superior to me but they shouldn't. They should feel inferior to me but they don't.

The psychic strategy here is very subtle. It is a means of judging others for what a person imagines to be true of himself. The result in the personality is a feeling of agitation. This disharmony becomes conceptualized as the state of true guilt.

To resolve this opposition, it is necessary to develop the capacity for symbolic regression. First, the person must be helped to see how, in his use of this strategy, the self is symbolically pitted against the energies of Being. Then, when the individual learns to relate to himself in symbolically regressive ways, he can let himself feel the needs of the child self and the organic self, as well as the cosmic self. The individual must come to realize that his real guilt is always the same message: "You are not being conscious; you are denying the awareness of your true needs as if you had no cosmic meaning or substance."

An example of the role of true guilt can be seen in the case of Larry. When Larry began discussing feelings of inferiority, he was asked to tell his father the nature of these feelings in intrapsychic dialogue. He couldn't tell his father he felt inferior. Instead, he realized he felt superior to his father. In order to maintain his imaginary position of inferiority, he had to isolate his father from imagination, thus treating the father as a person who had no meaning to him. He was challenged to feel guilty about this attitude toward his father and to listen to the message in the guilt. His true guilt lay in his inability to identify himself as the son of his father.

There are two kinds of anxiety, anxiety related to false guilt, and anxiety related to true guilt. In false guilt, the organic tension related to making choices cannot be discharged, and so the anxiety becomes circular and non-directive. It cannot be released in terms of choices and decisive actions, but is contained by psychic immobilization. Thus the anxiety builds and builds whether the individual is aware of it as guilt or not, and the individual becomes increasingly fixated on attempts to secure himself against bad authority images. The emotions involved in these states of tension continually mount up until the source of real guilt can be uncovered and dealt with.

On the other hand, anxiety feelings related to true guilt manifest the tension resulting from the opposition between the desire for mobilization and the fear of movement. This anxiety puts the individual in the position of making choices in which he cannot be sure he is being perfect. Such choices involve risk, the risk of relating to reality according to meaning without the full assurance that this relating is being done in an ideal or ultimate manner such as the fixated aspect of the personality demands. Authentic and mobilized living always involves the person's determination to endure the organismic tension caused by unresolved introjected demands. A non-idealizing strategy of life requires the capacity for courage and genuineness. When the person is relating out of a valid image of himself, the anxiety involved in his making a choice does not overwhelm him.

The two kinds of anxiety are qualitatively and ontologically distinct from each other. Only the latter one is based on the individual's ontological substance, his significance as a creature of time and space in a universe which is meaningful, for true guilt is a reality in this universe. In pathological strategizing, anxiety says to man that his needs are impossible because there is no dependable world except the idealized formulation to which he cannot commit himself. In natural symbolizing, man is aware of his tendency to idealize or to formulate a world which goes against the intrinsic nature of his being, but he is able to imagine his own meaning over against this tendency with such power that his idealization does not ensnare him.

Simply put, guilt is an image or concept related to dissonance; anxiety is the primary feeling of this dissonance. True guilt is ultimately related to taking one's consciousness or one's history as unimportant. It indicates a disruption of the process of symbolic regression. Therefore, in order fully to acknowledge the cosmic import of the self, we must deal with guilt as the underlying dynamic of all pathology. True guilt is the consequence of taking oneself as ultimately unimportant, and therefore acting in meaningless ways with the self.

Guilt and anxiety are directly related to all pathology. Yet guilt is not usually identified as such by the intellect, due to the pathological strategy. Usually a person cannot relate his guilt to his self-idealization and his symptomatic strategizing. Once he discovers that he has been trying to live without admitting the meaning of his deprivation, he can begin to understand his true guilt for his self-idealization and his symptomatic strategizing. One of the major tasks of therapy is to teach the person how he is guilty, rather than merely teaching him that he is guilty and shouldn't be. The individual needs to learn how he is already guilty and how he can transcend his self-conflicting state by relating himself to the ultimate authority of his being instead of to his fantastic self-idealized authority.

In true guilt the person uses a symptomatic strategy of life to shield himself from the grief which is his link to the meaning of his cosmic self. In this guilty strategizing he is idealizing himself in his relationships with others. In opposition to his true basic needs for cosmic relatedness, he makes whatever choices are necessary for him to maintain the self-idealization. The issue is how to interpret and use guilt so that it is meaningful for the person's quest for consciousness. Guilt is a signal that the organism is protecting itself against consciousness. The state of psychic immobility related to guilt is both positive and negative. It is negative to the degree that it is interpreted according to false authority introjects and is thus imagined to be without meaning. It is positive to the degree that the individual imagines its ultimate meaning and recognizes it as simply a defensive blockade against further destructive behavior. Psychic immobilization in the person is thus related to true guilt. The immobility is not the problem. The problem for therapy is the meaning of the immobility and how it relates to the whole of the person. True guilt comprises the tensions built up in the organism which have developed through a long series of reality choices based on fear rather than on faith in the intrinsic meaning of life. These tensions may be communicated somatically, psychically, or in attempts to coerce the outer situation to fit the strategy. Such tensions are often not recognized as guilt but are most often recognized as feelings of inferiority, inadequacy, superiority, or some other kind of insecure state. Guilt consists of these feelings at that level where they take expression as an image state.

Before a person can become aware of his need for change, he must admit the reality of his crime against being himself, and against being conscious of himself and of his cosmic meaning, and he must acknowledge his guilt for this violation of himself. It is true that the therapist is not responsible for inducing motivation. If, however, he is to help the person identify his true guilt, he cannot help but challenge him to be responsible for the crime of denying his own meaning as a personal and a cosmic being. This denial is a costly bargain that he has made with himself to cover over the deprivation, grief, and despair in his experience in exchange for an illusory sense of security. He disguises these needs in a symptomatic, idealizing life strategy. There are two elements of his guilt. Part of this guilt is for denying the pride he has invested in his idealizing; and part of it is for manipulating reality in order to maintain this pride system. Recovery of the capacity for symbolic regression removes the need for both elements of this elaborate and precarious kind of self organization.

In psychotherapy the person is first made aware of his true guilt so that the pain of grief, despair and other disappointing dimensions of self-awareness can be admitted. Self-idealizing imagizing and related psychic strategies of thinking, emoting and acting are only overcome by constant awareness of the true guilt which underlies all the person's thought modes, internalized sentences, and related behavior characteristics. The idealized imagizing expressed through such statements as "I feel inferior" hides the real guilt underlying one's unwillingness to relate. The individual is guilty for being irresponsible with himself about transcending these states. He is guilty for not facing and challenging his bad parental, sibling, and self-image fixations so that he might relate himself more harmoniously to his true nature. He may understand and explain this guilt as inferiority feelings or anxiety, but these feelings must be reinterpreted to him as self-idealizing imagizing. He must be taught to recognize such true guilt images and to move toward ultimate valid images of his being. The false guilt he feels when he relates positively to his own needs must be understood as his rationalizing away of the right to mobilize himself into responsible action. He is helped to understand that he uses such false guilt to avoid the pain of realistic and non-ideal self-striving. In many cases, there is no more important task in the effort towards consciousness than to reinterpret anxiety feelings and feelings of inferiority as symptoms of true guilt. In confronting the self-idealized images with the dynamics of true guilt underlying them, the therapist exerts the psychic leverage necessary to break the omnipotent demands of an idolatrous, introjected unreality.

When he beings to imagine the link between his real cosmic needs and his inner image realities, the individual can begin to transcend his depriving image fixations. When alternate images reflecting the true nature of Being become validated as not only more desirable but more real, the "shoulds," the inner perfectionistic demands, give way to admissions of true guilt. Thereby the symptoms related to the fantastical, omnipotent preoccupations of self-idealized imagizing can be acknowledged and given up. The "shoulds," which are related to self-idealizing imagizing, are neither truly moral nor truly social. These "shoulds" lack the kind of conviction that comes out of self-Being integrity. These "shoulds," however, do contain the perverted seeds of man's need to be related to his own ultimate cosmic essence. The seeds must be germinated into meaningful self-Being continuity by introducing the person to image ultimates which make his value system work toward integration with the natural world rather than in isolation from it. The goal of therapy is not to enable reason to prevail over imagination, but to allow reason to function in accord with imagination. Therapy is the effort to help the individual give up self idealization for self realization.

James came to therapy after ten years of not speaking to either of his parents, although he had lived with them during the whole of that time. At twenty-six years of age and holding a responsible position as a scientist, he found himself thoroughly depressed. His parents were his problem. With some initial support, he was finally able to move to his own place. He remained depressive, guilty, and cynical about life. He treated the therapist as if he were impotent to change him. He thought he had to be too ideal to confront the deprivation towards which he had taken an idolatrous stance. When confronted with the reality that he wanted to kill his mother, he broke into sobs and admitted his desire to kill her because she supported his father's impotence rather than her love for him. James was thus able to break with his idealization of deprivation and guilt so that he began to move toward more life-oriented symbolizing. He began to feel his need for good parents, for love, and for support. He was able to become angry at the deprived state with his parents and to move toward relationships which for the first time offered him anti-suicidal reality.

PATHOLOGY AND SYMBOLIC REGRESSION

The diverse pathological syndromes of classical nosology are particular manifestations of the elements of the pathological process described in this chapter. In applying this theory to the major classical categories of psychopathology, we shall focus on the relationship between the introjected family images involved with each particular syndrome and the element common to all pathology, the state of pathological anxiety.

When a person's actual parent or parent substitute—his employer, teacher, spouse, or other significant person—is directly or covertly hostile, then disturbing negative parent images are activated, and the person reacts to these frightening images with the responses that he learned as a child. Eventually he becomes fixated on such introjected parent images and this fixation mobilizes habitual strategies of defense against them. The given strategy which a person takes up to control or deny the anxiety which these negative images create determines what kind of pathology the person will manifest: neurosis, psychosis, perversion, or sociopathic disorder. Each of these is a variety of the unified, comprehensive dynamics of pathology which is outlined in this chapter. At the same time, each stands unique as a manifestation of the pathological process. A consideration of traditional nosological categories will show how this is so.

By general consensus, there are four major categories of neurosis. Each is a response to the anxiety provoked by introjected parent images: anxiety neurosis, anxiety hysteria, obsessive-compulsive neurosis, and conversion hysteria. First, anxiety neurosis is based on unconscious guilt for unconscious hostility towards the bad parent images. The person's symptomatic behavior consists of his attempts to overcome his "free floating" anxiety. That is, he is attempting to atone for the attitudes which the unacknowledged negative parent images evoke.

In anxiety hysteria, the person manifests symptomatic behavior as his attempt to avoid the objects or persons upon which he unconsciously displaces the bad parent images. The dangerous bad parents are identified with actual parents, objects, or situations, and they are assiduously avoided.

Obsessive-compulsive neurosis, another major type of neurosis, is the attempt to deal with the anxiety provoked by introjected parent images through excessive, even ritualized, control of the self and the environment. This controlling becomes manifested in obsessive thoughts, compulsive acts, or rigid disciplines.

Conversion hysteria consists of unconscious collaboration with the bad parent images in the effort to protect them from the person's defensive anger, thereby making them safe. Symptomatic behavior in this case is based on the person's succumbing to the power of the introjects in the attempt to deny that power through omnipotent, self-imposed castration.

Two of these strategies, anxiety neurosis and conversion hysteria, generally focus on the introjected father images and indicate a less severe mother deprivation because both atonement and self-castration strategies are guilt responses evoked by bad authority. This dynamic is in effect even when the bad father image is projected for the person by the attitude or actions of a mother figure.

On the other hand, anxiety hysteria and obsessive-compulsive neurosis focus more or less on the introjected mother image and indicate a more severe mother deprivation because strategies of avoidance or control are anxiety responses evoked by a negative or confusing nurturing environment. Likewise, this dynamic becomes effective even when the introjected mother image is mediated to the person by the influence of a father's hostility toward the mother.

Each of these four major neurotic strategies is a response to the threatening power of unconscious or partly conscious bad parent images. Each begins with fixation on the introjected bad parent and includes the person's self-idealization and omnipotence along with his sense of powerlessness and hopelessness. Yet each neurotic strategy--whether it is atonement, avoidance, control, or self-castration--is fundamentally characterized as a state of anxiety and therefore as a state of being cut off from symbolic regressive consciousness.

As in the neuroses, the fundamental motivation underlying the psychoses is the desire to escape the uncontrolled anxiety provoked by the repressed, poorly repressed, or unrepressed hostility embodied in the introjected bad parent images.

If neurosis is fundamentally an enactment of the person's anxiety at the power of his introjected hostile parent images, psychosis is an intensification of this condition, for psychosis is the behavior symptomatizing extreme alarm when the introjected parents become overwhelming and appear to threaten the person with annihilation. With this state, the introjected parent images flood into consciousness to distort or obliterate reality because these images become psychologically more real to the person than his natural images and the sensory material coming in from his environment. After the person's initial reaction of alarm at the overwhelming bad images, he reverts to the childhood level of adjustment at which he learned to secure his existence against the overwhelming images by one or the other of two responses: either omnipotent, uncontrollable rage, or impotent, passive dependency. Such childish modes of action enable the person to remain at a level where he can "take care of" the bad parental images and thus save himself from the feared parental annihilation.

The pathological process underlies all of the functioning psychoses. Each psychotic manifestation is a symptomatic reaction expressing this process. None of the psychoses need be regarded as a distinct disease entity embodying its own separate dynamics. Psychosis is always a desperate leap for survival against overwhelming attacks by inner bad father and bad mother images when these images have taken on cosmic proportions for the person. The type of psychotic symptoms manifested in a given individual depends upon three factors: the person's childhood success at handling introjected parent images; the strength of the personality's integration in defending itself against the introjected hostile parents; and the existence of positive actual interpersonal relationships which support the person's access to the natural inner parent images.

Schizophrenia is the individual's psychotic defense against closeness to other persons. The schizophrenic finds it almost impossible to contact the natural good father and good mother images within himself. The introjected bad parents with their symbolic cosmic proportions thwart this inner contact, making the schizophrenic react to persons in his experience as if these actual persons manifested the power of the introjects themselves.

The bad parent images underlying all schizophrenic conditions are always essentially the same. The type of symptoms in any given case depends on the strength with which the individual handles the attacks being made by his introjected bad parent images. In simple schizophrenia, hebephrenia, and paranoid schizophrenia, it seems that the person is temporarily able to handle these attacks to some degree of satisfaction; in catatonia and paranoidal depression, he is simply overwhelmed by them.

The manic depressive person never gets completely cut off from the natural inner good parents. The manic phase is his reaction to overwhelming bad father images, manifested as an aping or idealizing of some of the qualities of good father images. The depressive phase, on the other hand, is essentially a succumbing to overwhelming bad mother images, manifested as passivity, dejection,

Involutional psychosis is a person's being overwhelmed by bad parent images during advanced age when the vigor of youth declines and thus no longer sustains the person's contact with the good parental images at the surface level of conscious experience. Underlying neurotic elements are finally able to surface without resistance, and the person's reduced physiological efficiency works with his introjected bad parent images to produce the maladative regressive behavior usually associated with "second childhood" or senility.

The symptom is a type of symbol. It is a degraded symbolic state. It indicates that the person is blocked from realizing his full symbolizing capacities as a human being. Symptomatic styles and strategies of life rest upon an inadequate and untrue image of life and of one's self. Such strategies involve an attempt to survive in spite of a world in which a happy life is imagined to be impossible for the individual. Thus, since symptoms are degraded symbols, they communicate that the individual is in conflict with his own basic nature. They indicate that he is guilty of non-existence. This guilt is experienced as anxiety. Such experienced anxiety must be reinterpreted to the individual.

The symptomatic condition is not to be simply blamed, rejected, or treated as a nuisance. Indictment of surface symptoms is common practice, often without the therapist's even being aware that he is allowing the real issue to slip past him just as it has slipped past the client. Nowhere is this so apparent as in many of the case studies held up as model cures in many clinical settings. The symptom is a phenomenon most unique to the nature of man and it must be treated carefully so that its inner meaning can be brought out and not be lost. The symptomatic condition is always a distorted symbolic expression containing vital though distorted capacities and energies. The tranquillizing of symptoms before their depth meaning is understood is usually a compromise with the immediate crisis when true contact with the self would make confrontation with the deeper crisis possible.

The symptom is man's easiest way of immobilizing those dimensions of his existence which he cannot integrate with his own nature. The purpose of the symptom is to protect the individual from being aware of his deprivation because he imagines it to be meaningless. But more significantly, it also preserves the person's deepest capacities for future reclamation through the recovery of consciousness. The symptomatic man's way of being proclaims that in his world he has to be superhumanly weak or superhumanly strong to survive. In this alien world of his imagination he "knows" that he cannot be himself or openly explore his frustration unless he acts phony and isolates himself from himself, from others, and from the world as well.

NOTES

1. Max Scheler, Philosophical Perspectives, (Boston: Beacon Press, 1958), pp. 2-3.

2. Paul Tillich, Systematic Theology, vol. I, pp. 202-04.

3. Søren Kierkegaard, The Sickness Unto Death (Princeton, New Jersey: Princeton Univ. Press, 1968), and Concluding Unscientific Postscript, (Princeton, New Jersey: Princeton Univ. Press, 1968).

4. This is what Ronald D. Laing has described in The Divided Self: An Existential Study in Sanity and Madness, (Harmondsworth, England: Penguin Books, 1969), his existential analysis of pathology.

5. Donald R. Steiper and Daniel N. Weiner, Key Dimensions in Psychotherapy, (Chicago: Aldine Press, 1965).

6. Perry London, Modes and Morals of Psychotherapy, (New York: Holt, Rinehart & Winston, 1954).

7. Albert Camus, The Stranger, (New York: Knopf, 1946).

8. Max Scheler, p. 2.

9. Wilfried Daim, Depth Psychology and Salvation, (New York: Ungar, 1963).

10. Karen Horney, Our Inner Conflicts: A Constructive Theory of Neurosis, (New York: Norton, 1945), pp. 96-114.

11. Karen Horney, Neurosis and Human Growth: The Struggle Toward Self-Realization, (New York: Norton, 1950), pp. 43-45.

12. Fyodor Dostoyevsky, Notes from Underground, in Notes from Underground, Poor People, The Friend of the Family: Three Short Novels by Fyodor Dostoyevsky, (New York: Dell, 1960), p. 25.

13. Karl Abraham, referred to in J. Richard Wittenborn, "Depression," in Handbook of Clinical Psychology, ed. Benjamin B. Wolman, (New York: McGraw-Hill, 1965), p. 1043.

14. These are discussed in Wittenborn, pp. 1042-47.

15. Benjamin B. Wolman, in Wittenborn, p. 1044.

16. Edward Bibring, "The Mechanism of Depression," in *Affective Disorders*, ed. Phyllis Greenacre, (New York: International Universities Press, (1953).

17. Peter Shaffer, *Equus*, (New York: Avon Books, 1974).

Chapter VII: Genuineness

GENUINENESS IS THE HIDDEN DYNAMIC OF THERAPY

At the present time the theory of psychotherapy is in a state of confusion. Studies of the outcome of therapy are ambiguous because they lack either concreteness or depth. Normally, these studies have defined the changes brought about by psychotherapy in extremely broad terms such as the remission of major symptoms or general "feelings of improvement." Such categories are useless for determining what the individual has achieved in his search for meaning and fulfillment. Because of the lack of conceptual clarity in defining what the therapeutic task is all about, this research has necessarily been very vague. On the other hand, when these studies use one or another form of objective measurement, they repeatedly find that psychotherapy is ineffective. Further, such measurements fail to show any consistency in what takes place in the therapy process. Steiper and Weiner suggest that a reason for these difficulties in assessing therapies is that outcome research generally measures derivative or incidental factors which do not correspond to the nature of personality transformation.[1]

Moreover, theoretical conceptualizations have been found to be inadequate for determining the effectiveness of therapy in all of the schools of psychotherapeutic effort. This inadequacy is due to the fact that theories in themselves cannot be rooted in the ultimates which symbolize the meaning of man. Conceptualizations can only be life-serving: they must be rooted in man's intuitions of himself in his world. Theories of the mind, when considered apart from these intuitions, tend to degrade imagination rather than finding their basis in man's self-transcendence and in his being. Thus theories often overlook man's regressive dimensions as if they had no meaning.

Theory alone has to be confusing to both client and therapist: the mind of man is immediate and cannot be understood apart from man's ultimate intuitions. Measurements and theoretical goals in psychotherapy lose their heuristic function when they become severed from the immediate intuitions of cosmic meaning and Being upon which they must be founded.

When Steiper and Weiner describe psychotherapy as the quest for coherent integration, they point to a reality which transcends mere theory. Value congruence, the integration of experience and behavior which they posit as the goal of therapy, suggests a radically new orientation for therapy. The concept of value congruence implies that the person's most basic intuitions and assumptions about the world are what cause him to act as he does. When this concept is used as an indication of psychic change, psychotherapy can be seen as the attempt to help the individual to come to terms with the meaning of his life and actions. To extend this concept in terms of symbolic regression psychology, the lack of correlation between theory and effectiveness in psychotherapy is due to the almost total disregard of three factors which are the undergirdings of human psychology: man's cosmic meaning, the mythic-symbolic essence of human subjectivity made accessible through symbolic regression, and genuineness as the expression of this subjectivity in interpersonal behavior. Genuineness, as the interpersonal expression of the individual's groundedness in Being, is the most observable of these factors. Because genuineness is based on the person's sense of being truly at home in the world, it can be characterized in terms of authentic, non-manipulative relating to others.

Unlike empathy and warmth, genuineness is not a quality which can be taught as a set of techniques. Yet it can be evoked in a facilitating way in a clinical setting through the visualization or guided daydream, as the research of Darryl Freeland has shown.[2] In a relaxed state the client expresses his deepest images and accompanying feelings to the therapist. The visualization both sensitizes the client to his own imaginal functioning and supports him to bring his own subjectivity to immediate expression in his narration to the therapist. The experience is a profoundly integrating one which gives the client a foretaste of what he can come to claim for himself as he grows into his own genuineness.

The lack of correlation between the training of therapists of any particular school and the effectiveness of therapy suggests that the success of therapy depends on the extent to which the three factors underlying human psychology take expression in the therapist's relating to the client. The genuineness of the therapist is the crucial element which determines to what extent the dynamics of therapeutic personality change will be activated. All real achievements in therapy are based on the therapist's ability continually to relate out of his own genuineness in each moment of therapeutic encounter. The therapist's genuineness in relating to the client enables the client to orient himself to the situations in which his neurotic behavior has been acquired on a new, non-neurotic basis. The genuine responses of the therapist support the client to relate to these situations on the basis of his ultimate needs and thus on the basis of his cosmic legitimacy. The therapist's genuineness directly relates these needs to the images and values which are the conceptual and moral undergirdings for the person's evolving psychic commitments. The goal in this reorientation process is the value congruence which Steiper and Weiner have emphasized.

When the therapist relates to the client with genuineness, he is inviting the client to become grounded in Being as he is. As the client responds to the therapist's genuineness, his imagination is allowed to come into its ascendency and his renewed capacity for symbolic regression begins to make fixation on introjected images unnecessary. Eventually he comes to symbolize himself in terms of his cosmic meaning, and he feels a pervasive sense of his legitimacy in the world. Consequently, he does not attempt to placate, patronize, or manipulate the manifestations of Being with which he must deal. He has come to live in harmony with his own nature.

When the therapist's relating does not stand out for its genuineness, the client is not able to accomodate himself to the therapist's uncertainty and he is left obliviously to search on his own for genuineness—something he is not sure he can find and something he is not sure the therapist has found for himself. Yet when a therapist has become conscious of his own inner reality and therefore has begun to orient himself in relation to the ground of his own being, even if he has not become able to articulate these things, the therapist's depth with himself may be unconsciously communicated to the client as genuineness. The client in turn may begin to relate to this genuineness in ways that increase his own genuineness, even though the symbolic regressive dimensions of what has occurred are not made obvious to him.

It is no wonder that a great number of theories of therapy have done anything but focus on the inner life of the client, for it is impossible to concentrate on the distortions of the client's subjectivity without the therapist's first having apprehended his own inner life with ultimate seriousness and his having dealt with the grounding he does or does not have for his own sense of self. If his own inner life is not crucially related to anything of ultimate significance to him, the therapist is not in a position to sustain a process of therapy which has the power to lead another person into genuineness.

The overlooked role of the therapist's genuineness rests in part on the lack of attention the professional gives to his imagination and on his ignorance of the meaning of regression as the essence of his search for genuineness. The therapist's being must be related to the myth of his own meaning at the cosmic level. When he is rooted in cosmic realities, he articulates this relatedness in terms of his own symbolizing, and genuineness is brought to the encounter between therapist and client.

The therapist cannot be excused from the responsibilities to help the client to understand the meaning of his actions and to help the client take both the world and his own life story seriously. The client cannot be made not to think about meaning. In fact, psychic disorder is based on the person's inability to take his own life story seriously and thereby to find a real context for his subjectivity. The psychotic person cannot tie the present to the past, and he cannot tie the inward to the outward: he does not know about genuineness.

Because the criteria hitherto used to determine the nature of therapeutic interaction have had little significant relation to the client's subjective understanding of his images, these criteria have not taken into account the role of genuineness in the encounter. Without genuineness as the explicit foundation of the therapeutic relationship, the client cannot relate to the therapist's understanding of what is really going on in the therapist, and the client lacks any idea that the happiness he is seeking has to do with his ultimate nature as a human being.

A psychology based on genuineness in relating cannot be subordinated to any reality other than the person's subjectivity. The person cannot undergo fundamental change if he does not imagine that the conscious mind has something ultimate to deal with at the level of the cosmic-symbolic self. Thus at each stage therapy is a relating of the person to ultimate meaning and Being, and genuineness unfolds throughout the process of therapy. It follows that what might seem to be a random reconditioning is not random at all. Rather, this process is related to certain ultimate states of being in the person's imaginative life which form a sequence in the development of the capacity of symbolic regression.

The categories by which we measure therapeutic change have not yet been articulated as phases in the development of the capacity for symbolic regression. Yet, in the process of living, each person is constantly attempting and testing genuineness. This probing amounts to a search which either involves the person with symbolic regression or cuts him off from it. The symbolic regressive stance of the person and the phases of his symbolic regressive search must be studied in order to determine the meaning of the therapeutic process for that person. This focus indicates the need for precision about the realities which underlie the therapeutic process, especially the factor of genuineness. Therapy must be conceptualized in terms of this inner search for the ground of one's being as a basis for genuineness if we are to understand what happens in the interaction between therapist and client.

Conscious effort must be involved in attaining a symbolically regressed state of being. The process of therapy can only be understood and assessed when the different phases of the task of symbolic regression are made the criteria for knowing what is actually going on. Furthermore, an understanding of the phases in the development of symbolic regression enables the therapist to orient the person towards his genuineness with effectiveness at each point in his quest. Conscious understanding of the symbolic regressive phases through which a person must take himself and in which a therapist must relate to the person in the development of genuineness enables the therapist to direct the course of therapy in an optimum way.

Symbolic regression, as the process of re-symbolizing the person into genuineness, is the underlying principle which will finally render outcome studies intelligible. A clear articulation of the phases of the symbolic regressive process provides a helpful indication of what is occurring in therapy. A schematization of these phases will yield more reliable information about what goes on in therapy than any formulation so far suggested.

The heuristic mapping of these fundamental phases which follows will enable the therapist to assess where the client is in his therapeutic progress as well as how the therapist might articulate and support this development in the way which will be the most helpful for the client.

GENUINENESS DEVELOPS IN FOUR IMAGE PHASES

Genuineness develops in four phases of symbolizing: the need-awareness phase, the life-awareness phase, the identity-awareness phase, and the integration-awareness phase. Each of these phases involves the individual in the development of certain capacities for symbolic regression and each phase can be articulated in terms of specific symbolic regressive states.

The need awareness phase is undergirded by the complimentary images of the rescuing parent and the deprived child. Each person in the progress of his life has jettisoned his identification with the image of his child self. He has done this in order to take care of his parents and the world which has demanded that he "parent" it, that he validate it in order to survive. Faced with such survival demands, the child self with its inherent needs was jettisoned so that the person didn't have to face his child-deprivation in a mitigated way in his adult experience. Now it is this child self with its symbols and images which must be rescued. The individual begins the regressive journey into the states of the child self in order to recover the deprived child, to rescue the goodness of the child's needs, and thus to bring the child self and its images into an integrated state with his adult person. He must discover how to reclaim the feeling states, the body states, and the relational need states which were forsaken with the jettisoning of the child self.

The symbolic regressive task is to enable the person to retrieve the alienated child self. The phases of symbolic regression in the recovery of genuineness describe the various aspects of this task. The first stage is founded on the incipient re-symbolizing of the image of the father in the person's symbolic structure. This produces an inner atmosphere or expectation of good authority. Given this initial hope, the child is freed to deny the rejecting mother. Hitherto, the inner bad mother fixation has caused the individual to deny his needs, to idealize deprivation, and to see self-rejection as acceptance. The inner child must be supported by the individual's inner good authority to say no to what is poisonous for its welfare. This is the task of the first phase of symbolic regression: the establishing of the therapeutic relationship to provide an implicit good inner father state which can permit the child to admit the needs basic to his welfare.

The second or life-awareness phase of the symbolic regressive process makes it possible for the person to pursue life. In this phase the inner child has the encouragement of his inner authority to leave behind the resistance of the oppressive bad mother and to pursue the bountiful gifts of the good mother. Having learned to say "no" to what was bad for it in the first phase, the inner child learns in this phase to say "yes" to what is good for it. The good mother now appears as an ultimate image towards which the person can orient himself. She feeds, supports, and exudes the love energies which cause the individual to seek what is comforting in life. In addition, he learns to do this without guilt and without depriving himself. In this symbolic phase the good mother is retrieved for the child so that he can comfortably pursue life. Symbols of good food, gifts, love, and warmth appear in dreams. The individual tends to make changes in life which are good for him now that he does not have to make changes which are bad for him.

In the third or identity-awareness phase, that aspect of the symbolic father which has not been dealt with emerges as bad father. With the help of good mother, who energizes the will to live, the inner good child frees himself from his orientation toward the introjected bad father so that he might completely identify with good father authority. In this symbolic experience the individual develops personal autonomy. In this phase both poles of the good/bad authority continuum are resymbolized. The good father atmosphere can be trusted to support the person's autonomy only when the symbolic elements of the bad father have been personalized. Through this delimiting of bad authority over against the good authority inherent in the order of Being, personal identity is stabilized. The inner child has gained its individuality and is acceptable in its own right. The person is now free to live out of his own legitimacy and to claim his birthright as a cosmic child.

In the fourth or integration phase of the symbolic regressive search, the child self is integrated with the other elements of the emerging inner authority structure. The symbolic good parents unite to free the good child from the residual influence of the bad child, thus giving the good child its own place of authority in the inner family. In this experience, the person discovers his identification with the natural inner child and the child self is given its rightful place in the person's total inner symbolic structure. The person is whole. Let us now consider each of these phases in more detail.

THE NEED AWARENESS PHASE: THE PERSON ORIENTS HIMSELF TO THE THERAPEUTIC PROCESS AS A SYMBOLIC QUEST

The person approaching therapy is looking for the good authority who will help him discover his long-denied need states. By seeking therapy, he is attempting to relate himself to the supportive, good father dimension of his own symbolic being by which he can reject the need-denying, bad mother dimension. This is true regardless of whether the therapist is male or female. The person must ally himself with the therapist in a way that enables him to move toward those states of symbolic self meaning which will deliver him from his need-denying bad mothering states. The presenting stress given by the client involves him in a need-denying symbolic state. In this state, he experiences discomfort, the inability to deal with his needs, and a lack of the inner authority necessary to reject the need-denying, deprived existence into which he has locked himself. At the outset, the person must learn to take a symbolic regressive stance toward his needs and toward the therapeutic situation, for the therapeutic situation provides the kind of authority structure which makes it possible for him to discover the primary aspects of his being which are related to these basic need states.

To permit himself symbolically to regress into this authority structure and thereby to discover his needs and to reject his need-deprivation is a problem for the individual has learned to insist on a non-symbolic regressive stance toward life in his strategy of parenting himself. Thus at the outset of the need-awareness phase, the individual is denying those Being needs which are related to his primary processes. He is strategized against dimensions of his own symbolic self. He fears discovering the unknown dimensions of his own being which a developing symbolic regressive stance will bring to ascendency. Thus the therapeutic encounter should repeatedly emphasize the bad

GENUINENESS

state of affairs existing in the individual's life. This naming of "bad mother" may be the first experience with true comfort for him, for, at one level or another, his life ite has been filled with techniques to avoid admitting his pristine need states by taking a parenting attitude towards his existence.

The first task of therapy, then, is to enable the individual to regress into the ground of his being and to be simple and natural with himself. His symptoms, in fact, should be interpreted as devices to inform him that he is deprived—depriving himself and taking care of his world so as to stay out of trouble with himself at the expense of being genuine with himself. In initial sessions, the individual can be asked to communicate with the images of the past through intrapsychic dialogue. In this way he symbolizes his inner plight and becomes more effectively aware of his deprived need-state and of his difficulty in relating those needs which are basic to him to his inner parental states. Thus it becomes apparent to him that he is not able honestly to express the true nature of his difficulty with the parent, that he must in fact evade or deny the deprivation involved in his relationship with the parent. Then he becomes aware that in this strategy he is cutting off, or evading, or denying, or depriving himself of relating to a very essential aspect of his own being. The person becomes aware that his problem is in his imagination; it is rooted in his symbolic processes. The individual learns to experience that being very simple and almost primitive with himself is essential to his becoming more aware of himself.

When the individual is involved with the need awareness phase of his symbolic regressive capacities, he frequently attempts to patronize or manipulate the therapist so as to reinstate the need-depriving symbolic system through which he feels that he is in charge of the relationship. Through such parenting stances toward his inner reality, he is relieved of the requirements of consciousness and of his responsibility to maintain a symbolic regressive stance toward being.

The therapist's task is to permit his own self awareness to remain transparent both to himself and to the client in the therapeutic encounter. He himself must not parent the client. He must not patronize him or manipulate him. He must not in some way try to curry his favor. On the other hand, the therapist needs to be able to receive

genuine expressions of the client as they come out in his
attempts to reach himself. He needs to be able to perceive
the meaning which the symptoms that are brought to him can
have in reorienting the self. He needs to be able to be
unideal. That is, he needs to be able to present himself
in such a way both to himself and to the client that he is
relaxed about the person the client is for whatever that
may mean or be. Because he can approach the person as an
individual through his own inner cosmos, he is supporting
him and is giving him the necessary right to be the person
he is and to be conscious as the person he is. Thus, most
fundamentally, the therapist must be a de-parented person,
a person who lives because his inner cosmos is supportive
of him. Any success orientation or performance orientation
or parenting orientation on the part of the therapist will
be experienced inwardly by the client as that which produces
anxiety.

In the need-awareness phase of genuineness, the person
will be unable to find good food in his dreams. He will be
unable to get to those kinds of need-fulfilling situations
symbolized by good food, and he will be deprived of the
resolution such situations offer. Furthermore, in these
dreams, he will not be able to be given nor will he be able
to receive money or clothing. It is especially important
that the individual recognize the significance of these
depriving dreams and that he begin to see the possibility
for his states of sleep and dream to be much more rewarding,
much more relaxing for him. These need-depriving and frustrated dreams can be helpful to the person if they are
interpreted in precisely these terms. It should continually
be pointed out to him that as a person learns to become
simple with himself, to regress into the ground of his
being, his dreams will reflect this fundamental change in
stance toward his basic nature.

As the person moves toward need-awareness, it will
become obvious that the authority figures he must deal with
are not very helpful to him. The father image as it is
symbolized is frequently chasing or frightening him; the
mother image is frequently depriving or frustrating him.
Yet, as the stance of the individual toward his inner need
symbolism develops, these images will change toward more
comforting and helpful ones. As these images develop from
deeply frustrating images to images more harmonious with
his being, this transformation should be pointed out to the
individual and he should be encouraged to believe in the
possibilities of his inner nature. At this point, it is

GENUINENESS

important to discuss the idealization of deprivation that he is involved with and the strategies he uses with himself to deny his need states. It is also important to point out his inner movement away from self-deprivation as this process develops. He should be taught to confront the persons in his daily existence with the needs of his true being for love, for support, and for acceptance. He should be taught to say no to rejection wherever he is being rejected in his being.

Dreams at this stage are the major means by which the individual's inner deprived state can be made vivid to him. Bad dreams may be extended through meditative and directed visualization so that the outcome can be made meaningful to the person. The contents of all dreams can be related to the cosmic realities to which the person is responsive: the need for nurturance in the environment of Being, and the need for loving and supportive relationships within the need for loving and supportive relationships within the social environment. When the individual finishes telling the dream, he is often asked to close his eyes and to continue the dream so that he can look further into the dream for the meaning of that which he is denying himself.

MOTHER IMAGE

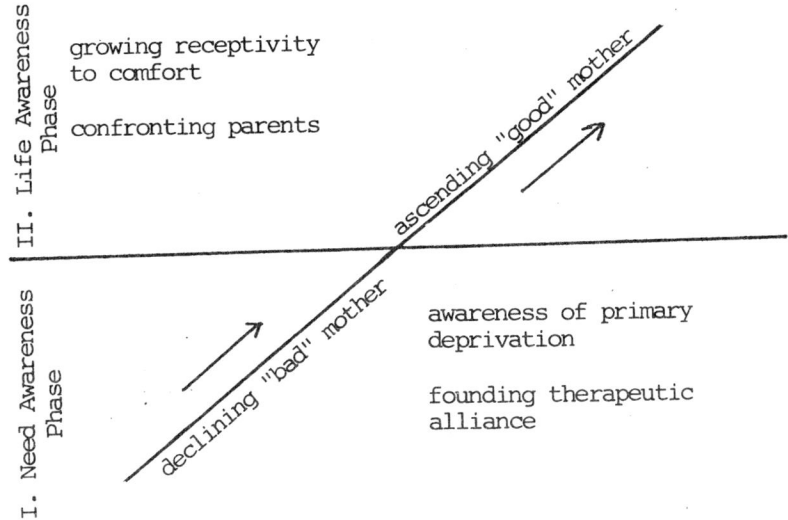

Figure 1

THE LIFE AWARENESS PHASE: THE PERSON SEEKS AND DISCOVERS A NURTURING WORLD

The second phase of the development of genuineness is the life awareness phase. As the person enters the life awareness phase of his own symbolic regressive capacity, he has learned to say "no" to that which is not good for him. However, the development of the capacity for good mother lies ahead for him. He really knows neither how to ask for what he needs nor how to receive as good what is given to him. He finds it hard to accept what is good. He has not yet developed the capacity for receptivity. This is the task of the life awareness phase: the development of the capacity to receive and to accept that which is good for the person. A crucial dimension of this phase can be seen in the way that the person relates to his parents when he first struggles to integrate the life awareness energies which have become available to him through his growing awareness, for this phase is marked by the beginning of the intense parental confrontation period. The only way that the individual can relate to his needs at depth and at the same time reject what he does not need is to work out the distinction in the context of the most primary regressive images of himself which rest in the images of the parents. These most central images are continually being validated or undermined by the existential relationship which he conducts with his real parents.

Initially the person will turn to his parents with his needs. The expression of his needs to his parents will still have the parenting aspect of his relating to them. This will manifest itself in a defiance of the old system or arrangement of communication by which he took care of them by repressing the legitimacy of his right to be loved by them. In other words, his first response in the life awareness phase is a reaction to the pathological aspects of his family life. In addition, his initial defiance will be combined with the demand that the parents change so that he can receive from them what he feels he needs by way of nurturance and love. This phase of reorienting himself to his life energies is a major life transition and it therefore requires enormous outputs of energy. Frequently, he fails in the attempt to change his environment so that it will nurture him. The energies he expends in defying the old order of existence do not immediately bring any further consciousness or light into his experience of his own being.

The period of parental confrontation is characterized by a great change in the parental relationship. The person is most frequently very sensitive to the way in which he has related himself to his parent and to the way in which the parent has related himself to him. He is very sensitive to the way in which his needs and his attitudes and opinions have been respected, listened to, or cared about by the parent. Given this sensitivity, he is learning to say "no" so that he will be able to say "yes" to what he really needs. Through this intense confrontation, the individual develops the ability to distinguish between his saying "no" to the parent and his saying "yes" to what he really needs with the parent. This crucial development is one of the most challenging demands ever to be made upon his existence.

For the individual to learn how to present himself to his parents in a way which leaves the parents free to be parents is indeed a task of utmost proportions. All of us have learned to take care of our parents in ways which are very deceptive to ourselves. At first, the challenge to the parent takes the form of demands that the parent become the ideal parent so that the individual can have his needs without encumbrance. The task of consciousness, however, is not that easy or simple and it is important that the individual learn that to remain conscious he must remain in a reality confrontation with both his authority images and his child images as these are embodied in the structure of his existential family.

It is hoped that the individual will decisively break with his mother symbiosis during this phase of the development of genuineness. The mother symbiosis is characterized by a mutually dependent life style in which the child takes care of his mother in order to maintain his sense of security and at the expense of remaining unconscious of himself. To break this, the individual must go through the anxieties of the separation from the parent and of emerging into a world where he can gain the comforts he more deeply needs. Many of these comforts may actually come from the parents if the parents are oriented to the person as he claims his autonomy. If not, he will learn to gain access to those comforts available in the good mothering aspects of his environment. The individual learns to receive from the environment of Being, and that it is natural for him to receive. He learns to give up demands that he receive from those aspects of his real environment, including his actual parents, which are not open to give to him what he needs. He asks for what through his own experience he knows is available to him in the way and at the place where it is available to him.

When parenting aspects of his life which have contained him in a state of unconsciousness are given up, he finds himself left in states of loneliness and aloneness. At first he is frightened by these because he has not yet yielded to the experience of the inner child. It is during this time, then, that the individual needs the direct support of others in the therapy process. He needs the support in a different way than he has needed it before: he is developing an understanding that, in order truly to live, he does need the real support of the child self of others. In other words, the inner child of the person can exist only as it is supported by honest interaction with the inner child of others. The development of an experiential definition of love through interaction with others is one of the most important experiences of this aspect of therapy. The inner child's consciousness is primarily focused on the spiritual-affectionate level of his environmental field, the qualities upon which he must depend for his primary sustenance. The meaning of the inner good mother to the inner child is a reality that reaches to all dimensions of the self, the cosmic and the organic as well as the personal.

The second part of this phase of growth into genuineness is the search for the nurturing world. This search includes learning to accept and to recognize that the world will not automatically give to the individual that which he so much needs and has a right to expect out of life: love and acceptance, those elements of existence which nourish and sustain the vital capacities of his being. Thus, in this part of the life awareness phase, the person learns to leave behind those relationships which do not succor or nurture him and to which he therefore cannot respond and to turn more decisively to those aspects of life which have vitality for him and to which he can respond. He learns how to receive from that which is truly a nurturing source of life for him and he learns how to respond and to be vulnerable and to be open to life's possibilities. In a few words, he learns what it is like to turn all his cards over and lay himself open to that which life has to give him. In doing this, he takes up a feeling of risk, he accepts a feeling of a certain kind of fear, but he also exults in the feeling of life, and he feels the intoxication of the exchange of energies which he has not before experienced.

Frequently, when some openness is really proffered by one person to another, the one who is on the receiving end in some way mitigates the full import of that input. He in some way evades it, pushes it aside, or does not make himself fully vulnerable to those life oriented energies which he so very much needs. In this phase the individual must be helped to see the strategies motivated by his fear of being vulnerable and of opening himself to life and receiving from it: he has pushed away the gifts of life offered him out of the consciousness of others, he has held himself in a state of non-vulnerability, and he has suspended the life energies and the vitality involved in open response.

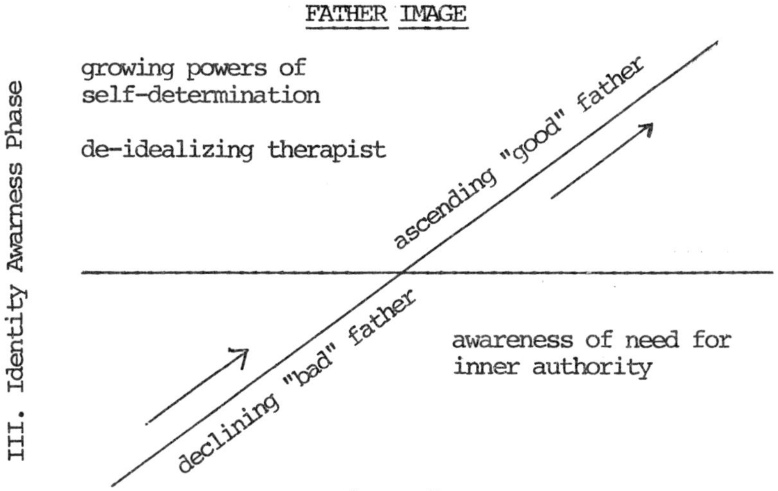

FATHER IMAGE

III. Identity Awarness Phase

growing powers of self-determination

de-idealizing therapist

ascending "good" father

declining "bad" father

awareness of need for inner authority

Figure 2

The three figures in this chapter, this one along with figure 1 on page 223 and figure 3 on page 229, schematically represent the sequence of image states through which the individual passes in the course of symbolic regression therapy. The individual advances from the state of consciousness represented at the bottom of each figure to that represented at the top and then on to the next figure as he progresses towards greater symbolic regression consciousness.

THE IDENTITY AWARENESS PHASE: THE PERSON IDENTIFIES WITH AUTONOMOUS, AFFIRMING AUTHORITY

The third phase of development into genuineness is marked by the appearance of the bad father image with its symbolism. With the support of good mother and implicit good father symbolism, the individual attempts to free himself from bad inner authority. In this attempt, the inner child is freed into his own identity. The individual becomes less ambivalent and more confident in his personal choices and in his perceptions about himself. The right to one's own authority among others' authority is important to the development of consciousness. With this claiming of this right, the person begins to give priority to how he wants to live rather than merely to what he must do to survive. And creativity begins to become his concern.

Frequently I observe that once an individual in therapy has begun to dream good mother dreams and has begun to confront life with his needs, he begins to confront me with what is not satisfying to him in his relationship with me. Because until this point he has not been autonomous with me, it has often been true that in many ways I had taken him for granted. Usually I am able to agree with him that something in the relationship needs to change. Here the person is dealing with his own authority. This emergent reality is involved with another development. The person now finds it easier to request of me rather than to demand of me. Demand has given way to expectation. He has begun to relax with his expectations that he be given his right to his own judgments. Although I would have listened to any requests the client might have made prior to this emergence, for the most part such requests are not addressed to me until the person is ready for this phase of his imagery development.

This phase is the time of the de-idealization of the therapist. The person begins to want a relationship which is truly human. He determines whether consulting with the therapist involves him in an ideally rigid role or whether it has some reality that can be described and mutually settled upon so that both he and the therapist can feel their own dignity and autonomy in the therapeutic relationship.

The therapy group becomes a place for defining one's personal autonomy in this phase. While during the first two phases the group functioned to support the self in the grip of bad mother symbolism and in the quest for good

GENUINENESS

mother symbolism, the person can now find his uniqueness by delimiting himself over against the group. This phase of the quest for genuineness brings the dimension of good father symbolism into the functioning of the group. Thus, frequently the individual will begin to differ from the group's perception and projections to assert his own unique stance toward reality. Moreover, in his individual sessions with the therapist, the person enters into a dialectic of mutuality in authority: the assessment of his perceptions is related to that of the therapist's. In a dream symbolizing this situation, a young man found himself in an office with the therapist. Both were behind desks, but his was behind the therapist's. Then he pushed his desk forward until it was in line with that of the therapist. They exchanged friendly glances, and he awoke.

Visualizations in this phase should be very spontaneous rather than closely directed, as the experience of personal autonomy is a most important aspect of the raising of the individual's consciousness at this time.

CHILD IMAGE

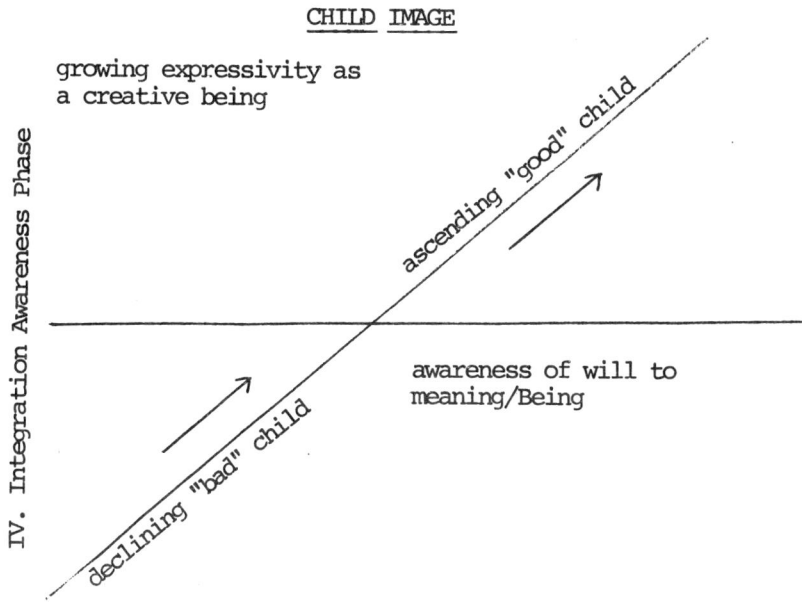

Figure 3

THE INTEGRATION AWARENESS PHASE:
THE PERSON DISCOVERS HIS CREATIVE POWERS AS A COSMIC BEING AND UNFOLDS THOSE POWERS IN SELF-REALIZATION

The fourth phase is the phase of personal integration. The good parents unite to free the child from the bad child within. The person begins to relate to his peers for purposes of advancing his consciousness and their consciousness. Competition for survival is given up and replaced by the struggle for self-expression. In this, survival becomes a by-product of a highly conscious existence. The individual gains a certain true confidence in his own self-sufficiency. He is almost totally concerned with the development of his creativity. He becomes productive socially because his contribution is uniquely his own. Yet this contribution may not be recognized by society because of its transpersonal quality. Nevertheless, it will sonner or later redound to the benefit of society. The contributions of many of the most conscious individuals in the world were not truly appreciated until these contributions were no longer a threat to society.

The dimensions of genuineness which indicate the integration of personality are directly related to the emergence in imagination of the symbolic good child. Good parental images free the inner child with the result of personal autonomy and feelings of legitimacy. The individual experiences freedom from the usual constraints of the introjected bad authority symbols into the world of his own uniqueness and personal meaning. Symptomatic living is given up for creative living. Fears of innovative living are traded for explorative living. The person becomes happy. Depression gives way to curiosity and interest in the unknown. The development into this quality of conscious existence is a culmination of the person's capacity to live at peace with himself. Many of the usual criteria of therapeutic success are those related to this phase of growth. The reason these criteria do not differentiate a successful from an unsuccessful therapeutic experience is because the treatment of the imagination and the resymbolization of personality must be measured to determine to what degree there has been actual inner change, and to what degree this change is one of depth. Almost everyone has certain happy moments, given the right encouragement. What must be measured is the individual's capacity to produce happiness in his environment. Some of the usual criteria that are related to the meaning of the inner child are self esteem, feelings of worth, and the ability to make choices. While these criteria are a measure of change and to some degree therapeutic success, the symbolic change itself, the actual self-images which undergird behavior, is what must be measured. It is not enough, for example, to measure assertiveness for the individual. Is assertiveness a competitive, introjected demand related to securing one's inner position against parental stated demands? Or is it an attempt to innovate and express a creative effort?

The symbolic child in his natural meaning develops as the person deals with introjected meaning. It is as if little by little the infant is born and the childhood capacities develop. As this occurs, the individual is said to have symbolically regressed into the ground of Being. It is this symbolic regression which is the measure of man's meaning.

NOTES

1. Steiper and Weiner, Key Dimensions in Psychotherapy.

2. Darryl C. Freeland, The Guided Daydream in Counselor Education, (Doctoral Dissertation, University of Southern California, 1972), Dissertation Abstracts International, 33 (1972), 567B.